Reflections
on
Life's Illusions
A Memoir of Culture and Consciousness

by Jane Gallagher

The purpose of this book, and its character as memoir, is to reflect on and artistically show, rather than scientifically describe, how the development of personal consciousness goes hand in hand with the development of the surrounding culture. The book's story highlights the ways I imagine my developing mind and emotions were affected by various personal interactions, political events, social movements and scientific discoveries that occurred over the course of my lifetime and the lifetimes of family members. Delving into memory using imagination as my primary tool, this memoir was written as a creative means to reflect on the development of personal opinions. Reflection on the memories and opinions this book contains was deepened through research into the cultural events that surrounded and informed their formation. The ideas of other authors influenced the development of the thoughts, opinions and emotional patterns at the heart of the story. As such, their inclusion is essential to the book's purpose and character. However, this book is a work of creative nonfiction and was never intended to supersede anything contained in the scholarly and journalistic works it refers to, all of which I commend to you as excellent resources for further exploration of the topics discussed.

Please direct inquiries to:
Reflections on Life's Illusions
P.O. Box 131
38 North Main Street
Waterbury, VT 05676
jane@reflectionsonlifesillusions.com

Paperback ISBN: 978-1-63337-907-7
E-Book ISBN: 978-1-63337-773-8

Printed in the United States of America
1 3 5 7 9 10 8 6 4 2

For Lilah and Clara

Contents

Introduction

We live in what feels like a cataclysmic time. Perhaps it feels that way for many at any given time, but as one raised to deeply trust the scientific method, this time of climate chaos feels especially so. This book rises in response to that feeling, conceived as a way to reflect on the forces that shaped my understanding of the world and the actions I took in response while creating the life I know. Written in a form designed to delve into the mysterious relationship between internal and external life systems, the narrative juxtaposes stories of personal experience characterizing various periods in my growing awareness and stories of key events that combine memory and research into what was simultaneously unfolding in the world around me. My aim in using this patchwork quilt writing process is to try to open the mind's door into wonder and imagination about the complex, integrated dance of inner and outer systems of thought and experience that shape every living moment. By doing so, I also hope to ultimately reveal a path of inspiration and energy that could lead the way through the inevitable challenges to come.

The worldview I know reveals itself here in part through the narrative structure, alternately moving from the inside out and the outside in. The threads of personal experience and cultural reporting are woven into the story in more or less sequential order, in depth in some places and skimming the surface in others, depending on how intimately or remotely they seem to have affected my developing consciousness. They also tend to weave back and forth within each time period like a developing or musing mind. Each story thread tells only what seems most essential in the voice that arose to tell it, with some that came to me years ago alongside more recent ones.

This project is also an experiment in letting the story write itself, as many authors claim they do. That writing process has been a revelation. I am profoundly grateful for all the encouragement received from friends and family as this book took shape, particularly from my husband, Bill Abel. Always my first editor, he has patiently listened and reflected with me during countless conversations, supporting the practice of thinking out loud, which helped sustain my focus to see this writing project through the seven years it took to complete.

Chapter One

Into the Mists of Time

There is a baby girl who lies screaming in the night. Her belly muscles spasm, squeezing tightly as they work to digest the canned milk received as nourishment. This baby girl has a mother who loves her but can't breastfeed because her nipples are inverted. There is no such thing as a breast pump in this mother's world. This baby girl's mother stops trying to nurse her child after two weeks because her child isn't growing as she should. Instead she follows the advice of her male doctor, feeding her baby watered-down canned milk.

There is a baby girl who lies dozing in a '52 Oldsmobile on a sunny June day outside a Howard Johnson's restaurant in Nebraska. The car windows are closed. The baby's young parents sit by the restaurant window in an air-conditioned booth. They eat lunch while keeping watch over their child, taking a break from the endless stress of sleepless nights. This baby girl sleeps, never making a whimper.

There is a baby girl whose parents hurry to return to their car after lunch because they notice she's crying. As they open the door, a rush of hot air blasts their faces. The car feels like an oven. The baby's face is as red as a little beet. This mother picks up her baby, hugging her, walking around in the shade of a tree to cool her, crooning, "Shhh, shhh, it's okay. Please don't cry. I love you."

There is a baby girl who lies screaming in the night as she does every night. Her parents take turns rocking her in their arms as they walk around their little apartment and feed her more from the warm bottle of canned milk, trying to calm her. The baby girl cries almost all night, only calming for a while when sucking or when walked and rocked or bounced on her stomach on her father's shoulder. She belches loudly then, releasing pain momentarily along with canned milk, which dribbles down her father's back. In the morning, exhausted from crying, her stomach finally calm, she sleeps through most of the day. The doctor calls this pattern colic and doesn't associate it with a physical reaction to the cow's milk she's being fed, which he also doesn't realize can sensitize a little body at this point in life, triggering a genetic propensity for allergic reactions. This situation persists for months. The baby girl feels afraid and angry when she cries, but she has no names for emotions. She just wants someone to hold her and stop the pain.

As this baby girl grows, her father learns to soothe her by rolling her from side to side in her baby buggy bed as he studies late into the night for the bar exam that will allow him to practice law in Washington, DC. The rhythmic movement eases the pain in her stomach and distracts her from her emotional reactions to it. She is quiet when she rocks. During the day when this baby cries, her mother wheels her onto the front lawn under the shade of a tree. Her crying stops as the soft breeze touches her skin. Her eyes learn to focus on dancing patterns of green leaves interlaced with moving sparkles of yellow sunlight and blue sky. She hears birdsong from the treetop. This baby finally begins to sleep at night for several hours. She is six months old.

This baby girl's mother starts to park her baby carriage regularly under a maple tree because the baby is happy there and her mother can enjoy half an hour of peace. Her baby seems fascinated and delighted by the caress of the wind and chirping of birds. Everywhere this baby looks, bright green leaves dance with glints of sunlight against blue sky. She discovers her toes with her chubby fingers and learns how they taste against the yellow–green–blue backdrop of sun, leaves, and sky.

When this little girl turns two, she begins to climb and move incessantly, never wanting movement to stop. She is comfortable when moving. When she is seven, this little girl is tall enough to jump up to hang by her hands from the first branch of a young maple tree. She pulls herself up with her strong, lanky arms. She hooks her knee over the branch above her head to aid her arms in pulling her body onto it. This little girl climbs high into the shelter of the green, dancing coolness she loves so much. Her mother encourages her to climb and explore, knowing, as her own mother taught her, that if you can climb up, you can also climb down.

At first this little girl's mother stands near the tree to give her advice about climbing. Before long, though, she goes back inside to attend to her projects, leaving the little girl to climb freely. She knows her daughter is agile, quite capable of carefully climbing up and down. This mother soon lets her daughter roam freely within firm boundaries of the neighborhood where she trusts her to stay. This girl's mother trusts her daughter's daring enthusiasm. As an artist, this mother is a keen observer. She sees her child's careful attention and well-coordinated body.

This mother watches her daughter grow while working full-time at home, creating a beautiful, comfortable, nourishing space where her family can live and grow, a space full of love, laughter, delicious food, wonderful stories, and plenty of beautiful music and art. When she can grab a few precious minutes of free time, this mother draws with charcoal on newsprint or paints with oil on canvas in the home studio on the attached sunporch, heating it with an electric heater in winter because there are windows in three outer walls and no insulation.

I'M SURE YOU KNOW that I was that little girl learning her first lessons about life in the mists of the green heaven where my family lived for most of my first nine years. I can really only imagine the beginning of consciousness growing in that small, developing body and its experiential environment because those physical cells have replaced themselves innumerable times since then, including the memory cells. Mysteriously, those experiences still form the deepest root of my perceptions, even though the mind that carried them from those days to this is not the same as the one that formed them from experience, and large parts of the story just told were remembered by others, mainly my parents.

Within the course of my lifetime scientists have discovered an astounding quantity of information about the structure and function of the human brain. However, the mystery of what constitutes the essence at the root of consciousness remains an enigma. The best any scientist can tell about the subject, even now, is to identify where in the brain various memories reside, rather than exactly how it's possible for them to be there, given continuous cell replacement happening all the time. What constitutes the essence informed by those memories, however, the essence that gives rise to internal organizing patterns of thought and emotion called "myself," still lies deep in the realm of mystery.

HARVARD PROFESSOR OF EXPRIMENTAL PSYCHOLOGY Steven Pinker, in his 2011 book *The Better Angels of Our Nature*, describes the whole era in which we in the "baby boom" lived as a time characterized by a rising conflagration of social movements and a dying back of all-out war in support of empire, an era of surging technological growth and innovation alongside growing consciousness and concern about the extinction of increasing numbers of plant and animal species.[1] These trends characterized the swirling soup in which a seed of awareness began to grow in the mind and body of the little girl we just met crying in the night. The multiplicity of cultural upheavals over the course of her lifetime increasingly challenged the way humanity, particularly those of European descent such as I, were accustomed to perceiving themselves, and *their* world, for generations.

The fallout from those roiling, coalescing cultural forces has made Earth seem a much smaller planet than anyone could earlier have imagined. Pinker points out that human life spans everywhere have lengthened and populations have exponentially expanded on all continents, intensifying perception of Earth's physical limits among all who pay attention to the planetary view of life. Everything, including cultural upheaval, seems to be speeding up, reflected ultimately in rapidly changing climate patterns.

The dominant old stories about how life came to be, told in different ways in different cultures, generally include a thread about the unique creation and imagined importance of human life above and beyond other species. Such ancient stories are being yelled louder and held ever more firmly and inflexibly by some who seem to deeply fear the increasing speed of change on all fronts, feeling personally threatened as institutionalized cultural traditions are continuously challenged.

As a result of these mounting, unifying forces of change on so many levels, we humans now find ourselves in a time between starkly competing foundational stories, some based on religious tradition, some based on science, and very many held with a surfeit of certainty. In the past, some cultures at impasses like this discovered a unique capacity to tell new, more inclusive stories to inspire innovative approaches to shared problems, while others clung tightly to old treasured ones. Civilizations that flexed and changed continued on, while those that sought to enforce adherence to old ways eventually became archeological relics. Of course the stories of any culture are only one force affecting its resilience. Weather, volcanos, disease, and more lethal weapons owned by enemies are at least as determinative. Stories, however, inform the ways in which each culture uses the knowledge and tools available to it to motivate people's responses to external threats.

The stories now being questioned have been understood by many as reliable and meaningful, as stabilizing cultural elements moving all of Earth's cultures along a path toward more complex civilizational structures, a linear progression long understood as a good thing in most places. However, the stories that sustained and inspired humanity to make it this far are now clashing with increasing bile and bitterness with newer tales, which ironically rose from the scientific discoveries and embodied experiences that surfaced as a result of the wondrous advances made possible by the old stories.

Each of us who reads and tells cultural stories, along with our own uniquely personal ones, is inevitably nourished by the soil in which we were planted, using the water and sun available there as well as the emotional and psychological space within that particular living environment. The mystery behind life, that which rhythmically inflates our lungs and sets our hearts pumping regardless of conscious choice, first inspires instinctive reactions to the world around us (as is true for every mammal), reactions that can be seen as life reaching for attention and care from whoever can provide sustenance for survival. In the case of humanity, that eventually includes their stories. Everyone's story is important because every being is unique, even as we are all fully integrated into the continuous flow of Earth's living process.

SOME WOULD HAVE CALLED my distant great-grandfather a scoundrel and a thief. He was in fact a pirate. Others would have called him a privateer, a patriot and hardworking merchant in a wild new country because he gave a portion of his stolen bounties to the Continental Congress. These cultural stories, or memes,[i] use the same facts to tell different tales depending on who employs them. They elicit different emotions and spark different actions in people who place their faith in the truth of one story over the other.

---

i. A meme is a unit of cultural information, such as a cultural practice or idea, that is transmitted verbally or by repeated action from one person to another, spreading cultural information in a similar way to the physical spread of genetic information in the replication of genes within families.

My distant great-grandfather's descendant, my father, was a war hero, having successfully completed all fifty-two missions as an air force navigator during World War II. Only half of such men survived the war. He was also considered too dangerous to hire after graduating from Antioch College and Columbia Law School in the 1950s—Senator Joseph McCarthy's day—when a blacklist of communist sympathizers told a cultural tale that dominated US hiring practices. That was the tale the State Department still adhered to near the end of that era, the summer of 1954, when Dad was offered a job there. In order to accept it, he relinquished his position as Associate Professor of Law at the University of Nebraska and temporarily moved his young wife and new baby (me) into his in-laws' home in Lakewood, Ohio.

When Dad arrived in Washington, DC, at the appointed time to begin his dream career, the outer office secretary for his new boss told him that she was sorry, but she had no record of an appointment for him in her calendar. When he politely argued that there must be some mistake, the secretary firmly but kindly refuted him, although she didn't object to his waiting in the outer office for her boss to emerge from his inner sanctum. After several hours, the man who had hired my father from afar finally opened his office door and much to his chagrin encountered Dad. The man responded to Dad's polite self-introduction and statement of his dilemma by coldly repeating his secretary's story: he was sorry, but he had never heard of him, following which he brushed briskly past and headed down the hall without another word, despite Dad's fervent protest that there must be some mistake.

My father never quite figured out what false fears had motivated his prospective boss to connect him with Senator McCarthy's tale of communists infiltrating the US government through the international law division of the State Department, or perhaps he never wanted to imagine how that storyline had become attached to him. Luckily for me and for our family, the story that falsely marked Dad that day was not one that he or anyone who knew him accepted, which allowed him ultimately to achieve a long and successful career as an international corporate lawyer. Dad's story of that experience became a very personal warning for me, however, about the dangers of placing trust in the authority of institutions. I learned of its impact on my family as a high school freshman, when Richard Nixon, a former member of Joseph McCarthy's House Un-American Activities Committee, was campaigning against Hubert Humphrey in the 1968 presidential election.

Despite the shock of the changed circumstances that utterly altered his career, forcing Dad to cool his heels, and his young family to move into Dad's stepmother's vacation cottage for a year, he was well aware that his luck was far better than most whose lives and careers were not only changed but destroyed by the cultural story of the "Red Scare." Dad finally accepted the one job offer that came his way at the end of that year, after firmly resisting the idea of redirecting his career away from international diplomacy toward corporate law initially. An earlier graduate of Antioch College offered him the job he accepted in New Jersey, as a contract lawyer for Johnson & Johnson.

Throughout that hair-raising time for their young family Mom was adamant that Dad must not be too attached to his career vision or to place, either of which could have made him unemployable if held too tightly. She gently and persistently insisted that he must go wherever there was a reasonable job offer that would allow him to use his law degree to restore hope of realizing their shared dream of a stable, happy family. My parents were ahead of their time in ways I later came to understand, connected as they were in an equal partnership at the root of their relationship. As a result, Dad ultimately listened to Mom's advice and we moved to New Jersey, where he worked for Johnson & Johnson for several years, including a year when we lived in New York City while he was studying for the New York bar exam. Dad's story about his career derailment was my introduction to the power of cultural stories, or memes, which pass along the known facts of a tale, while also sustaining the life of the emotional resonance the story elicits across generations. Memes I learned about other family members had a similar effect.

My Great-aunt Mame, on my mother's side, was a bohemian radical according to many in her day. She was an accomplished sculptress and smoked a pipe at a time when polite, educated society women, such as she, were trained to live as delicately as hothouse flowers. Taught never to challenge the status quo, in which their husbands were the sole decision-makers and owners of property, these women were also defined as little more than property under the law. That's the extent of what I know about Aunt Mame, based on well-known history and memes passed down from my parents.

Aunt Mame's sister, my maternal grandmother, was always very quiet, gentle, and proper during the time I knew her. She was also a flapper and a suffragette in roaring twenties New York City, according to Mom. Grandma received an art teaching certificate from Pratt Institute in 1913 and passed down to Mom a lovely white, lightweight cotton halter dress with a wide ruffle hitting just below the knee. It was decorated with small navy blue polka dots. Mom passed it on to me in the early '70s when retro clothing styles became popular. That dress became my symbolic proof of Mom's tale about her mother. Amazingly, the dress lasted long enough for me to pass it on again to my older daughter during the next generational wave of retro clothing styles in the '90s.

My maternal grandfather served as an ambulance driver in World War I after graduating from Dartmouth College in Hanover, New Hampshire. After the war he married my grandmother, who was by then an art teacher in Ohio where she grew up. A very gregarious, playful, kind, and friendly person, Granddad also had very conservative ideas about a woman's place in life, which I discovered when his beloved Dartmouth decided to admit women for the first time in 1972, the year I graduated from high school. He was adamantly opposed to the idea. Because Mom was very quiet about her opinions, as was her mother, I was left to imagine that my beloved Granddad's conservative idea about women had something to do with their reticent silence. Later I came to understand that all of them were caught in a web of conditioning that held the still point of cultural balance intact partly by silencing women.

My paternal grandmother could take an ambulance apart and put it back together again, according to Dad, a reputed requirement for acceptance into the World War I ambulance corps. However, as a woman, she was not allowed to apply, shipping out instead as a nurse due to the dominant story about women in those days, which held that they lacked the physical, mental, and emotional stamina to act rationally under pressure. Another result of that cultural tall tale was that all three of the high-spirited, college-educated women just described—Aunt Mame and both my grandmothers—were nearly thirty when US law finally allowed them to vote, following public outrage over the violent abuse that had rained down on thousands of peacefully protesting suffragettes in numerous marches held around the country. My maternal grandmother was likely one of the marchers in the huge protest held in New York City in 1912 while she was studying at Pratt. A photo of her in an old Pratt yearbook suggests that possibility. She sits in a group photo, dressed all in white beside another woman dressed the same way, the "uniform" of the suffragettes. They sit beside several other women and men dressed in street clothes.

Despite the hard-fought voting-rights victory, made possible for *white* women as a result of many years of continuous protest by suffragettes like my grandmother, both women and men from ethnic backgrounds with dark skin remained disenfranchised even then, due to the dominant European cultural story that defined all living, breathing beings as part of a God-given hierarchy, in which brown skin placed a person at the bottom of humanity's top tier of life's hierarchical pinnacle. For far too long that place was widely believed to be only a few steps above animals, a view forcibly imposed on society by institutionalized memes from as far back as the Roman Empire.

What effect did these cultural memes about my immediate ancestors have on my growing understanding of the adult world? When I first heard them as a youngster I felt a visceral sense of sympathy for my grandmothers and their sisters, who had pushed against the restrictions of what I knew to be patently false cultural stories. I was proud they had the hutzpah to realize much of their potential despite those restrictions, although at that point I didn't realize how the social privilege they enjoyed was also essential to their ability to do so. Their stories nevertheless hold a quality of courageous resilience that continues to inspire me to be true to myself within whatever cultural balancing act I may find myself performing. Like all stories, however, those tales can be viewed through many different lenses, creating very different interpretations in different minds.

Conditioning of course happened in both mind and body as I grew, and as many of us in healthy, loving households are lucky enough to do between the ages of four and ten, I learned that my body had the capacity to move in many interesting ways. I also learned that its range and capacity for movement was often greater than others'. For a long time I assumed that everyone shared the same interest in and capacity for physical movement and the particular kind of engagement with life it affords. I did my best to encourage siblings and playmates to equally experience the satisfying thrill of reaching the top of various climbing trees and rooftops or experimenting with tumbling and twisting tricks on the grass, on the empty bar of the backyard grape arbor, or on the poles supporting the swing set. Eventually I realized that somehow I had lucked out in the physical realm, having been born into a body that was more elastic and able to coordinate its movements in an unconsciously accurate way, capable of taking me to places where lots of others couldn't or wouldn't go (by the time high school graduation rolled around, I had learned there were many more with far greater physical capacities than mine). However, beginning life's journey in a body that effectively engaged the world around it, while almost daily being released and/or shooed into natural environments with my mother's unspoken trust to effectively negotiate physical challenges and also keep the younger children safe, gave me early self-confidence. That confidence became deeply rooted in freely connecting with the natural world. As a result, nature became a primary and treasured friend. Communing alone with its physical language has often proved at least as helpful as anything a human friend could offer me in times of confusion or grief.

I quickly became a proud tree hugger. Climbing trees was by far my favorite activity until about age fourteen, when dancing superseded the drive to climb and a wide variety of climbing trees was no longer available. Three experiences stand out from a multitude of ventures into tree branches—especially the two young, sturdy maples and the huge old willow tree in my front yard—when I was between the ages of five and nine. The most gentle of these memories happened one day when I could locate no playmates. I decided to climb into my favorite maple tree in its summer leafing-out because there was nothing better to do. Reaching a comfortable perch in the crook of a branch two-thirds of the way up and looking around at the leaves, I realized that no one could see me from the street, or anywhere else except directly under the branches if they stood by the trunk and looked straight up. A gentle, cooling wind rustled the leaves, touching my face and riffling my hair, which felt wonderful on that hot day. The trunk and branches stood firm in the breeze, except at the very top and outer edges where new growth was pushing toward the sun. When the wind blew, shafts of sunlight danced momentarily into the emerald green bower where I sat, creating brief openings of robin's-egg-blue sky through the electric green of the sun-kissed leaves.

I sensed the tree holding and befriending me through a mutual love of the living moment and a joyful connection to the whole experience that required different physical capacities of the tree and of me. My heart softened and opened to a feeling so safe, warm, and happy that I began to sing, working my way through a number of folk songs I grew up singing with my mother and noticing how the movement of the air through my body while I sang heightened my physical connection to the moment and its peaceful, solitary joy.

Another time, when I was about eight or nine, I climbed to the top of a very tall pine tree in a friend's front yard because it looked so easy to do. While I was ascending it—with its so many branches to choose from, all ordered just so—I realized it was almost like a spiraling ladder to heights far beyond any I'd reached before. After climbing as high as possible without venturing onto branches too thin to support my weight, I looked down at my friend who had refused to venture into the tree at all. From that height she seemed only a third of an inch tall, at most. Her mother, who had joined her at the base of the trunk, looked not much larger.

Just then, the wind began blowing in sharp gusts and the pine tree started bending this way and that, taking me with it. Clinging to its branches with all my strength, fear of falling surfaced for the first time in any climbing experience. I could easily see how close I was to tumbling all the way to the ground. I would have to be extremely careful climbing down, which I urgently wanted to do because the wind gusts were strengthening and growing closer together.

That situation focused my attention on physical awareness in each second. While holding as tightly as possible to branches small enough to get each hand around, sitting on those large enough to support my weight, and remaining stock-still with my body pressed tightly against the trunk, I endured each movement of the tree as it careened with the wind. It bent alternately in directions that tipped me backward or sideways, followed by the tree's trunk swinging forward or to the other side in graceful, terrifying arcs interspersed with periods of stillness. It was clear that if I fell to the ground from that height I would die, a thought that strangely made me feel more alive than I had ever felt before.

Clinging tightly to the tree with each gust of wind, waiting until it ebbed before carefully moving one foot, then one hand, followed by another foot and another hand, and keeping firmly planted with all the other limbs as I moved just one, I climbed slowly and steadily down in the brief, windless pauses. Shifting down only a branch or two at a time, I sunk into another safe nook or cranny where I could securely press against the tree when the wind began to blow again. In order to calm my fear enough to prevent panic, which I knew would further endanger me, I made a determined effort to sustain a very sharp focus on one movement at a time once it became safe enough to risk one. As I did so, I reminded myself that if you can climb up on your own, you can also climb down, as my mother had taught me. Staying starkly focused on each of my movements and those of the tree allowed me to gradually make my way safely to the ground. During that whole perilous descent, I knew I would get no help from anyone else. I was the one who had gotten myself into that mess, so I was the one who had to get myself out.

In the end, I learned there were some very different and unexpected elements to climbing pine trees that can't be learned from climbing maples and willows. Later I learned why. Pine trees grow very tall very quickly, making them enticing to inveterate tree climbers, but because they grow tall so fast, they don't grow very wide. That enables them to bend in the wind almost like huge blades of grass and very unlike maples and willows, which grow much more slowly and stand much more firmly in the wind.

Another important lesson I internalized from that experience, although I had little or no capacity to articulate it at the time, was that fear can be used to focus attention in a way that enables you to consciously choose where and how to direct your thoughts. Wise actions can then follow that may save your life. Discovering that I could use that strategy to get myself out of physical danger, having put all my tree-climbing skills to the test, felt utterly exhilarating. After surviving the terror of the descent and jumping to the ground with immense relief, receiving no more physical harm than a bit of sap on my hands, I also decided that climbing tall pine trees was not something I wanted to do again. The lessons learned from that experience were seared into my cells in such a way that I can mysteriously recall them in minute detail more than fifty years later.

The third tree-climbing story is one of falling hard from the branches of a dearly loved old willow, the most majestic tree in the neighborhood, which grew right outside the front door of the tiny Cape Cod style house where we lived. That fall was the result of my taking balance for granted while sitting comfortably astride a crook in one of the first divisions of its trunk, not far from the base though still at least five feet from the ground. That branching trunk division was so wide in the crook where I sat, like sitting astride a broad-backed horse, that I could put my fully extended arms only partway around the trunk in front of me. The thickly ribbed bark, however, allowed small fingers to hook into its crevices, giving an unwarranted sense of secure handholds.

Perceiving the perch to be low in the tree and feeling confident of balancing there, I was not paying close attention to body position in relation to activity. While I stood astride the very wide branching and leaned down to loudly defend my sister in an argument with another child, the angle of that lean, coupled with gravity, pulled my arm away from the trunk and tumbled me headfirst into a front flip. I landed smack on my back, and the wind was knocked hard from my lungs. Considerable pain accompanied any attempt to rise. After finally lifting to a half-bent stance and walking while crying into the house in search of Mom, I feared a broken back.

Coming to the door as I entered, Mom calmly explained that my back was not broken and described in simple language what happens when you fall hard enough to drive air from your lungs, and she helped me to lie down on the living room sofa. As she sat to comfort me and hear my story, I saw no sign of fear or panic on her face, only compassion, concern, and a slight irritation that I had not paid enough attention to know what would happen if I leaned that far out of the tree. It wasn't the only time I fell hard from the big willow, which is probably why I usually enjoyed its shady branches from the ground, preferring to instead climb the maples, whose branches could easily be encircled by one small hand.

These physical tree-climbing experiences taught me mental concepts that grew and spread enough to later provide imaginary handholds for climbing out of other, very different kinds of challenging situations, some mainly physical and others mainly emotional.

One theory that makes sense to me, about why these memories are so clearly stamped in my brain more than fifty years later, is that several qualitative elements of these experiences were deeply ingrained enough in my physical/psychic being to later transfer their mental constructs and inform my escape from very different challenges, compounding each time and reinforcing the minute details of the experiences in a positive memory feedback loop.

I've learned over the years that getting stuck emotionally—as happens to me from time to time when I find myself unable to shake off an emotional quality that in small or large ways hampers effective engagement with living—often indicates something deeper lurking beneath, something the conscious mind would rather avoid, like sadness, fear, pain, or anger.

Having long been comforted by trees and having learned respect for them after falling from their branches and failing to pay attention to the risks in favor of the thrill of the experience also initiated a deep psychological root system that positively connects me emotionally with forested environments. All those experiences were my first lessons in learning the value of slowing down. Sometimes slowing down may appear to others, and often oneself, as slacking off, but it's crystal clear now that those who can't slack off a little in favor of their own emotional/mental/physical health risk creating even more dangerous situations for themselves and others down the road.

ANY STORIES WE TELL OURSELVES ABOUT WHO WE ARE have a critical effect on how we understand and react or respond to every contact we have with both society and nature. Stories also evolve directly from the way we each develop into conscious beings focused on well-defined selves, balanced at that still point of awareness between whatever ignites a natural sense of wonder and inspiration and the human cultural matrix in which it emerges. If a child grew up in a privileged, *white*[ii], European-derived, Western culture during the 1950s and '60s, as I did, consciousness of self—as communicated through cultural stories, even those of my outdoor-loving family—did not include the concept of being an integral part of nature.

Everyone uses orientations to the outer world that are embedded at birth in the unique genetic and environmental mix feeding their access to intelligence. Over time, I've learned that, for me, the motivation to explore a new concept, mentally, first makes itself known within a chain of awareness that begins with physical experience, moving from there into emotions and finally into thoughts and words. Once the perception has reached the level of thoughtful analysis, the words that emerge to describe experience must often be either spoken to a sympathetic listener or written using stream of consciousness expression in order to translate the physical/emotional knowing into wording that others can easily understand. Expressing concepts first through movement, such as dance, facilitates translation into effective verbal communication for me. Listeners to my speech are generally treated to subconsciously emerging hand movements as a result, and often I use words more effectively while walking. For many others, the direction of that progression, involving physical awareness, emotion, and rational thought, seems to move in exactly the opposite direction.

---

ii. I italicize the words *white* and *black* throughout this book when they refer to people, because these words draw distinctions based on a cultural construct of racism, which defines a false hierarchy of human value based on skin pigmentation.

Chapter Two

Mind Over Matter

The deeply rooted, pervasive concept of mind over matter, with its lenthy historical development, dominated Western cultural attitudes between 1910 and 1980, the time now referred to as "the modern era." Because that time encompassed most of the twentieth century, its commonly held belief systems are still the most prevalent at all levels of Western culture today, in 2024. Similarly, the most prevalent belief systems that dominated Western culture during the first two generations of "the moderns" (aka, the modern era) originated in the Victorian era. The influence of modernism became especially apparent in the roaring twenties when young people like my grandparents took its premises to heart, challenging their parents' cultural perspectives. The second generation of "modern" young people gave birth to baby boomers, who initiated the cultural perspective of "postmodernism," a term still difficult to broadly define beyond a vaguely generalized sense of relativism. The most distinguishing characteristic can perhaps be described as valuing situational ethics over institutionalized codes of conduct.

Modernism spread farther and wider than Victorianism did by using the communication tools made possible by the technological and industrial focus at the heart of its value system.

Modern values now dictate most cultural norms in some form nearly everywhere on the planet, not just in Western culture. It's hard to say in any exact way where the hierarchical story thread of valuing mind over matter—the heart of the modernist approach to life—actually began. There are many stories holding pieces of the truth, as with any story about human history. However, the following quick overview, though hardly the whole truth from an archeological and anthropological perspective, approaches a reasonable enough synopsis for the purposes of this story.

Lynne Kelly's 2017 book *The Memory Code* is a good place to start. It explores what Western archeologists and anthropologists uncovered in the twenty-first century about the surprisingly accurate and comprehensive ways in which knowledge was transferred in ancient, nonliterate societies whose oral histories have long been thought to be as unreliable as the game of "telephone," in which a whispered phrase becomes unrecognizable after having been passed from ear to ear around a circle of players. By contrast, Kelly documents unique forms of memory devices capable of accurately transmitting oral histories over centuries. Their methods for recalling historical details, which included the use of memory devices (explained below) and training in how to use them, are still in use today in remote places around the globe.

Kelly describes how such memory devices included various combinations of landscape features, drawings, dances, and songs linked to each other, which served as surprisingly intricate systems to record and remember traditional oral histories for those initiated into their use. By means of these devices, which included specific land features, such as significant rocks, hills or water bodies, the most skilled minds were taught to memorize detailed information about food, medicine, animal behavior, taxonomy, astronomy, etc. Using colorful, imaginative dances, songs, and stories triggered by each land feature, cultural memes and the social value of wisdom were transferred among those with the longest memories within these nomadic tribes, who were also revered as the wisest. Her research suggests that such societies valued human bodies and the earth because aspects of both could be used to augment the societies' ability to memorize reams of data unavailable to modern Western minds without the aid of books or computers. The closest parallel today is the practice of competing in memory competitions, for fun, using what are called "memory palaces."

The gender of those gifted with wisdom made no difference in ancient days, according to Kelly. What mattered was the extent to which the mind could be cultivated through rigorous memory training. Those who were adept at this form of memorization were able to retain huge amounts of information without written words by associating stories with specific sight, sound, smell, and touch experiences available in particular places. These experiences could also be sparked using portable items carved or painted with geometric designs that recalled such places to these skilled keepers of cultural knowledge.[1]

It's still widely believed by the general public and many anthropologists, whether or not it's actually true, that when techniques of agriculture arose, nomadic tribes began to establish and sustain communities in particular places, an evolutionary theory explored in Jared Diamond's book *Guns, Germs, and Steel*, originally published in 1997. In this way of conceiving prehistory, power in many such social structures began to shift away from women and men gifted in the ways uncovered by Kelly's research, transferring instead to those able to amass material wealth in one place and to protect it using violent defense. Diamond describes the importance of this shift as lying in the association of violence, rather than wisdom, with power, establishing violence as a key initiating element in social structures featuring an ultimate metaphysical power at the apex of a massive, God-given hierarchy of life. Those who were more vulnerable, such as women, children, and elders, were gradually demoted in such societies. Similarly, the earth and all its creatures gradually lost their sacred value, except in terms of their value to support human life.

In this way, the power to determine the course of history shifted in many societies to those with the ability to accumulate wealth, and the most violently powerful among them were seen as blessed by one or more supernatural beings, understood to rule the world using a mysterious set of laws that only the most powerful could decipher and publicly interpret. Diamond describes how this structure can be seen in some form across early agrarian civilizations of all kinds. Generally, some people in each civilization played roles of defense for the blessed wealthy, spending their lives in a warrior class of some type. Others began to spend their lives communing with the ultimate power in enclaves separated from society, unsullied by the violent use of weapons, except indirectly under the protection of the politically powerful. The words they used told stories of their deep relationship with the ultimate power, understood to be speaking uniquely to and through them as the designated priestly class.[2]

Religions of all varieties came to govern hand in hand with political and military systems as a result of the burgeoning of hierarchical social structures. Men gradually came to dominate these spheres because of their natural physical strength and capacity for violence. Women in turn began to be valued mainly for their ability to produce heirs. They were also seen and described in cultural stories about value as deeply connected with the earth because their bodies were the source of human life, just as the earth was the source of animal and plant life, increasingly understood as mere material resources for feeding, housing, and clothing society. This increasingly entrenched belief system held that men's bodies had been created in the physical image of the dominant god and charged with the responsibility to mediate between divine and material realms. In such societies, women were understood to be possessions of men (due to women's immersion in the messy material world of blood, babies, and human milk), over which women had no control beyond the quality of their relationship with their children's father.

As a result of this developing thought system, women's bodies were increasingly seen as either the seductive, enticing, entertaining, and necessary release valves for men's stress or the mysteriously sacred producers of human life. As such, women's bodies were to be used and valued mainly for men's sensual pleasure or put on a highly protected pedestal of sacred, virtuous motherhood unsullied by sex for pleasure. An inherent contradiction arose as a result, creating cultural stories to describe women's bodies—and bodies in general—as impure, material distractions from the mental/spiritual purity necessary to connect with the realms of the divine.

Maintaining control over women's bodies and their sensual allure became an essential tool for maintaining the power of the mighty, which also came to mean that the women who were most docile, beautiful, and capable of bearing healthy children became highly valued possessions of wealthy men. Those same men sought out secret interludes with passionate women willing to use the sensuality of their bodies in hidden, dangerous ways, often because they had lost life-sustaining support through the death of husbands, fathers, or whatever males had formerly fed and housed them, so they used their bodies as the only means available to feed themselves and their children in societies that saw women as possessions. As monotheistic societies developed, men who focused their lives on spiritual connection to the divine strove to remain "pure" through the practice of celibacy and came to be understood as closer to god as a result of their ability to control what had come to be imagined as debased physical urges, a stark example of the mind over matter value system.

This perspective reigned in various forms throughout history until modernist cultural constructs began to rise in the West in concert with the science of evolution and the dawn of the industrial revolution in the mid-1800s. Modernism dramatically caught fire in the early twentieth century when my grandparents were children. Science rose in value, due in large part to increasingly profitable business ventures made possible by the mechanization of labor. Rational, evidence-based analysis began to replace subjective, belief-centered understanding as the cultural norm of the ruling elite. Scientific discoveries began to increasingly contradict religious belief systems that had long rationalized entrenched hierarchies of power. The story of mind over matter that led to the advancement of science was, however, spawned by the hierarchical belief system that had reigned since the beginning of agriculture. Valuing mind over matter, rational analysis, and mental constructs over bodies, earth, nature, and emotional experience still forms a context unconsciously internalized by people the world over as the basis for human identity.

MY PERSONAL INTRODUCTION to cultural consciousness began with *Life*[3] magazine, which arrived on the living room coffee table in our little Cape-style house in suburban New Jersey promptly at three o'clock every Friday afternoon. Memories of this time date back to 1959, the year I turned five. The mailman took the iconic magazine out of his great leather sack and deposited it in the mailbox on his daily walking route. I would sometimes reach for and leaf through it, either because it was too dark to play outside and dinner was nearly ready or because my younger sister needed help putting on her jacket and couldn't find her mittens before we climbed into the big round, heavy Oldsmobile to drive to the commuter rail station to pick up my father. He arrived there around 7:00 p.m. after working all day in a corporate law office in New York City.

The mailman and the weekly copy of *Life* were part of a predictable, comfortable rhythm that supported the flow of living I took for granted, never imagining any other pattern as possible. This was just the way life was. That regularly repeating pattern also included the milkman who delivered quart-sized glass bottles of milk with cream floating on top to our doorstep every Monday morning. He collected the empties my mother left in a small insulated metal flip-top box outside the front door and left fresh bottles in their place. Sometimes the Fuller Brush man would come to the door to show my mother his suitcase full of new brushes designed for all kinds of different uses, from cleaning milk bottles to smoothing hair. Sometimes an encyclopedia salesman would show up and once we even bought a set, with twenty-six volumes that contained a wealth of easily digestible information about nearly every topic I could imagine. I referred to it when researching any school project all the way through high school.

On Sunday mornings, my younger sister and I would sit on the living room rug in our full-skirted dresses, sometimes with fluffy petticoats beneath, bobby socks with ruffles at the top under our best shoes, with straps instead of laces, and so much nicer than the usual pair of brown Oxfords we wore to school. We sat on the rug feeling pretty, holding our ears close to the cabinet-sized Magnavox radio and listening to fairy tales and songs presented by "The Singing Lady" before heading out in the Oldsmobile to Quaker meeting at the local library. There, a seed was planted in the fertile ground of my open, curious child's mind, which began to send out tiny roots. Those roots connected to a concept that was reinforced weekly by this gathering of maybe fifty adults and a few children: that the mystery at the heart of life, named God, was not a man with a white beard sitting on a cloud somewhere, as the Bible stories my father read to us in first day school (Sunday school) seemed to imply. God was instead something wholly mysterious that permeated everything and spoke to everyone through their own hearts. Sitting quietly, my father explained, one might hear what he described as a "call," and the only time anyone said anything in Sunday meeting was when they felt called to do so by that mysterious internal voice. That idea was totally confusing and wonderful at the same time. It was very comforting to know that God was right there with me all the time and that I could learn somehow to hear the mysterious voice calling me to do or say things. Unfortunately, like most children, I had a very difficult time sitting still for the twenty minutes we children remained with the adults. Usually I did what I could to get a seat next to the bookcases so that I could read book titles when I got so bored I wanted to jump out of my skin. I deeply trusted and loved my playful father, though, so the seed of the Quaker concept of God became my root understanding of the mystery everyone referred to as spirit.

The steady rhythm of this pattern of living kept my fears and periodic nightmares in check, providing comfort through numerous bouts of tonsillitis and one round each of measles, mumps, and chicken pox, which were normal hazards for most US children before 1964. The central axis of my world was my mother, who stayed home to care for us and make a home for our family in the same way that every other mother I encountered also did.

Mom loved to paint, cook, and garden and never seemed to stop calmly and steadily moving. The cozy house my younger sister and I shared with my parents was nestled into a neighborhood of grassy hills to roll and sled down, trees to climb, and small wooded areas to explore. It also had backyards where you could sleep outside under the summer stars with only a pillow, a sleeping bag, and a good friend. Our backyard had a large sandbox my father built for baking mud pies. Our basement held a huge box of brightly colored, flowing cast-off clothes and shoes to enhance characters we created with our friends in hundreds of games of make-believe, and the plays staged on our backyard patio that sometimes emerged from them. These were performed for whomever we could coax into serving as audience, usually our mothers, though sometimes also a few fathers if a play developed on a sunny weekend.

My best friend and I walked about a mile to school, climbing what we called "the big hill," or rode a school bus to the next town, depending on the year. My sister and I listened to bedtime stories nearly every night, read by my father with great enthusiasm, then listened to him play piano sonatas, the notes wafting up from the basement where he practiced, as we drifted off to sleep in the finished half of the attic two floors above. We built snowmen and snow forts in the great white piles winter brought. We raked leaves into mounds and jumped out of front yard trees into them, laughing and rolling around before they became the final piles that all neighborhood fathers burned in their yards with great fanfare on early fall evenings. Pungent, crackling bonfires lined the streets as darkness fell and threw the aroma of autumn into every breath of the cold, crisp air.

By the time I turned ten, however, life as I knew it had begun to tilt, opening into a much larger, more unpredictable world. I was a nine-year-old fourth grader the day President John F. Kennedy was assassinated. The day had begun as usual with a kiss and hug for my mother and a walk in the sunshine up the hill to school with my best friend. By midday I was sitting at my desk in Mrs. May's classroom and learning French words when an announcement interrupted us from the intercom box on the wall, saying that the president had been shot and school was canceled. Everything just stopped right in the middle of class! Being released suddenly from school due to a tragic event in the outside world was a never-considered impossibility until it happened. Unbeknownst to me, that earthshaking jolt to my imagination opened a deep psychological chasm for me—and for multitudes of others—which began to change the inner and outer contours of everything we had formerly imagined as dependably repeating natural patterns of human life.

In a November 1981 article in the *New York Times*, "The 50's Family and Today's," Andrew Cherlin describes how the decade of the 1950s was often held up by *American*[i] traditionalists of European descent as the standard by which individual character and the quality of family life in the United States should be measured.[4] That was a natural enough assumption for those whose ancestors came from Europe and whose stories of history and cultural values had defined the foundations of this country's social and political institutions for centuries. From the country's founding until the 1960s, such stories were institutionalized in ways that continuously suppressed or erased knowledge of contradictory accounts. The truncated story of history that was accepted as common knowledge was therefore the only one available to most of those who either began to grow up or began to rear children in the '50s, including all of my nuclear family, except my youngest sister, born in 1963. By the time the 1960s began to come into view, however, many elements of US culture had begun to change and have continued on that new trajectory ever since. The divorce rate, for example, more than doubled as statistical trends returned to the trajectory they had long been on before the post war years of the 1950s briefly interrupted them. Simultaneously, the average age of first marriage rose and birth rates dropped.[5]

Comparisons between the '50s, as somehow representative of US cultural patterns, and patterns seen in succeeding decades leaves a mistaken impression of typical patterns of marriage and

---

i. I italicize the word *American*, in many places where its use refers to the country also known as the USA because the people who lived in this land before the colonists arrived never fully joined the union or legally ceded their territory, North America, to the colonists, even though the colonists began to call themselves American.

childbearing, however. Family life in the '50s, which seemed like an Edenic capstone to the country's growing worldwide significance to those of European descent, was actually far different from anything that had ever existed before in the US.[6] As a result, the experience of children like me, who grew up as members of the baby boom generation, was historically unique with an unusual set of joys, expectations, and stresses.

When considered in historical context, what truly characterized US society in the 1950s were stark cultural aberrations. A primary family pattern mourned by *American* cultural traditionalists of European descent who consider themselves politically conservative, for instance, concerns the age at which women have historically married in the US. In the late 1950s, about three-quarters of the US population of women between the ages of twenty and twenty-four were already married, while in 1981 that was generally true for only about half of US women.[7] Such statistics have often been erroneously used as evidence to suggest that young adults were increasingly rejecting the traditional age of marriage in response to rebellious baby boomers like me, who in one way or another initiated and fed what came to be known as the counterculture. Confronting that inaccuracy is essential to telling a more resilient story of what happened to US culture in the '60s. The truth is that only half of young people were married by the age of twenty-four in the late '70s, which was a similar number of married young people at that age in the US between 1890 and 1940.[8] In that context, marriage could only be seen as increasingly postponed in the decades afterward through an extremely narrow comparative lens, juxtaposing the number of young people typically married by age twenty-four in the decades before and after the '50s, fifty percent, to the number typically married by that age in the decade of the '50s, seventy-five percent.[9]

The one- or two-child family size that also became very common during the '50s was the size of the one I began to raise in the early '80s. That small family size is also consistent with long-term fertility trends in the United States but not with family sizes in the 1950s, which typically had at least three children, as the one in which I was raised did, and often more, like that of my second husband.[10]

There were also fewer divorces in the '50s than historical statistical patterns projected. In the protected bubble in which I grew, for example, there were no single parents at all, and I was aware of only two divorces of any adults I'd ever heard of or encountered by the end of high school. Divorce, however, had been on the rise in the US since at least the Civil War. Increases in divorce rates in the '50s were unusually small when the long view of changes to US families is taken into account. The number of divorces during the '60s and early '70s was large only in comparison to the uniquely slow rate of increase in the '50s.[11]

Conservative media pundits in the late 1970s, who held the views that Cherlin's research counters, predicted a return to the trends of the 1950s once the country could be rid of the countercultural self-absorption inflicted on the broader population by young hippies in the flaming '60s. In their estimation, baby boomers would eventually settle down to more conservative lifestyles when the instinctual urge to raise families kicked in. As a result, those pundits characterized such things as rock 'n' roll music as passing fads. Many of us in the first wave of the baby boom, those born between the mid-1940s and mid-1950s, knew better.[ii] Instead we began to cultivate what we imagined to be more just, equitable, interdependent, and ecologically nourishing ways to live, which we've continued to work toward over the full course of our lives.

---

ii. This definition of the time period defining the baby boom is my personal view of its vague boundaries, based on the people I have known and the common conditioning we all received.

Chapter Three

Nature and Nurture

On September 27, 1962, when I was an eight-year-old reveling in the natural world and continually opening to new levels of heartfelt connection between body and environment, society's consciousness about nature also began to open in ways that would profoundly influence the direction of my life. That was the date when a gifted marine biologist, author, and beacon of courageous inspiration, Rachel Carson, catalyzed the modern environmental movement with the publication of her book *Silent Spring*. The book contained a transformational exposé of the pesticide industry from a deeply scientific point of view using unusually lyrical language to describe the problem. She intentionally used that writing style to catch and hold the attention of a much wider audience than typical scientific writing ever could.

In that poetic style, *Silent Spring* laid out an irrefutable case for life's interconnectedness for millions of people. Its story stunned their moral imagination, waking them up to the perils of industrial chemicals. Until then the military industrial complex had been honored by most people as the leading edge of scientific progress by virtue of the heroic success its technological systems had employed to defeat Nazi Germany in WWII. An unprecedented level of citizen concern about air and water pollution rose with this new understanding, planting the seed that grew into the environmental movement. Eventually, Rachel Carson's words and the public reactions they spawned moved the hearts and minds of federal legislators enough to institute a new federal agency to oversee industrial activities, calling it the Environmental Protection Agency.[1]

The environmental movement gave birth in turn to Earth Day in 1970, a national celebration intended to keep memory and attention alive to the interconnected flow of earthly life. During the spring that bloomed as my sophomore year in high school neared completion, the celebratory concept and the colorful, public, outdoor fair-like gatherings it spawned in cities and towns throughout the country had music and food along with educational booths and presentations, providing a bright spot of community-centered joy and healing amid continuous images of caskets coming home from Vietnam in my go-to news source, *Life* magazine.

From the first time I encountered Rachel Carson's writing, not long after I graduated from college, her example repeatedly cropped up, always providing a badly needed flash of hope. She was a courageous, intelligent, passionate woman and a single mother (after adopting her niece's son following her niece's death), a culturally challenging position to sustain, which also became mine several decades later. She approached her challenges with qualities of imagination and heart to which I aspired and strove to emulate in the small ways I could. That admiration led me to delve more deeply into her life story each time her name surfaced, inspiring me yet again. A woman of great courage, Rachel Carson challenged the full military industrial complex in full-throated public protest at great personal risk. She also died from a disease directly associated with the lack of understanding and deliberate corporate obfuscation of the link between industrial agricultural practices, cancer, and medical treatments focused on symptoms of disease rather than their prevention through health-sustaining practices from farm to table.

Long before she wrote *Silent Spring*, Rachel Carson had been following the science of pesticides and their deadly effects on nature, which had been consistently and carefully glossed over by the chemical and agricultural industries that worked diligently to keep knowledge of those effects out of public view. [2] She believed after years of research that the new, powerful pesticides these industries had developed provided a very profitable way to adapt surplus wartime chemicals for peacetime purposes, especially DDT, which had first been put to widespread use in a powdered form on the skin of military troops fighting in WWII, successfully using it as a means to control the spread of disease carried by the lice that tormented them.[3]

Corporate titans, who had jumped on surplus DDT when WWII ended, built huge businesses and employed thousands of people to repurpose that chemical for use by gardeners and farmers. DDT and other army surplus chemicals began to be used everywhere without reserve, from the '50s through the early '60s, to control any aspect of nature imagined to be impeding the booming postwar economy. The wide use of DDT also supported the development of industrial-scale farming, designed by these same economic overlords to ensure that farmers would become consistent customers dependent on the insecticides, herbicides, fertilizers, and ever larger farm machinery their corporations produced. Those corporations deliberately kept public focus away from the ill effects that the chemicals and machines began to have on people, plants, animals, and the land and instead trumpeted the short-term growth of the bottom line in the corporate accounting books of farm machinery and fertilizer companies. That short-term bottom line was all that mattered to eager young executives who climbed the corporate ladder by selling whatever product their employers produced in order to increase profits. Few if any of them were aware of the extent of potential ill effects for the natural world that those products contained.

At the time *Silent Spring* was published, Carson had already made a name for herself as the most popular and widely respected science writer in the country through the magazine articles and books she had written about the ocean. In *Silent Spring* she used that prominent voice to capture the imagination of readers and hold the federal government accountable for the abuses of power that had foisted these chemicals on the unsuspecting public, assaulting people and the natural world under the guise of useful products produced by the military industrial complex. "Knowing what I do, there would be no future peace for me if I kept silent," she wrote to her dearest friend after sending the manuscript for *Silent Spring* to a publisher.[4] She was well aware at the time that speaking out against the pesticide industry would subject her to a barrage of cruel attacks by corporate and government interests, which is exactly what happened. She saw no moral alternative, nevertheless, to making a concerted attempt to shock humanity into a new kind of awareness about its relationship with and responsibility to life on Earth, due to the fundamental love she experienced for the natural world, the source of all her writing.[5]

Rachel Carson's iconic writing style gave *Silent Spring* the transformational ability to awaken public perception from docile acceptance into clear knowledge of the perils to both nature and health posed by substances deceptively marketed as panaceas to improve human life. Through her writing, she also challenged government institutions to take responsibility for regulating these chemicals, warning that corporate language used to package and commercialize them as consumer products also separated them from the research findings of several scientific disciplines, effectively erasing the truth. Strictly bounded research niches in academia at that time created virtual tunnel vision for most scientists studying various aspects of the deeply intertwined and deadly effects of these chemicals.[6]

When citizen protests took the risk of challenging these enmeshed systemic forces with incontestable evidence, Rachel Carson declared that they were "fed little tranquilizing pills of half-truth." In a striking statement that resonates even more deeply over a half century later, she pleaded, "We urgently need an end to these false assurances, to the sugar coating of unpalatable facts." Above all, she faulted the short-term focus of commercial interests for these deceitful practices. Carson countered the pesticide industry's messages with her description of "consequences remote in time and place" from poisons permeating a delicate and interdependent ecosystem from which no living thing can be isolated from any other within the continuous flow of time.[7]

It's a sad truth that due to her doctor's willful negligence, in addition to the cultural blindness of the medical community to the role played by toxic chemicals in catalyzing cancer, Rachel Carson was diagnosed with metastatic cancer in 1960, long after the disease had already spread beyond any possible help from the

medical community.[8] In June 1962, just before the first install-
ment of *Silent Spring* was published in *The New Yorker*, she heroically took to the sky to fly across the country for the first and last
time using some of her waning strength, knowing she faced death
in the next couple of years. She made the trip to fulfill a promise
she made before realizing the state of her illness, to deliver the
commencement address to that year's graduating class of Scripps
College, an all women's college in California, providing a clear
example of her faith in the power of women to change the world.
In her speech she handed the baton of the environment's defense
to the baby boom generation, telling graduates:

> Your generation must come to terms with the environ-
> ment. You must face realities instead of taking refuge
> in ignorance and evasion of truth. Yours is a grave and
> sobering responsibility, but it is also a shining oppor-
> tunity. You go out into a world where mankind is chal-
> lenged as it has never been challenged before to prove
> its maturity and its mastery, not of nature, but of itself.
> Therein lies our hope and our destiny.[9]

In 1963 President John F. Kennedy read *Silent Spring* and
demanded a congressional hearing to investigate and regulate
the use of pesticides. Despite her progressing terminal disease,
Rachel Carson didn't hesitate to go to Washington, DC, to
testify, an especially significant choice when you consider that
she was experiencing debilitating pain and exhaustion from
the radiation treatments she was receiving while her disease
relentlessly destroyed her body. With her testimony, President
Kennedy and his Science Advisory Committee were finally able

to invalidate the vicious verbal and print attacks against her arguments and her person. Heeding instead Carson's call for reason over unfounded emotional reaction, the first federal US policies were enacted to protect the natural environment upon which all life depends. [10]

Rachel Carson's story still inspires me on so many levels, especially considering that she was a woman scientist without a PhD or academic affiliation who nevertheless became the most powerful voice of resistance against ruinous public policy in a time when no one else was speaking up. She heroically endured simultaneous attacks from both cancer and powerful corporate and political critics. A spirited and deeply knowledgeable idealist, Rachel Carson was posthumously awarded the Presidential Medal of Freedom and died before the sea change in public awareness and resulting public policies ignited by *Silent Spring* came into being. Today a new crop of political and corporate institutions are once again threatening her hard-won legacy in different ways, but the energy she inspired lives on and continues to grow within a worldwide intersectional movement calling for climate justice.

There is an eight-year-old girl who loves to dance. Her best friend is taking ballet lessons. She wants to learn too. This girl visits her friend's dance class. She loves the way the girls are learning to move so gracefully, so precisely. She tells her mother with great enthusiasm about what she saw and how she too longs to learn to move that way. Her mother says no, she will hurt her legs if she takes ballet. Her legs and feet will turn out forever and her bones will not grow properly if she does.

This girl cries and begs her mother to change her mind. She stamps her foot, but still her mother says no and sends her to her room to calm down. This girl learns that dancing can be bad for her body. She learns that what her heart most wants to do can be bad for her healthy growth. She begins to understand also that her heart's desire is not always important. She also begins to question her heart's call.

This girl finds out about menstruation a year later from a friend. She tells her friend that her friend's mother must have some kind of disease because this girl's mother had never told her about menstruation. This girl can't believe that her mother would keep a secret from her about how girls' bodies work, a secret that is so important to her own life. When she returns home, this girl's mother tells her that her friend's mother does not have a disease. All women bleed once a month.

This girl gets very angry with her mother. How could she keep from her something so awful, so basic about her own body? Her mother apologizes and doesn't know what to say. She doesn't tell her that the blood gives women a special power. She doesn't explain that there are benefits that go along with it, wonderful feelings she has never had before. She never tells her anything about sex except the mechanics of it, which strikes the girl as disgusting. This girl does not want to grow up. She begins to question her mother's advice.

There is a ten-year-old girl who is learning to play the drums. She wants to play the snare drum in the marching band someday, yearning to make that impressive, loud, rhythmic noise that makes her toes tap and legs bounce whenever she hears it. She practices her drumroll endlessly on the little rubber practice pad she was given in school. Her drumsticks are her treasures. It sends shivers up her spine to think of marching with the high school band in those snazzy uniforms and rolling out the beat. She doesn't need to be told to practice, not the way she always has while learning to play the piano.

This girl is hurt and confused when her mother tells her that she will have to choose between the drums and the piano, but it would be a shame to quit the piano after seven years of hard work. This girl doesn't want to quit the piano. She knows how her playing pleases her parents. She doesn't understand why she's being asked to choose because she doesn't neglect her homework or piano practice to practice drumming. Instead she gives up precious hours of outdoor playtime.

Drumming makes this girl happy. She loses herself in the rhythm she can already create. She's been raving to her parents about how much she likes drumming and how quickly she's learning. Now she argues and pleads with her mother to no avail. Her mother tells her she just doesn't have time for both and will have to choose. It's her choice her mother tells her.

This girl feels very angry. She doesn't want to quit drumming, but she knows that's what will please her parents. She is not strong enough to stand up for herself. She needs their love. She quits drumming and two years later quits piano too.

THOUGH THE IMPACT on my consciousness was indirect, President Kennedy's shooting in 1963, which happened in the middle of the time period described above, refocused my attention onto the wider world. A continuous question rose about what was going on out beyond the cozy neighborhood where I lived. Many questions about politics and about power of all kinds, including that of my parents, began to hold and shape my attention deep beneath everything else on the surface of life.

The development of the human ego, which increasingly guides decision-making as we grow, evolves in a balancing exercise between physical and emotional life and the defining boundaries of our particular field of perception. Very young children naturally play with the experience of the moment when allowed to do so. They notice what's there and react without self-consciousness or any sense of *should*. Tiny babies have not yet experienced visual depth of field or boundaries of any kind when they first open their eyes. It's in learning physical boundaries that we conceptualize reality and discover how to manipulate *things*. While doing so, we are innocently and inexorably drawn into constructing a mental concept of body as *self*, something we increasingly learn to operate using our developing ego, which is inevitably influenced by the culture in which we were born.

ON AUGUST 28, 1963, a couple of months after I turned nine and while I was still learning to balance in climbing trees and walking atop backyard patio railings, Martin Luther King Jr. gave his famous "I Have a Dream" speech at the Lincoln Memorial in Washington, DC, to an unprecedented crowd of 250,000 nonviolent protesters whose appearance that day was another momentous event of the year 1963.[11] With that speech, given to a massive crowd, bigger than any seen before in the nation's capital, the balancing point maintained by force between *black* and *white Americans* began to tip within the country's cultural story. Systemic racism as a means to maintain power and control over institutionalized social structures started to wobble. That speech also marked a high point in the civil rights movement, which had begun to spread across the country in 1954, the year I was born, after the National Association for the Advancement of Colored People's (NAACP) legal strategy to end segregated education culminated in an affirming Supreme Court ruling. That 1954 case, *Brown v. Board of Education*, also ignited viciously violent resistance from *white* southerners in particular, but not only in the South.[12] Boston, the perceived bastion of liberalism and the hub of life in New England where I've spent the majority of my adult years, saw its own violent race riots in the mid-'70s as a new state law began to be implemented, which required busing students from *black* neighborhoods to schools in *white* neighborhoods, which my second husband encountered firsthand as a seminarian in the Boston University School of Theology.

Violent southern resistance to lawful integration in 1954 empowered the all-*white* male leaders of southern states to use a variety of tactics, such as lynching *black* men for any or no reason, to avoid the law's intended effect. Elected officials often participated in this horror. In the summer of 1955, fourteen-year-old Emmett Till was kidnapped and brutally murdered as part of this surge of anti-*black* violence. Loud, peaceful protests, which included both *black* and *white* participants, broke out all over the country in response, spawning the nationwide civil rights movement by December of that year.

Civil rights protests erupting all over the country began to coalesce as a movement in December 1955, when Rosa Parks, a seamstress and also secretary of the local chapter of the NAACP, was arrested. Her crime, under Southern Jim Crow laws, was refusing to move farther back from the first row of the back section of a bus, set aside for riders of color, in Montgomery, Alabama. She had been asked to do so by the bus driver because all seats in the front section, set aside for *white* passengers, had been filled. Rosa Parks' arrest that day led, five days later, to the formation of the Montgomery Improvement Association (MIA), which began planning a citywide bus boycott that continued for a year. Although the widely accepted story of that boycott today only gives her credit for refusing to move farther back on a racially segregated bus after a tiring workday, the truth is more nuanced. It can easily be imagined that Rosa Parks was making a deliberate personal protest in her role as a local civil rights leader, in addition to being tired. She knew of course that despite what the *white* bus driver wanted her to do, she had not breached the officially established racist color barrier for bus seating sections, and she had been harassed by the same bus driver in the past, so presumably she was also angry. As a result of her arrest following her refusal to change seats, she joined a group of other *black* civil rights leaders to form the executive committee that created the MIA, electing another member to be the organization's president, Dr. Martin Luther King Jr. As an executive committee member, she also worked briefly as a dispatcher for MIA's Transportation Committee, which created the volunteer transportation system that made the bus boycott possible, connecting people who usually needed to use the bus system to get to work with people who owned private cars and also with drivers of church-owned station wagons, resolving the transportation problems associated with the bus boycott. [13]

As I was turning six in 1960, NAACP Youth Council chapters held sit-ins at *whites*-only lunch counters in the South. I remember the pictures from those protests published in *Life* magazine as clearly now as they appeared in my six-year-old awareness. There was no need to read more than the photograph captions I could decipher because the pictures said it all. Those lunch counter protests inspired a wave of nonviolent direct action during John F. Kennedy's presidency. Large black-and-white photographs in *Life* depicted the 1961 Freedom Rides, in which *white* and *black* teenagers rode together on buses across the South, an unheard-of abomination in the eyes of many southerners. The students endured brutal violence nearly everywhere they stopped and *Life's* photographers caught those horrors on film, embedding more pictures and concepts about the outside world into my young memory. I also saw how the young people persisted, nevertheless, gaining more participants as they continued their Freedom Rides despite the violent pushback.

My parents supported the efforts of the protesters, calling them courageous. They briefly explained a little more about what was happening in answer to my *why* questions. Their words were introductory lessons in the awful truth of institutionalized injustice. Hundreds of demonstrations erupted in cities and towns across the nation in response to the violence levied against the young, peaceful protesters. National and international media coverage of police using fire hoses and attack dogs against *black* child protesters stunned the Kennedy administration and deeply impacted young readers like me. President Kennedy called in federal troops to quell the bombings and riots that followed in Birmingham, Alabama, on May 11, 1963, just before I turned nine, and on June 19, 1963, he sent a comprehensive civil rights bill to Congress. Public support for the bill grew significantly as a result of the March on Washington for Jobs and Freedom on August 28, 1963. After Kennedy's assassination on November 22nd, his vice president, Lyndon Baines Johnson, became president, [14] ultimately signing the bill into law on July 2, 1964.

LIFE'S PREDICTABLE RHYTHM and what I imagined it meant were permanently altered by Kennedy's assassination, as they were for millions of others. The tears gathering on the lids of my beloved fourth grade teacher's eyes as she dismissed us so early from school told me that something very important was very wrong. Mrs. May had always been a tower of kind certainty and cheerful strength. Equally jarring was the realization that I had never seen her, or any other adult, cry.

My father stayed home from work the day of President Kennedy's funeral. He also brought the television up to the living room from its banishment in the basement, another unheard-of event, especially since none of us was sick, it was daytime, and the whole family was actually encouraged to gather in front of it. Black-and-white images of the president's cortege crawled across the screen as a somber parade made its way through throngs of people who were also pausing their lives in Washington, DC. It seemed very strange to spend the day watching something so distant, sad, and ultimately boring, but I paid attention, mostly out of curiosity about my father's behavior. He had stayed home from work to watch television! He said we were watching in order to honor the president. That was confusing and impressive since the president and his family wouldn't have any way of knowing we were doing it.

Walter Cronkite, the grandfatherly voice of reason who delivered all kinds of bad news during my youth, narrated the gruesome details of how Caroline Kennedy and her little brother, John Jr., had lost their father. Caroline, I realized, was the same age as my younger sister, and someone had shot her father through the head, splattering her beautiful mother with blood and brains. I felt so sad for her and for her very little brother, losing their father, especially in that violent, public way, when they were even younger than I was, all of which seemed inconceivable. I couldn't understand why anyone would even think of perpetrating such a heinous act against any young family, especially not that of a very popular president. My protected bubble world had been pricked and had begun to seriously deflate.

When I repeatedly asked why it had happened as we watched the lugubrious procession, my father said he couldn't explain it either but told me a little about power, politics, and government and how and why the rules we live by in our country are made. It was shocking to think that a fight about the rules my father described could be so intense that a very popular young president, one even nine-year-old children like me knew something about, could be killed in cold blood right in front of news cameras. Yes, he was riding in the back seat of an open-topped car with his beautiful wife, but huge throngs of well-wishers lined the sidewalks of Dallas, Texas, and lots of men surrounded the president to protect him. Even *Life* couldn't explain the assassination when I checked it out later, though I carefully examined all the pictures of what had happened, scanning them intently for something the authorities might have missed. From then on I paid close attention to everything I came across about power and politics, well before I had any real idea of what those words meant.

Another jolt to my perception of life came when our family moved to Princeton, New Jersey, in the middle of the fall term of my fifth-grade year, 1964, leaving behind the cozy neighborhood I loved. The move dropped us into a bigger town and a brand-new house in a brand-new housing development. Mud and partially constructed houses now provided the venues we used as climbing apparatus when workmen were not around, and created the background for our imaginitive play. In a new town with a new school and different children, a different life altogether began to unfold. I also had a new little sister who was only a year old.

At first the move seemed like a grand adventure, but soon the new situation left me with my first real sense of loss. My best friend was too far away to keep up with, and none of the new friends I began to make could replace the special bond we'd had. The new bi-level house never quite felt like home either. For the first time I had a bedroom of my own, but it was on the finished half-basement level while the rest of the family slept upstairs. Because the house had been built into a hill, giving the illusion of a slightly smaller house from the front, my bedroom on the lower floor also opened at ground level to the backyard from the family room, adjacent to my bedroom. At the other end of the hall was the door to the garage and the short flight of stairs to the rest of the house. My room had three windows in the front of the house at about eye level for me, looking out at the level of the lawn.

The rest of the family had rooms adjoining one hallway upstairs, which led to the living room and kitchen. My room was the largest bedroom, or maybe the size of my parents', but it was set apart from the family by two sets of five or six stairs. One set went down from the kitchen to the landing at the front door and another descended to its end directly opposite the laundry room. Family life, for the most part, took place upstairs. As much as I tried to make the best of my new situation, pretending I liked it by consciously projecting what I imagined was confident independence, I never felt at home in that room, even after I was allowed to paint it lavender. As much as I tried not to notice, I felt separated and alienated, and I missed the company of the sister I'd shared a room with in the old house.

In the years after the move I still reached for *Life* as it lay on the coffee table but with increasingly less sense of its power to reflect a fascinating world. A vague trepidation about the adult culture I would too soon have to enter replaced it. *Life*'s pictures and accompanying stories were short enough for an active preteen to sit still to consider, but they raised many more questions than they answered as they brought home iconic images of the mid-sixties. In addition to the civil rights movement, there were photos of the Vietnam War and the growing protests against it and images of the women's liberation movement, pictures that were shaping much more than the backdrop of memory along the way. As ever more of those stories and pictures unfolded, it became clear that although the times were changing, as Bob Dylan informed young people, they weren't likely getting better and would probably get worse before I became an adult. Nevertheless, I would somehow have to find a path into adult responsibility and leave home, as every previous child in my family had done for generations.

Despite grave misgivings about the realities hidden in the outside world, I was also hungry for adventure and desperate to find out who I was outside the enmeshed cocoon of safety my parents had created. I fretted in near panic later, however, underneath the veneer of high school success as a cheerleader, multisport athlete, and school and community service youth leader, wondering how I'd ever find a way to live happily in an adult world that had brought the assassinations not only of President Kennedy but in all too quick succession the two remaining idols of my generation, Martin Luther King Jr. and Robert F. Kennedy, the torchbearers of hope after JFK's death. It seemed increasingly unlikely that our country's story would be able to somehow right itself and begin moving toward the just world that everyone under thirty seemed to be crying out for in the plethora of protest movements rolling out all over the country.

As a young adult, I never stopped wondering what it was about the civilization I had been born into that would give birth to the despicable acts pictured in *Life* magazine during that time and on what grounds anyone in their right mind would want to become part of that world or willingly take positions of decision-making responsibility within it. From where I stood, it all looked like a demented time bomb that every adult had to somehow dance around in order to make a living. That question about modern society haunted me even as I did my best to push it away and carry on.

BETTY FRIEDAN'S BOOK *The Feminine Mystique* was another seminal event of 1963, my ninth year. Of course I read about it in *Life*, and although I didn't read the book until much later, simply reading the article as the curious girl that I was, seeking the best path into womanhood, imprinted my awareness with a message that would powerfully affect the conscious balance I later struck as an adult, between lived experience and social perception. Published on February 17, 1963, *The Feminine Mystique* is often credited with igniting second-wave feminism by revealing a psychological landscape of hidden pain behind the widespread ideal of feminine domesticity in the rationalized world of post-World War II US ideology. Freidan asserted that the stifling of career opportunities for middle-class women like my mother who wanted to marry and raise children—by closing the door to careers in anything other than "homemaking"—was causing deep and widespread discontent in many households. Her research delineated how women were subtly and not so subtly coerced into serving in the homemaking role through institutionally enforced cultural structures that were constantly echoed in women's magazines and advertising, as well as by the Freudian psychologists and college professors women turned to for advice. Friedan's research revealed that all these cultural resources reflected and served to perpetuate a domestic ideal that left women deeply unhappy, if not clinically depressed, across the economic and racial spectrum.[15]

Reverberations from the findings in *The Feminine Mystique* had a powerful effect on girls like me who were on the brink of puberty and paying increasing attention to cultural messages about how to become women we could respect. Friedan began *The Feminine Mystique* with a survey conducted among her former Smith College classmates, through which she discovered that many felt depressed even though they possessed the 1950s cultural ideal of a feminine life. All of them had husbands, beautiful homes, and children. "What more could they possibly want?" was the question often asked if they complained about their life circumstances. Expanding her study, Friedan identified a pervasive sense of depression shared by a great many women from every walk of life—"the problem that has no name"—which is not a class- and race-based problem as it is still described in some circles. Instead she found that it existed among women throughout all sectors of society. Significantly, she was the first to say that by suppressing women's personal growth, society was losing a vast reservoir of human potential.[16]

The impact of *The Feminine Mystique* was cataclysmic because it directed young women's attention away from their personal situations as the primary cause of their distress, reorienting it toward a societal basis of their psychological problems. That realization stirred many fresh out of college in the early '60s to engage in political and social activism, hoping to realize more opportunities to advance into professional careers rather than remain mired in the secretarial pool, on the hospital nursing staff, or in the K–12 teaching pool, the few places educated women could find work at the time as long as they remained unmarried.

Friedan faced some negative reactions from women who enjoyed their roles as mothers and homemakers who understood their work as a vocation and a critically important, creative form of meaningful employment (despite its lack of financial remuneration), a view that career professionals (men) who benefited from their wives' work at home gave lip service to, all while masking their unspoken perception that such work entailed only drudgery. Friedan also received hundreds of letters from women describing how *The Feminine Mystique* had changed their lives. Her book has sold over two million copies since 1963 and has been translated into many languages. Thousands of copies are still being sold today.[17]

THERE IS A TWELVE-YEAR-OLD GIRL whose body is changing. She doesn't want to grow up. She doesn't want to become a woman. Women don't climb trees and run around outside. Women don't do handstands or balance on fences. She doesn't want to do what her mother does. She feels emotions like fire on the prairie where she was born. Try as she does to contain them in order to please her parents, they burn so strongly that she is often reprimanded for too much expression—of joy, anger, pain.

This girl comes to think of her feelings as handicaps in the world of people. She begins to believe that the world is ruled by the brain, not the heart. This girl now feels truly free only in the mountains, in the woods, and by the ocean. These are safe places to unleash her fire with abandon, to feel alive again, but this girl can only get to a little patch of woods sometimes after school when she's not too busy. She sees the ocean once a year and the mountains hardly at all.

There is a thirteen-year-old girl who wears a bra for the first time. This girl feels like the bra is made of neon. After dinner she runs downstairs and rips it off, putting on an old, loose sweatshirt to hide her chest lumps. She is forced to wear the bra again a couple of weeks later so that the boys won't stare at her nipples, but she feels as though she's wearing some kind of elaborate engineering construction, not a piece of clothing. She hates it.

This girl can't understand why her friends are so happy to be on the brink of womanhood. When she first needs to wear a menstrual pad, she feels as though she's wearing a football between her legs. She cries about it so much that her mother gives her tampons for her second period. They help but constantly leak. This girl hates the business of becoming a woman, and she's so embarrassed around boys that she can hardly speak to them. They seem like Martians.

There is a fourteen-year-old girl who has friends who are boys. She wants to connect with them, but her mother tells her that she can't call them on the phone about anything because they will think she's trying to get them to go on dates with her. Her mother tells her that these boys won't be her friends anymore if she calls them. Her mother's words don't seem right to this girl, but she worries a lot about what the boys might think and doesn't call them.

This girl and her mother have many arguments about hemlines and leg shaving, ear piercing, and stockings. Her mother doesn't want this girl to have anything to do with miniskirts or any of the other things teenage girls are beginning to wear to make themselves feel stylish and pretty. Her mother especially doesn't want her to wear makeup. Her father never touches her anymore, except for a stiff hug when he gets home from work. This girl misses the physical games they played when she was little. She hates her body. She gets the message that her sexuality is bad somehow, something dangerous and dirty, something that nice girls hide.

There is a fifteen-year-old girl who sees that there are plenty of nice girls who dress stylishly and attractively, use makeup, shave their legs, and wear reasonably short skirts while still gaining respect, getting good grades, and achieving social popularity among their peers. This girl starts to be more successful in standing up to her parents. She starts to build a suit of emotional armor that thickens and solidifies, closing in and protecting the hurt little wild spirit inside. This girl still tries to please her parents by behaving mostly as they wish. She needs their approval and love to feel good about herself.

There is a sixteen-year-old girl who is beginning to feel very confused about who she is because she knows very well that the things her heart most desires are not always acceptable and generally not important. They are just for fun and some of them are dangerous and will get her into trouble if she lets them out of the shadows. Sometimes they slip out anyway, and this girl has a wild adventure that feels risky and electrically intense because it contains forbidden elements of passion she must usually deny. She tells herself that these times don't count; they aren't really who she is. This girl strengthens her armor after any such episode, especially if her parents find out.

There is an eighteen-year-old woman who doesn't know who she is. She's heading off to college in a couple of months and has no idea what she wants out of life, except a husband and children for company. She believes she can't make a living as a dancer or drummer, a gym teacher, artist, or novelist because these things aren't really important. They are recreation. She can't seem to find something important that she also likes to do. She knows she loves the outdoors. Maybe geology would be a good subject to focus on, but she hasn't enjoyed science and math since junior high school due to teaching strategies that served only to undermine her interest. She shrugs with frustration when she thinks about careers, telling herself that she'll figure it out later and heads for the beach to ride the waves and scout the sand for boyfriends. This girl is always too shy to talk to new boys, but she dreams of a white knight in surfer's clothing who'll sweep her off her feet and show her how to live happily ever after.

Chapter Four

Social Protest
with a Backbeat of Funk

Anyone who has lived long enough experiences how cultural change happens in unpredictable ways, playing out in a similar dynamic to the one unfolding within their personal experiences of psychological and physical development, or even in weather patterns that change in small, unnoticed shifts, building momentum in unseen ways that ultimately lead to major, dramatic changes affecting everyone. A mythical butterfly flaps its wings on one side of the planet, moving a tiny breeze that goes on to blend with innumerable others to become a storm by the time it reaches the opposite side.

The culture-challenging events associated with the sixties could be imagined as a huge flock of butterflies beginning to flap its wings in countries all over the globe, especially in the West. Endless questioning by young people opened everything to examination in ways that had never been possible before. Those butterfly wings grew exponentially in number as the sixties moved into the early seventies, just as I was graduating from high school. In Charles Dickens' famous opening words from *A Tale of Two Cities*, "It was the best of times, it was the worst of times," a sentiment that is so often true and certainly felt that way to baby boomers. Partly as a result of that feeling, a widespread loss of faith in traditional Western authority structures ignited within a cacophony of youthful questioning.

Traditional authority structures in the West had until then succeeded in maintaining wide acceptance of cultural institutions, especially the military industrial complex, which had been built and expanded so effectively to support the Allies in WWII that it began to take on a life of its own in the war's aftermath, reshaping and rigidifying thought systems embedded in its authority structure and recasting every occupation as some kind of "industry." The rationalized value underlying that view—conceiving of life as a huge mechanized system—promoted the idea that the efficiency of mass production could be applied to nearly every form of human work and in its broadest sense could be used as a key measurement to determine the health of national economies. The quality of life for those who worked the production line was not much of a concern to those at the apex of the economic hierarchy, except to ensure workers' willingness to keep working at their mind-numbing jobs. It was widely believed that those working the bottom rungs of the cultural ladder held their jobs because of the level of merit they each brought to their work and that if those workers had possessed more intelligence and initiative, they would have been able to "pull themselves up by their bootstraps" without anyone's help, something that even the titans of industry believed they had done, ignoring the institutionalized cultural context crucial to their success.

By the mid-sixties, baby boomers began to question as never before the continuous confidence in the authority of government, patriarchy, progress, capitalism, and the concept of violent punishment as a reasonable solution to problems believed to stem from "character" (such as addiction and homosexuality), as well as acceptance of *white*, European-derived cultural superiority. A template was also taking shape for organizing and implementing peaceful, sustained protests, strongly igniting activism nationally and internationally. The simple, powerful actions and courage demonstrated by Rosa Parks as she worked as a member of the executive committee of the Montgomery Improvement Association to plan and personally initiate the Montgomery, Alabama, bus boycott set a precedent that was further developed and expanded under Dr. Martin Luther King Jr.'s leadership. The example set by the MIA in its successful bid to integrate the buses in Montgomery caused civil rights organizing to explode across the US in the mid-sixties—as I was beginning to pay attention to politics as a preteen—informing activists of all stripes about effective grassroots organizing tactics.

People young and old, of every skin color, were inspired to stand up in multiple ways against institutionalized Jim Crow policies via the huge protests organized and led by Dr. King. The civil rights movement gave birth to and blended with the anti–Vietnam War movement, especially among baby boomers, those both directly and indirectly affected by the military draft. Nearly everyone had relatives, friends, or classmates drafted into military service against their will. The huge waves of protest that began to roll out everywhere in the US also ignited violent rioting in cities across the country, particularly in the wake of Dr. King's assassination. As the anti–Vietnam War protests built alongside the civil rights movement, college students began to take over administration buildings for weeks at a time, halting any possibility of normal functioning until student demands were met. Ubiquitous among their demands was the removal of military recruitment offices and ROTC classes from college campuses.

All these protests had a backbeat of funk and a melody enhanced for the first time by electronic amplification, not only voices with microphones but also instruments. In an era without the Internet, when transistor radios were the new technology and music was not yet a corporately controlled monolith, the new, loud, demanding music spread the story of protest to millions of ears through easily understood lyrics. Guitarists began to play dissonant, slashing chords, and drums could be heard from miles away. In what had earlier been dubbed "a good beat you can dance to" by teenagers on the '50s television program *American Bandstand*, the top forty most popular songs were broadcast in a "hit parade" that changed from week to week, with the top ten or twenty playing over and over along with humorous, enthusiastic, and often edgy commentary from popular DJs like Wolfman Jack in Chicago and Cousin Brucie in New York City, the DJ I listened to throughout high school whenever I could get control of a radio.

Folk protest ballads from the '30s and '40s, written and sung by Woodie Guthrie and Pete Seeger to energize the labor movement, began to be repurposed and widely popularized by a new generation, including Joan Baez, Bob Dylan, Arlo Guthrie, and Peter, Paul and Mary, among many others as the '60s unfolded. These were not mere love songs or the sweet, melancholy tributes to the exigencies of life that had characterized popular music in the past. They were calls to action, anthems for a generation no longer willing to simply buy into the status quo that was killing so many of their own, in Vietnam and through racist brutality everywhere.

Sitting on the sixth-grade playground one sunny spring day in 1965, I was thrilled at the opportunity to learn the words to Bob Dylan's "Blowin' in the Wind" and "Mr. Tambourine Man," which laid down deep tracks in my young heart. One of the most powerful of the songs that became '60s anthems—"We Shall Overcome"—which still galvanizes hope, vision, and commitment in discouraging times, was first sung by Lucille Simmons as she led a tobacco workers' protest against a South Carolina cigar factory in 1945. "Where Have All the Flowers Gone" was another protest song that gained new life. Written by Pete Seeger in 1955 and popularized by Peter, Paul and Mary a decade later, it was a song that nearly every young person learned in the '60s. The words and melodies to both songs are permanently embedded in my memory. I learned them on the same playground where I enjoyed swinging as high as I could on the wonderful swing set there, pumping the swing on its long chain high enough for the chain to jerk for a second at the top of its arc to make me laugh. I later sang the same songs with my daughters whenever we took long car trips. Aretha Franklin's "Respect" and songs by Marvin Gaye, including "What's Going On?," were two of hundreds more songs that came later and kept the protest element alive in rock 'n' roll.

In 1964, the year before I began to learn those songs, my family had just moved to Princeton and the Beatles had become my major musical touchstone. I was able to listen to their music instead of simply reading about them in *Life* magazine that year because I made fast friends with a girl two houses up the street who also had a younger sister the same age as mine and a brother in between. They were not only allowed to listen to the Beatles on their home stereo, their parents actually enjoyed rock music. Since both parents also worked during the day and their young babysitter liked the music too, we could play all the records we wanted and turn up the stereo's volume as far as our ears could stand. We couldn't get enough of the Beatles, Herman's Hermits, and all the groups from "the British Invasion." Belting out the lyrics along with the records, learning how to do every popular dance step our friends could teach us—including the Twist, the Jerk, and the Swim—and being energized by the drumbeats and clanging electric guitar chords inspired jubilant, rambunctious dancing.

When I was in seventh grade, my parents finally acquiesced to my constant begging for a radio, allowing me to listen to the music I loved somewhere other than in the upstairs living room where the family stereo lived. They still did not countenance rock 'n' roll music but had come to understand that it was not going away for young people. Perhaps Dad convinced Mom that my sister and I should be allowed to listen to our music since he had been a big fan of Benny Goodman and popular jazz in his day. Although he'd played piano in a jazz band he'd organized in college, by this time he'd settled down to listening mostly to classical music and sometimes songs from the Broadway musicals he loved. The radio I received for my birthday in 1967 was not the little red transistor I craved, however. It was instead a large clock variety with an alarm you could set to the music of any radio station. It plugged into a wall and could not be carried around outside on a loop around the wrist the way a transistor radio could.

Although the clock radio was a big disappointment, I was happy to have at least some way to play rock music at home, so I tried hard not to show my feelings when I received it. I began to use the radio to keep me company in my basement bedroom while I got ready for school after waking up to Cousin Brucie. When stuck in my room to clean it up on a sunny Saturday, or for other disciplinary reasons, the radio made the stay more palatable. I generally had little desire to hang out in my room just for fun, however, even with the addition of the radio. The outdoors was far and away a more powerful draw. After the clock radio arrived, I still spent most of my free time outside or at my friend's house. At home I had to shut my bedroom door and turn the volume down if I listened to the radio or the record player I later received.

After the record player entered the scene, I began to buy 45 RPM records with one song on each side. I used my allowance of fifty cents, received weekly after fervent and persistent negotiation. In high school, babysitting for neighbors and mowing our family's lawn gained me another few dollars here and there. One of the first long-playing albums I bought with my savings was *Sgt. Pepper's Lonely Hearts Club Band* by the Beatles. "All You Need is Love" and "Can't Buy Me Love," from their earlier albums, had by then become rules of the road to adulthood for me, even as I continued to sing about never growing up from the musical version of *Peter Pan* and about daring to dream big in the song "Somewhere Over the Rainbow" from *The Wizard of Oz* (both of which my family had annually watched on television while eating popcorn together on the ratty sofa in the basement of the little Cape house we'd lived in before moving to Princeton).

By the late '60s, when I was in high school and the *Sgt. Pepper's* album landed in my lavender-painted bedroom, the musical background of life also included the long string of hits that had begun rolling out of Detroit's Motown music studios in the late '50s. Social commentary about alienation contained in other songs like "The Sounds of Silence" by Simon and Garfunkel and "Teach Your Children" by Crosby, Stills, Nash and Young describe the outlines of the huge generation gap that was opening ever wider at the time. The rebellious story told in many other songs was further amplified in a song called "San Francisco (Be Sure to Wear Flowers in Your Hair)," written by John Phillips for Scott McKenzie. That song, advertising the 1967 Monterey Pop Festival, became a smash hit, so popular that it was later called the unofficial anthem of all the movements in the late '60s, known collectively by now as "the counterculture." The Fifth Dimension cut a single mash-up of two other songs from the Broadway musical *Hair*, entitled "Age of Aquarius/Let the Sunshine In," which had a similar effect. Those calling to give peace and love a chance, as these massively broadcast hits did, were dubbed hippies, and many embraced that term as they descended in unheard-of numbers on San Francisco's Golden Gate Park to create a unique kind of summerlong war protest, which they called "a Human Be-In."

I was thirteen then, teetering on the brink of high school. The music was my lifeline to joy, connection, and identity as it constantly played in the back of my mind or when I sang loudly and danced with friends at sleepover parties. Young people only a few years older than I was flocked to San Francisco to camp in Golden Gate Park, which sounded like a wild adventure. An iconic photo appeared in *Life* that summer, of a young woman with a long, flowing skirt and long blonde hair crowned by a ring of flowers. She was poised to place the stem of a daisy into the barrel of a rifle aimed directly at her face from a line of young National Guard troops called out to confront peaceful protesters.

Soon, darker songs began erupting into the top forty hit list, including "The Eve of Destruction" and "Ohio," a song memorializing the death of four students shot during a peaceful protest at Kent State University by National Guard soldiers sent there on President Nixon's order to break up the long-standing takeover of the college's administration building. Music brought their story to life especially intensely for those of us who were between fourteen and twenty-four. The picture of a dying young man not much older than I was, lying helpless and bleeding on the sidewalk at Kent State next to a screaming friend who squatted beside him, her long brown hair falling to her waist, hit our coffee table in the pages of *Life*, clearly depicting what the song "Ohio" was about. The bravery and rebellion in that image of two embattled innocents became another instant symbol for the massive number of college students standing up nationwide to the unimaginably powerful foe of the federal government.

THE WORLD I READ ABOUT in *Life* magazine was still somewhat removed from my experiences throughout the '60s, even as the breeze escaping the bubble of illusion surrounding my early childhood had grown stronger by the year. By the time I entered high school, it was a strong wind. That explosive year, 1968, was also the first year I couldn't avoid full acknowledgement that growing into adulthood was happening whether I liked it or not. That visceral truth increased the impact of the year's tragic events on my psyche as I looked ever more closely at what was happening in the wider world where adults couldn't avoid taking their share of responsibility for society's behavior.

The events of 1968 hit hard, even if indirectly. Every baby boomer was marked by them. The students in my high school joined that year's national student protest moratoriums against the escalation of the Vietnam War, for example, walking out of classes at ten o'clock one bright fall morning. That act was ostensibly intended to create a giant sit-in to protest the war. Teach-ins, organized and led by juniors and seniors, were held in the auditorium and outside on the football field in front of the bleachers. Princeton High needed both venues if every student walked out of class and attended because about twelve hundred students would be involved.

The aim of the high school moratorium was to teach the tactics of direct democracy, educating each other about the war, hierarchical authority, and how to organize opposition. With my heart in my mouth, I joined the majority of the student body that walked out of class that day, communicating our disgust with the way adults were handling their responsibilities to their children and to humanity in general and with the appalling example they were setting. That was the first publicly rebellious act I'd ever engaged in, and it required more courage from me than you might expect. Disobeying school rules was not my style, and the teacher of the class I was in that morning urged us not to join the protest. After walking out, however, I didn't attend the sit-in or the teach-in but simply walked home, figuring that those events wouldn't really have a direct effect on anything and the act of shutting down the school was the most important aspect of the protest.

It felt very good—and far more important than any math or history class—to take part in a mass protest, demonstrating to adults that even those of us three or four years younger than draft age were paying close attention to what our elders were up to and did not approve. Of course my mother did not approve of what I had done when I got home, either, but that just told me how badly our little protest was needed. We succeeded in shutting down the school that day, which taught me a lesson I never forgot about the power of those at the bottom of any power structure to send a strong message by educating each other, organizing, and standing up together for a heartfelt cause.

As it turned out, the high school moratorium made a few demands of the school's administration that were more pertinent to my life than I'd expected. The most visible was the end of the long-standing dress code, formerly requiring girls to wear dresses or skirts and boys to wear button-down shirts, nice pants, and often neckties. That dress code applied at many public schools in those days. In the spring following the student moratorium, students at Princeton High were suddenly allowed to wear whatever we liked, including ripped jeans and flimsy Indian bedspreads as saris, which one student regularly began to choose as her outfit. I greatly appreciated the dress code change, especially on cold winter days when I could now wear pants instead of leggings worn beneath miniskirts, which often required awkward removal in school hallways in order to avoid tardiness to class, and thankfully pantyhose also came on the scene shortly thereafter.

Although my psyche was increasingly politicized in 1968 and 1969—my freshman and sophomore years in high school—the structure of my daily life hardly reflected any hint of that transformation, and my life continued to be shaped by a promise I'd made to myself as a bored fourteen-year-old riding my bike aimlessly around town during the summer following eighth grade. I had vowed that day that I would volunteer for every opportunity to engage in school-sponsored activities when I entered high school, as a way to try new things and meet new people in the huge student body. Hopefully that would give me enough to do to avoid the deadly boredom I was feeling that day. That commitment also led me away from the environment presided over by Mom, replacing it with a focus on sports, particularly gymnastics, which I had practiced informally since I could run and climb. Artistically decorating bulletin boards and participating in various forms of student government were also part of the mix. Involvement in multiple after-school activities, along with homework, also kept me too busy to pay detailed attention to the wider world. Nevertheless, the rock music of the late '60s and early '70s kept the nationwide explosion of emotional pain front and center, and the free-form dancing that went with it became a celebratory refuge from all my growing pains and provided opportunities to playfully connect and blow off steam in the process.

THE TERMS "hip" and "hep" were part of the slang of Jive, which dominated *black* popular culture in New York City's Harlem neighborhood in the 1940s. Both terms meant sophisticated, fashionable, and up to date.[1] Swing dancers in the '40s were encouraged to be "hep to the jive." The Beats (members of the Beat movement) adopted the term *hip* along with a preference for jazz, in the '50s, which began to break down the wall between *white* and *black* cultures, and the wall further crumbled as the late '50s gave way to the '60s and the rise of Motown Records in the "Motor City," Detroit, Michigan. Motown raised a steady string of *black* musicians to stardom and wide popularity among young people of all ethnicities, including the Four Tops, the Temptations, Smokey Robinson and the Miracles, the Supremes, and the Shondells among others. A new collection of young people followed in the wake of the Beats, a group that began to be called hippies, a diminutive form of the term hip. Hippies not only took up Beat slang, they also had similar musical preferences and countercultural values, adding new elements of their own that crystalized in the huge anti–Vietnam War protest mentioned earlier, the Human Be-In. That protest attracted between twenty thousand and thirty thousand participants, demonstrating that hippies were likely not the tiny minority of confused young people the older generation had assumed; otherwise, so many would never have materialized at the drop of a hat, or better stated, at the call of a song lyric.[2]

Many of those who descended upon San Francisco stayed on and were joined by tens of thousands more as the summer unfolded, turning the Haight-Ashbury neighborhood into a mecca of hippie culture still evident today. The Human Be-In was infused with rock music and a sense of community-building centered around spiritual love, which was thought of as a natural gift available to every human heart and best accessed in whatever way felt most authentic. Eastern spiritual practices began to spread throughout that gathering and beyond. Also, as the primary means to growing the grass roots of a more loving culture, participating in and supporting social and ecological reform was embraced by many in attendance. Many hippies believed that culture would soon transform because who wouldn't want more peace, love, and understanding? Mediation to solve disagreements, deep listening practices of multiple varieties, communal living, ecological awareness, and mental disciplines believed to strengthen access to a higher, more loving consciousness, including various forms of meditation, yoga, and psychedelic drugs, were all experimented with by hippies as countercultural means to build a more compassionate social structure.[3]

Seeking to promote a vision of possibility, rather than simply protesting the war in Vietnam, was part of what made hippie culture so appealing to young people discouraged by the dissonance between the Judeo-Christian values of kindness and forgiveness they were taught at home, at school, and in churches or synagogues and what they saw playing out in society through the burgeoning news media. It was clear that something beyond protest was needed to really "give peace a chance." That "something" certainly seemed to require love of a kind that appeared nowhere in the political sphere into which young adults were now flooding in huge numbers.

The June 1967 Monterey Pop Festival grew out of the Human Be-In and became an essential element of California's "Summer of Love." That nationally publicized, three-day-long concert at the Monterey County Fairgrounds in Monterey, California, had an unusual lineup of musicians—including the Jimi Hendrix Experience, the Who, Ravi Shankar, Janis Joplin, and Otis Redding—who were making their first major US appearance, which immediately catapulted all of them to fame. The concert's music popularized hippie culture among young people throughout the country, ultimately spreading the spirit of the Summer of Love throughout the country and internationally, spawning a movement to organize what became the 1969 Woodstock Art and Music Festival.

Hippie fashions and values permeated the popular music world as a result of these events and began to flow into television, film, literature, and fine art. The religious and cultural diversity hippies espoused went on to gain widespread acceptance in liberal political circles in the decades that followed. Reinterpreted versions of various Asian spiritual concepts and practices that hippies explored, derived from Taoism, Buddhism, and Hinduism, included meditation, mindfulness, and yoga, which have now become mainstream alternative sources of inner peace, replacing institutionalized religious practices for many throughout the US and the world.[4]

Hippies also experimented with many kinds of alternative art, such as street theater and improvisational barefoot dancing in large groups that didn't require any form or partnering and accepted any and all varieties of dance expression. Rock 'n' roll, rhythm and blues, and folk music were essential aspects of life in hippie culture. All these artistic means were used as methods to access embodied joy and authenticity. Body-centered spirituality beyond religious dogma also served that purpose. Accessing emotions and using these methods to create a dynamic, peaceful, shared energy of protest against society's conventional systems lay at the heart of all these expressions. Freely offered public events called "happenings" also aimed to inject a celebratory energy into hippie community-building experiments, seeking to displace and transform the wider culture's angry power politics by bringing people together through joy and sharing instead of fear and hate. A favorite Beatles song from my early high school days, "All You Need Is Love," expressed the central concept of the hippie value system.

There were, of course, immense challenges that reared their heads from deep within the psychological conditioning that every participant inevitably brought to these idealistic efforts, which ultimately resulted in the breakup of many communes and relationships after a few years. Nevertheless, new conceptual tracks had been laid down for a pathway out of the cultural quagmire of the Vietnam War and systemic racism, suggesting another way to approach living that began to reverberate broadly within Western culture.

Over the years that followed the Summer of Love and the explosive cultural upheavals of 1967, rock music of all kinds became a constant background melody for my days, buoying my spirits and inspiring an affinity for social action. The rock concerts I attended also embodied hope, as thousands of hearts celebrated their togetherness, opening to the beauty of a life-sustaining vision right alongside the heartbreaking pain of the realities described in many of the song lyrics. The mystery of how life held it all was implied in the harmony and dissonance of the music itself.

Chapter Five

Spirit, Heart, and Institution

As I turned fourteen in May 1968, I read about a high-pro-file trial taking place in Boston. It revealed another element of that era's culture that doesn't get as much attention as the civil rights movement and combined youth rebellions. The trial reflected a growing cultural undercurrent that revealed a resurgence of conservative Christianity, which was quietly gaining ground across the US. It began in the pews of mainline Protestant churches as a reaction to the continuous and widespread protests to so many formerly unquestioned cultural conventions.

The trial caught my attention as I perused *Life* magazine. It revolved around five men charged with conspiracy for encouraging young men to evade the military draft. Presbyterian minister and Yale University chaplain William Sloane Coffin Jr. was one of them. He and many ministers, both *black* and *white*, from multiple Protestant denominations, vehemently opposed the Vietnam War while many of their parishioners fully trusted their elected leaders to determine public policy and military strategy once elected. As such, those parishioners supported the Vietnam War and opposed any changes to operative social structures, including racist Jim Crow laws, which many *whites* saw as not their personal business. In the minds of such people, the racist Jim Crow system was out of their hands, an issue to be dealt with by state government officials as they saw fit.[1]

Nevertheless, church communities and whole Christian denominations were becoming deeply divided over the Johnson administration's conduct of the Vietnam War. The war had become a personal moral crisis for young people, young *American* men in particular. Many had by then begun to realize that they were being drafted into military service by the tens of thousands for a war that was not only unwinnable but also unpopular with the Vietnamese people for whose benefit those men and their friends and siblings were traveling halfway around the globe to fight and often die.

A divide began to deepen between those who were intent on upholding conventional institutional authority, including a hierarchy of decision-making and anticommunist values, and the young men who sought and found support from Protestant ministers who sympathized with their fear and loathing of the Vietnam War. Many conservative Protestants began to feel alienated from the teachings of their ministers who supported these young men. As a result, those Protestants became increasingly unwilling to bridge the newly widened ravine that stretched beyond the traditional political gap that formerly allowed for gentlemanly disagreement between them and their more liberal fellow churchgoers. As a result, churchgoers in the late '60s saw conservative families beginning to abandon mainline Protestant churches in what became an unprecedented wave of defection over the course of the next fifteen years. They flocked instead to growing evangelical Christian congregations whose ministers supported the war. That fallout began to construct a new version of conservative

Christianity in the US, strengthening the disparate political undercurrents that had always existed but were formerly laid at the feet of elected decision-makers to resolve through mutually agreed-upon institutions of political authority.[2]

William Sloane Coffin Jr. was a prominent figure in mainline Protestantism in 1968. Mainline Protestantism refers to European-derived Protestant denominations brought to the US by huge waves of immigrants from Europe in the 1700s. Such denominations grew to include the churches attended in 1968 by people in the middle- and upper-class political and cultural establishment. The Coffins were an upper-class New York City family, and William Sloane Coffin Jr. had an upbringing typical of sons raised in elite families like his, including easy access to influential leadership circles that overlapped governmental, academic, and religious spheres. Coffin's father, for example, was the president of the board of trustees of the Metropolitan Museum of Art in New York City, and his uncle, Henry, had been one of the most famous ministers in the United States. Earlier in his own career, Coffin had been a CIA officer during the Korean War. He also became Yale University's chaplain upon his graduation from Yale. Using his authority in that position, he legitimized opposition to the war through his actions and sermons, which led to his becoming a defendant in the trial I read about in *Life* in May 1968.[3]

Coffin's arrest, indictment, and criminal trial were fallout from a 1967 antiwar rally in Boston, during which he collected the draft cards of men who refused to serve in Vietnam, a federal crime. He publicized his activities at the protest in order to *seek* arrest and force a national debate about the morality of the military draft. He was charged with incitement to unlawful conduct for encouraging young men to refuse or evade military registration, a crime punishable by imprisonment for up to five years. Reverend Coffin was not the only Protestant minister to oppose the Vietnam War. Many ministers began criticizing US policy in Vietnam in the mid-sixties in a blatant departure from their former public stance upholding the separation of church and state. This criticism of the Vietnam War from mainline Protestant ministers grew particularly strong in early 1968, the year I began high school, catalyzed by the results of North Vietnam's Tet Offensive, the large-scale surprise attack by the Viet Cong on targets throughout South Vietnam, including the US embassy. Those attacks were ultimately unsuccessful in defeating US troops, even though they created a devastating setback for the US military, killed many thousands of US and South Vietnamese soldiers, and led many *Americans* to doubt President Lyndon Johnson's continuing assurances that the war's end was in sight.[4]

Leading Protestant journals began sharply criticizing the war in the wake of the Tet Offensive. For instance, the *Christian Century*, a widely read nondenominational magazine supporting the values of mainline Protestantism, published an article condemning the war and maintaining that the spiritual integrity of the United States was in grave jeopardy as a result of the country's Vietnam policies. These ministers followed William Sloane Coffin Jr.'s example, matching practical activism and civil disobedience with the words they preached on Sundays, inspired by Dr. Martin Luther King Jr.[5]

Many teenagers like me, and particularly those a few years older, were catalyzed into activism by these shifts, both for and against the war. However, the support given antiwar protesters by mainline church leaders—ministers who each Sunday preached ethical, loving behavior and who were willing to protest shoulder to shoulder with civil rights leaders and hippies—bordered on heresy and sedition in the eyes of the cultural institutionalists in their pews.

At the time, seminarians of draft age who were studying the evolution of Protestantism in the US were wrestling with their consciences about whether or not to risk jail time to align their deep faith and their politics by becoming conscientious objectors. The man who much later became the love of my life saw the actions of the protesting ministers as deeply courageous, uniting their core spiritual beliefs with the active, peaceful confrontation of long-held destructive social norms. These church leaders whom these students carefully watched felt that unwavering adherence to social norms on the part of so many Christians was one of the main problems taking society utterly off the rails. Remaining true to convention in the way that conservative Christians of the time were beginning to do required an untenably blind obedience in the eyes of the seminarians as well, an obedience that ignored the death and destruction it unnecessarily caused—to their friends, siblings, and potentially themselves—under the leadership of a set of particularly corrupt, power-hungry politicians in the Nixon administration. My future husband was studying at the Boston University School of Theology at the time, the same school from which Dr. Martin Luther King Jr. graduated a generation earlier.

Many evangelical Christians believed that supporting the war was a morally defensible position because it was a way to prevent the spread of communism, a viewpoint that echoed the fears inflamed by Senator Joseph McCarthy that had derailed my father's career. These church members were unshakably convinced that communism would create an unstoppable domino effect—spreading Godless communism across the globe—if any hint of its possible spread wasn't immediately snuffed out using military force. Conservative Christians adamantly supported this narrative while simultaneously ignoring or minimizing something else that was becoming clear to anyone reading *Life* magazine, as I continued to do. Soldiers fighting in Vietnam were not only following orders to attack Viet Cong soldiers and military personnel, they were also instigating and carrying out repeated massacres of Vietnamese civilians using the excuse that enemy combatants were indistinguishable from anyone else in Vietnam. One egregious example of the twisted, traumatic expression of that insurmountably tragic confusion was the My Lai Massacre carried out by US troops and photographically documented in *Life* and other publications by reporters who were free to move within war zones as they saw fit in those days (the perspective of war correspondents today is much more aligned with military policy because they are no longer free to travel at will in war zones, embedded instead within military units of volunteer soldiers).

A compounding issue driving conservative Christians away from mainline pews beginning in 1968 was that this was not the first time prominent Protestant ministers had set themselves at odds with their churchgoers. A division had already existed between liberal Protestant leaders and conservative mainline churchgoers over those church leaders' involvement in the civil rights movement. Many liberal ministers championed the movement and interfaith cooperation between Protestants, Catholics, and Jews, policies that were staunchly opposed by many of their conservative congregants. It was ministers preaching against US military policy, however, that led many parishioners to finally conclude that their values were not aligned with those of the leaders of the churches their families had attended for generations.[6]

There were few personal consequences for William Sloane Coffin Jr. due to his status as an elite *white* man within the structurally embedded systemic racism of the time, still very visible today for those who care to look. He was found guilty as charged at his trial in Boston, but his conviction was overturned on appeal and he returned to Yale as a hero of sorts. He became minister of New York's nondenominational Riverside Church in Manhattan as his career unfolded. Mainline Protestant denominations, however, lost nearly one in six members between 1970 and 1985, feeding the growth of conservative evangelical churches, which grew rapidly during the same period.[7]

WE ARE ALL BORN into a certain time and place and embodied as a result of the unique physical integration of two lines of genetic heritage, which alter each other as they intermingle in an emotional, psychological, and physically intimate act within a family, community, and cultural context unique to that particular moment. Those educated in biological and other physical sciences will tell you that at a molecular level we are primarily made of water. When focusing an even stronger lens on the world of matter, we discover that we are mostly space, commonly perceived as similar to air. Air and water, two constantly flowing, changing, interconnecting systems, shift in relationship to one another when heated or cooled. Boiling water rises to become steam, easily blending with the surrounding air, and warm air full of steamy humidity cools during summer evenings, separating more tangibly to become dewdrops on leaf tips.

This description of life stands on the scientific foundation laid by Charles Darwin's *Origin of Species*. Written in 1859, it created a heated controversy in religious circles that has raged continuously ever since. Although rarely recognized, especially in public conversations, scientific ideas about a natural process of evolution go all the way back to Greek philosophers in the fifth century BCE, a time when Taoists were thinking in similar ways in Asia. It is little known or taught that Christian theologians in the fourth century also entertained these ideas, as did Thomas Aquinas in the thirteenth century. The controversy that continues to play out in political efforts to inject Creationism (the concept that God created everything on Earth six thousand years ago) into public school classrooms, insisting that it be taught as an equally valid "theory" to evolution, originated in Europe and North America not long after Darwin's seminal book was published.[8]

By the late nineteenth century, discoveries in geology had established a generally accepted consensus that included both perspectives, understanding Earth to be far more ancient than previously believed. Fossilized remains serving as demonstrable proof of past biological extinctions had won over adherents to anti-evolutionary beliefs—as long as the evolution of humanity was not in the mix. Enthusiasm for the scientific concept of evolution gained its strongest foothold among Quakers and Unitarians, the two Protestant denominations to which my parents exposed me and my sisters while we were growing up. Those denominations lay at the fringes of nineteenth-century cultural conventions, however.[9]

In the late 1800s, science professors at universities in the northeastern US very quickly embraced Darwin's theory of evolution and introduced it to their students. Conversely, many living in the southern and western United States were heavily influenced by the preaching of Christian fundamentalist evangelical ministers, coupled with very limited access to higher education in those places at that time, a situation that generally resulted in wholesale rejection of evolutionary theory as immoral.[10]

New England had known increasing numbers of universities offering ever-expanding varieties of academic disciplines since the founding of Harvard University in 1636, the first US school of higher education. With the advent of the nineteenth century, there was a burgeoning of land grant colleges across the US for the first time. These new educational institutions were established primarily as a way to spread practical knowledge about new agricultural and engineering technologies rather than to introduce philosophically and religiously fraught scientific ideas like evolutionary theory.[11]

Darwin's theory took on intense political overtones in the US following WWI, when public schools began teaching Darwin's theory of natural selection and connecting it with the evolution of humanity. In response to that shift, the state of Tennessee passed the Butler Act of 1925, which prohibited the teaching of any theory of humankind's origins that contradicted biblical teachings. That was the same year my mother had her first birthday and my father turned two years old. My grandparents were in their early thirties. The law was immediately tested in court in the highly publicized Scopes trial and was subsequently upheld by the Tennessee Supreme Court. That law remained on the books until 1967, when my parents were in their early forties and I had entered eighth grade.

In 1968, the US Supreme Court ruled in *Epperson v. Arkansas* that specific theories of human origins could not be banned because doing so had a religious purpose at its core—whether for or against the teaching of evolution—which contradicts the establishment clause of the First Amendment to the Constitution, which separates issues governed by churches from those over which secular government has jurisdiction, such as public education. In further cases before the court, this legal interpretation came to mean that neither theory could be banned from school curricula and, conversely, that no requirement to teach them both could be established either.

Almost twenty years earlier, in 1942, Julian Huxley's book *Evolution: The Modern Synthesis* was published. That was the year my father turned nineteen and was awaiting his call into the US Air Force. Huxley took Darwin's ideas to a whole new level, popularizing a new notion of a wide synthesis of many scientific disciplines and transforming humanism into a virtual religion by claiming that religious thought must be drastically reordered, centering it on evolutionary patterns instead of a mythical god. He advocated expansion of scientific inquiry to augment human capacities.[12] Public opinion polls of that time suggested, however, that most Americans either believed that God created human beings outright or had somehow guided the evolutionary process. Membership in churches preaching ever more literal interpretations of Christian scripture steadily rose in the southern and western US, especially in churches within the Southern Baptist Convention and Lutheran Church–Missouri Synod. As they grew, these churches became increasingly effective in delivering their Creationist message by founding colleges, schools, publishing houses, and broadcast media companies to push it into mainstream culture.[13]

Scientists studying evolution and its implications in 1968, along with their families, joined the throngs leaving the pews of mainline Protestant churches. This movement proceeded in the opposite direction from the one chosen by those leaving to join evangelical Christian churches, however—the scientists moved away from church altogether. As these families left, firm opposition to the Creationist education movement transferred out of the pews of mainline Christian churches into secular social circles with inherently less influence over Christian audiences. As a result, anti-evolutionary forces gained strength in many congregations that survived both exoduses. Those who continued to participate in these churches, long central to community life, popularized an accommodating position in regard to Creationist ideology, which eventually resulted in reducing the number of school districts teaching from standard biology textbooks that described evolution as fact. With this cultural shift moving in the background, the secular court system was able to limit the spread of Creationist ideology only by preventing outright religious instruction in public schools.[14]

Prevention of outright religious instruction in public schools might today seem almost a laughable side note; however, public schools were very different in that respect when I was young. Every morning in my fourth grade public school classroom in 1962 in Basking Ridge, New Jersey, the ritual beginning of each school day involved first standing to recite the Pledge of Allegiance, followed by a different child chosen each day for the honor of reading a passage from the Bible, mainly the psalms as I recall, followed by a moment of silence during which students were encouraged to pray. I grew to love the twenty-third psalm as a result: "Yea though I walk through the valley of the shadow of death, I shall fear no evil, for thou art with me . . ." (Ps. 23:4)

At home, a different story was playing out. Many ideas from Huxley's modern synthesis were growing a taproot into my parents' developing worldview. Nevertheless, they vehemently opposed eugenics theory, understanding it as pseudoscientific prejudice layered on top of replicable scientific studies. Both my parents had become avowed humanists by the time I was in high school and I grew up understanding evolutionary humanism as basic truth. In that conceptual view, genetics, developmental physiology, ecology, systematics, paleontology, cytology, and mathematical analysis of biology are deeply entwined and inter-related. My parents modeled this approach to living, encouraging their daughters to ask questions and answering them as best they could, all while continuously encouraging us to discover what was true for ourselves. No question was ever considered a dumb question in our home.

The vision of evolutionary humanism arose in the wider culture as a result of extending the ideas behind the modern synthesis into a system of ethics that included a meaningful place for humankind in the ongoing evolutionary process of life, grounded in a unified theory that included progressive evolutionary improvement, species by species, with humanity at the summit. Natural selection under this interpretation was "a fact of nature capable of verification by observation and experimentation." A "period of synthesis" was noted by Huxley as taking place during the course of the 1920s and 1930s, when my grandparents were young. The understanding of a deep interrelationship of scientific disciplines became more widely evident during that time, embedding a new scientific and cultural perspective that rivalled physics in its impact on technological progress.[15]

After my father's death, I discovered a book he appeared to have studied intently called *This View of Life* by George Gaylord Simpson, a respected mid-twentieth-century scientific polymath. The book's cover enfolded a stash of articles Dad had carefully extracted or photocopied from the journal *Science*, among others, which fell out as I opened the book's cover. That book and collection of articles were published between 1963, the year I turned nine and first began discussing philosophy with Dad, and 1972, the year I graduated from high school. They all analyzed Darwin's theory of evolution from different angles. That book and all the articles between its covers confirmed what I had long suspected, that Dad had sought for years to reconcile the scientific truth he believed about life with his heartfelt love of the goodness and beauty contained in the liberal Christian religious tradition in which he had been raised.

The long philosophical talks Dad and I had about life's origin and meaning during my teenage and young adult years later led me to conclude that the wonder embodied in his experience of liberal Christianity provided solace for him as a pre-teenage boy whose mother had died. When I was in college, however, he told me point-blank that rationally one could only say, from the evidence, that we all return to dust when we die and nothing more. Scientific observation was his most trusted source of information, so he had finally adopted the *dust to dust* theory hook, line, and sinker, although he was still intrigued in a bemused sort of way by other imagined possibilities I proposed. While conceding that science could not completely eradicate the mystery of life's origins, he never again wavered from his stated position in our discussions. Nevertheless, Dad never lost enthusiasm for church attendance and hymn singing in the Unitarian tradition, finding comfort in the ritual of Sunday services, especially when his mind increasingly failed at the end of his life. Finding Simpson's book, and finally reading it along with the accompanying articles these many years later, confirmed that Dad, like so many other young people of the '40s and '50s, began to question the story that had formed the basis of everything he knew from his cultural inheritance. Scientific discoveries in his lifetime had begun to unfold for him a kind of irrefutable, double-blind-tested truth that had never been available before, as they also did for many others like him.

E. O. Wilson, the American biologist known as the father of biodiversity (the number and variety of life forms in a region that interact with each other to create and foster an ecosystem) taught at Harvard University from 1956 until retiring in 1996 and extended the concept of scientific synthesis that had inspired young thinkers like Dad and Mom in the '60s. His research and writings created a whole new field of study, first called sociobiology with his 1975 book, *Sociobiology: The New Synthesis*. That book introduced the concept that tendencies in living organisms could explain the creation of hierarchical social organization among humans by taking into account the inheritance of such tendencies through families as part of an evolutionary cultural process inextricably associated with physical evolution. His book

On Human Nature, published three years later, further addressed the role that biological inheritance plays in human cultural evolution. The Pulitzer Prize for General Nonfiction was awarded to Wilson for that seminal work.[16]

For decades, Wilson studied the intricately interlacing web of systems within systems that Dad and I loved to discuss on the many walks we took under the stars with various family dogs. Wilson's work greatly expanded the new science of ecology as it developed. As a result of Wilson's work, humanity has evidence that it takes only the destruction of an ecosystem's keystone species to create deep and widespread destruction of biodiversity. *Keystone species* is a term referring to the way certain species are similar within their ecosystems to the keystone at the apex of an architectural arch. The keystone in an arch balances the forces of physics to maintain the arch, just as the keystone species balances the forces of nature in an ecosystem to maintain its biodiversity. "Even though these species may be only a handful out of thousands in a particular ecosystem, they are needed in good health to maintain the whole ecosystem," [17] Wilson explained. His talks and writings on the topic often pointed to the example of the American marine otter.

When marine otters were hunted along the North American Pacific Coast for their fur, their populations were decimated to near extinction, causing sea urchins to lose their only natural predator. Sea urchins then multiplied until they nearly caused ecosystem collapse, destroying the balance centered on an intricately interdependent system of biodiversity rooted in the ecology of vast kelp forests, which had evolved into nurseries for numerous marine creatures, in a close-to-catastrophic change. When otters were finally allowed to repopulate, the kelp forests and sea creatures dependent on them slowly regenerated. Many other examples of this phenomenon exist all across the globe. Perhaps Dad's fascination with the science of interrelated natural systems partly explains why he strongly defended the wild fields bordering our yards, in both Basking Ridge and Princeton, New Jersey, impressing upon my young mind the importance of even the smallest wild places to the health of nature, including humanity.

The exponentially multiplying and intertwining scientific discoveries that rolled out of universities over the course of my adult life, while Wilson and others systematically studied their interrelationships, documented the increasingly irrefutable fact that we are not the unique and separate individual, physical beings we appear to be. Instead we are moving systems within larger moving systems. According to the stories most modern scientists tell, based on facts they have the means to prove, these interwoven systems don't end at the boundary of Earth's atmosphere either. They spiral out far beyond this planet into outer space, as far as the mind can imagine and farther still. Some notable astrophysicists postulate that outer space is far larger than anyone can conceive and contains multiverses. The single universe was itself an unimaginable, earthshaking discovery only a few decades before I was born. When my parents were young, the perimeter of the Milky Way galaxy, Earth's home galaxy, was thought to be the absolute *edge* of outer space.

IN HER 2014 BOOK, *Minding the Earth, Mending the World*, Susan Murphy describes a spiritual experience, as a youngster, of being flooded with light for an indeterminate amount of time with the intense feeling that everything was wonderful and whole and perfect, even though everything was not as everyone imagined it *should* be.[18] Reading about that image brought back another turning point for me during my high school years, 1968 to 1972, a time when I lost my mental balance as a sleepless teenager. For two weeks I lay awake all night and sleepwalked through my days, unable to focus or attend school, anxiously following my mother everywhere. I became lost in a mind unable to move in its normal patterns, feeling utterly and frighteningly stuck.

It was the fall term of high school, 1970. I had spent two months of the preceding summer in England and Switzerland with the family of my mother's oldest friend who needed babysitting support for the family's nine-year-old son and four-year-old daughter. It had been an eye-opening, wonderful, and challenging experience, which in retrospect clearly affected my experience of the beginning of junior year. My time spent with that family in England had been lovely, but the local teenagers to whom I was introduced had an unexpected impact on my sense of self.

As it had been explained to me, most of the English girls I met attended what we in the US would call a private school, although in England it was deemed a public school that focused all efforts on sending students to universities upon graduation. Students attending such schools were required to pass a rigorous "O level" test at the end of eighth grade. If they did well enough on the test, they were put on a university-bound track in high school. Those who didn't fare as well, whether from test anxiety, bad study habits, or lack of intellectual acuity, were funneled off into a more technical high school track, never to have another chance at college, at least in England.

A girl my age in the family next door to my mom's old friend had not passed this rigorous test with high enough grades. I thought nothing of that and felt quite comfortable with her, truly enjoying one brief afternoon spent together after encountering each other outside when no one else was around. She told me that her grades in school had always been strong but that she had major test anxiety, a situation I could relate to, having had the same problem on any final exam in math in high school. Unfortunately, I was discouraged from befriending her for reasons I couldn't fathom, and I had no further opportunities to contradict that advice.

Instead, I was introduced to the friends of a girl I had met before traveling to England. She was the same age as I was and the daughter of friends of my mother's old friend in England. I had met her when she stayed for a couple of nights with us in Princeton on her way to California. She was taking a similarly arranged trip to the one I was about to make to England. Since my family was halfway between England and California, this friendly, cheerful girl stayed with us in order to adjust to jet lag. Although she seemed more grown-up and reserved than girls I was used to, I put her behavior down to shyness in a new country. She was also kind and interested in everything, which made conversation easy. She warned me to avoid invitations to socialize with one particular girl associated with her friends back in England, to whom she anticipated I would be introduced, describing that girl as a first-class snob. I took note of her advice but thought little more about it.

After arriving in England, however, there was little to do other than help my mom's friend with her household chores and keep the younger children occupied, which I enjoyed but which wasn't really enough to fill all the time I had on my hands. Mom's dear friend had long ago accepted the role of godmother to me, in order to please my paternal grandfather who had wanted me to be baptized in the little church he attended in Rhode Island while we were briefly living in the borrowed cottage owned by his wife. In later years she laughed when I mentioned that title because she was a very unconventional godmother, not being a churchgoing person herself, although she set a strong example of the importance of loving family, and having emotional resilience and courage.

That summer in England brought me the joy of reading. I read fourteen books before returning home, including everything I could lay my hands on by writers of historical literary fiction and international spy novels. These books provided exciting, fascinating distractions from the unavoidable loneliness of a lack of friends my own age. The political intrigue and historical narratives, particularly those set near or within the timeframe of WWII, fed my growing interest in politics and power and added an international perspective to it in keeping with where I found myself as I read.

Eventually, I was invited to a teenage party held by the family of the girl I had been warned to avoid. By then, however, I was desperate to meet anyone my own age and figured I could be polite to her while staying out of her way, so I said nothing to my godmother about the warning I had received. After arriving at the party, I was shocked to find that the small unsupervised group gathering, held in a renovated garage next to the house, included perhaps four other sixteen-year-old girls and a similar number of young men in their mid-twenties.

As a sixteen-year-old, I was still interested in climbing trees and playing capture the flag on barefoot summer nights at home.

I had minimal experience with dating, having politely accepted a couple of invitations to participate in daytime activities with a boy with whom I was friendly but nothing more. I had no experience involving young men ten years my senior and had never sought it. That more serious kind of relationship, potentially a prelude to romance, was totally out of my league. As a result, I mainly hung out with the younger brother of the girl I was trying to avoid. He was only one year younger than I and much more fun from my perspective—a totally uncool way of sizing up the situation from the point of view of the other girls at the party.

There was one tall, devastatingly handsome young man I couldn't help noticing, however, despite my shyness. He had wavy, longish blond hair, blue eyes, and a slim, athletic build. To my utter amazement, he walked over and initiated conversation with me at one point. I discovered that he was from Scandinavia and was also visiting somewhere nearby for the summer. He was kind and curious about me, which was overwhelming because of his age and good looks, although of course I was thrilled that he had any desire to talk with the likes of me for even the short time we did.

There was another party several weeks later, to which I was again invited by the girl I had been warned to avoid. She had made no move at her own party to get to know me, except by speaking to me briefly and with great reserve when I first arrived. I accepted this second invitation as, once again, the only way to interact with any young people. However, when we arrived at the party's venue, I found myself completely at a loss in a massive gathering at some kind of country club where tables were arranged, a bar was set up, and a band was playing. I had accepted a ride to the party in the company of this girl, who clearly had no intention of befriending me. She had been polite while remaining emotionally distant and cool as we sat together in the back seat of her family's car. After her parents departed, however, she quickly began to ignore me, as did her friends with whom we claimed a table for the evening. I made a couple of feeble attempts to join their conversation, which received very cool responses, so I finally chose to leave the group and wander around the larger space where the party was taking place. Perhaps I could explore a little, I thought, and maybe even walk outside somewhere to get a grip on feeling completely lost emotionally.

Not long after I began my little exploration, the handsome young man from the earlier party—clearly a person of interest among the girls in the group I'd left—tapped me on the shoulder and asked if I was all right. Unable to hold in my sadness, I explained exactly how I felt, barely holding back tears, and he told me that he found those girls insufferable too, which made me laugh. He then asked me to dance, which was a thrill. It was a fast dance in the free-form rock 'n' roll style I loved, which had become and remains one of my favorite ways to blow off steam.

Several more fast dances followed, which we also enjoyed together. Those dances are the reason I remember the party with any pleasure at all. When the band finally struck up a slow dance, neither of us was really interested, so we returned together to the group at the table. My return with the man of the hour stunned the other girls, which was clear from the looks on their faces and the halt in their conversation. That gave me courage, as did the fact that my ally and I remained together in a united front for the remainder of the evening. With this kind young man as escort, I was grudgingly accepted but had no interest in participating in the group conversation and was very relieved to finally return to my godmother's house.

Getting ready for bed that night, I dissolved into tears in the bathroom, which drew my godmother's knock on the door. I explained what had happened and asked her not to accept any more such invitations on my behalf. I was content to read spy novels and play in the backyard with my nine- and four-year-old charges as entertainment from then on. Nevertheless, there were a couple of other interactions with young people that summer, which were much more pleasant though still challenging. During one visit with a kind, friendly girl who had not attended the parties—although she was also a friend of the English girl I had met before traveling to England—I discovered another disconcerting fact: it had been the right choice for me to quit piano lessons several years before, not only out of protest, but because I had no talent for reading music.

This girl said she was very sorry to hear that I had endured the company of the girl who invited me to the parties, saying she avoided her at all cost. She also told me she mostly kept to herself and read or played piano rather than socializing, and she asked whether I ever played piano. I told her about my seven years of lessons, and she suggested we share some playing together. I warned her that I was quite rusty, having long stopped practicing, but told her I'd be happy to hear her play. It amazed me to discover that she could sit in front of a piece of music she had never seen before and play it flawlessly, from my perspective, purely by sight-reading the music, a feat so far beyond my ability as to be laughable.

Later in Switzerland that same summer, on vacation with my godmother's family, I met some young people who spoke only French, with whom I struggled to communicate with my very limited command of that language. We laughed nervously together in each other's company on a few occasions but were unable to communicate in any meaningful way.

I returned home a much more reserved and less confident girl than I had been when I set out. It had been an eye-opening adventure with a lot to remember as wonderful, even though it took a psychological toll that soon brought unwanted, ungovernable feelings to the surface. In addition to the social challenges I had faced while visiting, I had also been ruminating on the responsibilities I would have to take on after returning to the States. Those included a heavier load of homework, researching and applying to colleges, participating in three varsity sports, and two community leadership commitments. In the back of my mind, I was anxiously trying to figure out how I would fit everything in while effectively giving each role my all, particularly while applying to college and striving to continue to excel in my studies, at least to a B+ level.

Following my flight home, after having a bit of a laugh as customs agents pawed through my luggage, I was happily surprised to discover that without realizing it I had picked up a slight English accent. That brought back some sense of confidence, along with the great relief to be home with my family again. The customs officials had done exactly what they should have, though it made me smile. They had no way of knowing that, despite my appearance, I was as far from importing a load of drugs in my luggage as anyone could get. Their decision to pull me aside and rifle through my bags before letting me enter the country was triggered by my determination to look stylish in the popular "Mod" English fashion while traveling alone, mainly to give an aura of debonair independence while bolstering my self-confidence. However, to the customs authorities, I was clearly a hippie. My long, straight, honey-blonde hair reached the middle of my back. It hadn't been trimmed in quite a while and was topped with a brown felt fedora sporting a colorfully braided leather hatband. My pants were my favorite light green paisley-covered bell-bottoms, which hugged my thighs and flared in huge bells from the knee down. They were made of a thin cotton Indian bedspread-type material. The top I wore, also of a thin, loose-knit Indian cotton, was a white Nehru-style collarless long-sleeved blouse with teal blue embroidery around the slit at the neck and at the ends of the sleeves.

When asked by customs officials whether I had anything to declare, I told them I had some cheese from Switzerland. They immediately directed me to place all my luggage on their metal table and proceeded to take everything out of my suitcase, carry-on bag, and purse to examine it closely, finding only a couple of large blocks of cheese, just as I had said. When I finally walked away toward the main concourse, it dawned on me that the outfit I was wearing must have triggered their search. At that time there was a large flow of teenagers on the run from parents everywhere, often carrying concealed marijuana or hashish while seeking to join communes or travel to exotic places where illicit drugs were freely used.

Once I had reunited with my family, I regaled them with this story, which made them all laugh. A couple of days later, the English girl I had met at the start of the summer stayed with us again for a couple of days before heading back to England. It was a bit of a shock to notice how she had relaxed into very casual, sprawling ways of sitting while talking about everything she was thinking and feeling, and I, by contrast, was now behaving in a much stiffer, reserved manner than ever before. We were surprised by how our experiences over a couple of months in different cultures had so quickly affected our behavior and casts of mind. This story is relevant not only for the experiences themselves but for what arose a couple of months later when that spinning thought pattern about all my impending responsibilities finally got the better of me. Perhaps what happened was partly due to the lost confidence I experienced during that summer abroad.

After waking my parents almost nightly for those two sleepless weeks when they tried everything they could think of to help me to sleep and get me back on track, without success, one very early morning a physical experience flooded my senses with something I can only describe as a kind of living fire. As I lay awake at four in the morning with the continuous cycle of panic spinning in my brain, suddenly all mental and physical experience morphed into a surreal inferno of leaping yellow, orange, and red flames devoid of heat while containing physical–emotional ecstasy. Those ecstatic flames completely engulfed every sense organ and seemed to pour in, out, and through every living cell in a leaping, constantly shifting movement that erased any sense of self, body, world, or experience beyond itself. The yellow–orange–red color of this all-consuming *fire* expunged every sense of identity and replaced it with a bottomless joy.

After an indeterminate length of time, perhaps a minute, perhaps an hour, the experience abruptly ended. Consciousness returned to the body in my bed in my room at home, leaving me with a powerful amazement at the sheer opportunity to be alive and able only to exclaim into the dark, "WHAT WAS THAT?!?!"

Leaping out of bed and grabbing a pencil and paper, I began to write, not something I had ever done before without prompting. There was such a strong need to somehow remember and record the experience that pencil and paper were the natural tools I reached for to free the words that flooded out into a poem, to my great surprise. My painfully trapped brain had been liberated, bringing me back to reality and allowing me to do what I could to fulfill all my commitments, even though I knew that if I didn't have so many, I would be able to do a much better job with each one. From then on, however, I became intent on doing *what I could* and psychologically accepting whatever limit existed at any given time, rather than following my parents' advice to always do *the best I could*, which wasn't always possible.

Key words from the poem that flowed out of that unique experience remain beside my picture in the senior yearbook from the Princeton High School class of 1972 because that was by far the most stunningly memorable experience of my high school days. Those words also became my life's credo: "To live is to love, laugh, dance, help, hope, and create, and to give of oneself to the utmost is to be satisfied." Writing poetry became a go-to outlet for exploring the meaning behind the strong emotions I experienced, a trusted form of sculpting mental handholds to grip reality and maintain the necessary inner balance to move into whatever the future might hold.

Chapter Six

Don't Trust Anyone
Over Thirty

Every parent teaches their children about the relationship of spirit to life, whether it's described in religious terms or not, and no matter what name they give to that source of inspirational energy. Parents teach, if only through unconscious example and tradition, how to focus and sustain spirit, inspiration, enthusiasm, or whatever word you use to describe positive, energetic engagement with life. Mom and Dad's orientation toward spirit led to my religious education in the Quaker meeting, from age five through ten, followed by membership in the local Unitarian church. Other aspects of the way they led their lives demonstrated the heart of their spiritual understanding, such as a deep commitment to the long-held ancestral value that we should always leave things better than they were when we found them.

Both my parents were privileged to have been raised to think critically by college-educated parents. Their parents also knew how to find and create pathways to joy, even in times of sorrow, and reveled in good songs and stories of mystery, enchantment, and humor, even as they attended to disturbing events in their own lives and the wider world, thus ensuring through their example that attention was paid to both aspects of the dual nature of any moment. When we were young enough to be read to, Dad's bedtime stories always included scary, imaginary, evil beings whose doings kept us on tenterhooks, wondering whether the courage and wisdom of the protagonist would be enough for them to save themselves in the end. The villains came vividly to life in his telling, just as clearly and energetically as did the fairy godmothers in the same stories. Although I deeply loved *Grimm's Fairy Tales* and similar books read to us by my father as we snuggled next to him in our pajamas, the stories they contained also produced some vivid nightmares still clear in memory, as well as the ability to terrify myself and my sister with scary stories invented and told after we were tucked in for sleep.

WHAT CAN ONLY BE TERMED spiritual development plays out simultaneously with physical, emotional, psychological, and cultural development, all nourished or truncated by the natural circumstances in which living rises. Just as babies in the womb are affected by the chemical environments in which they are suspended, mothers are equally affected by every aspect of their living environments. While a child is gestating in the womb, mother and child are a growing, changing unit affected by everything their unified system encounters, as well as the ways in which it responds to those stimuli, physically as well as mentally and emotionally, informing various aspects of their developmental growth. Whatever emotions a mother feels, the food, drink, air, and water available to her, and any pathogens that cross through the umbilical cord or breach the placental barrier between the baby's tiny pond and the ocean of life surrounding the island of the mother's body, connect their whole living system to the much wider ocean of life where they come together into being and which itself is changing and growing all the time.

How can one identify what constitutes spiritual growth, especially at a cultural level? It seems that Albert Schweitzer's term, reverence for life, must be a key value when seeking an answer, acknowledging as it does the imminence and wondrous mystery held within everything and every moment of living. Is it possible to collaboratively grow cultural systems that ensure healthy enough physical, psychological, and emotional development to imbue the wider ocean of human consciousness with a reverence for life? How can a sense of reverence for life become the most important cultural value?

Those questions raise a few more: Can acceptance of all that *is* become the grounding force to finally allow humanity to see the wonder and beauty present in each unlikely moment of living on Earth, right alongside the ugliness and pain that can never be expunged, making it possible to deepen a sense of faith in life's unity and resilience? Can we increase consensus around what constitutes culturally acceptable practices, raising awareness and giving broad support to philosophical development deep enough to allow wide understanding to quickly emerge about humanity's full interdependence within the whole wondrous ocean of moving, dancing, living Earth? Remembering the patience required for any significant learning process to unfold and cultivating the ability to deeply appreciate how highly improbable it is to have the amazing opportunity to experience life as a human being at all seem necessary to the development of humanity's resilience. Learning to trust that the ineffable mystery within life itself, beneath the chemistry and biology that can be measured, is what ultimately guides any developmental process.

A LITTLE-RECOGNIZED CULTURAL LEGACY from the hippies of the '60s and '70s is the normalization of travel to exotic places for more people from every walk of life than had ever made such trips before. Thousands of rebellious European, American, and Australian baby boomers from every socioeconomic strata threw caution to the wind to travel, by whatever inexpensive means they could identify, along an overland route through Asia, altering history in the process. Jack Kerouac, a cultural icon of the Beat generation, may have had something to do with it. *On the Road*, Kerouac's 1957 book, documents his experience of taking to the open road in order to test himself against the unknown in a journey of self-discovery. That inspiration was compounded when Beat poet Allen Ginsberg moved to Varanasi, India, in 1962 and began expounding on the wonders of Eastern philosophy. Soon afterward the Beatles traveled to Rishikesh, India, to spend time with the Maharishi Mahesh Yogi. Cat Stevens, later called Yusuf Islam, went to Kathmandu. The Ray Charles version the song "Hit the Road Jack" rose to wide popularity on the hit parade, soon joined by John Denver and Peter, Paul and Mary singing two versions of Denver's song "Leaving on a Jet Plane." The overland route through Asia came to be seen by those drawn to hippie culture as the path to a more enlightened future capable of fully and equitably realizing human potential and shifting Western cultural norms away from war and planetary destruction toward peace, love, and understanding.[1]

Hippies who set out in search of life's meaning quit their jobs in order to do so, rejecting the conventional values of money and materialism as they sought other ways to define themselves and discover who they naturally were beyond cultural conditioning. They were drawn to reports of the deeply embodied spirituality of Eastern religious practices and imagined that those practices could provide the exotic oases they needed in order to challenge their conditioning and jump-start new insights. Previous generations in the West, more often than not, had held a touch of fear about anything new and different, from cultures, food, and people to any custom they'd never encountered. The hippies who flooded into public squares throughout the West, however, summarily rejected those commonly held fears, which had long ensured adherence to traditional cultural norms. This rowdy group of young people, who rose to the sociopolitical moment with long hair, artistically expressive clothes, wildly colorful art, song, and story, and playful fearlessness, defined a leading edge for the shift in consciousness rumbling beneath the surface of young psyches everywhere.[2]

Nearly all baby boomers were influenced in one way or another by the hippie movement as it progressed and began to define what was fashionable, from hairstyles to clothes, music, dancing, humor, and a plethora of other cultural signals to those under thirty. An important key to their approach to life was challenging social norms by intentionally putting themselves into situations where they couldn't help but experience the unknown. Young people had been seeking out and experimenting with Eastern cultural practices like yoga and meditation for some time by 1971, the year I began my senior year in high school. Meditation had also started to gain a following after its introduction in California by Shunryu Suzuki, whose book *Zen Mind Beginner's Mind*, along with the Alan Watts book *The Wisdom of Insecurity*, began to circulate widely among young protesters during the explosive years of 1967 and 1968.

In Cambridge, Massachusetts, where students were taking over university administration buildings, a Korean Zen master named Sueng Sahn began teaching a group of young meditators. His students included Jon Kabat Zinn, a PhD student at MIT, and Larry Rosenberg, an assistant professor in Harvard's psychiatry department, who likely attended meditation sittings along with the man I would much later marry. Jon Kabat Zinn went on to create the internationally acclaimed approach to managing chronic illness called Mindfulness Based Stress Reduction. Larry Rosenberg went on to found the Cambridge Insight Meditation Center, where years later I studied regularly. My future husband went on to become a leader in the deinstitutionalization movement for people with developmental disabilities, his chosen ministry grounded in what he learned as a seminarian at Boston University and the philosophy and practices taught by Seung Sahn and others from a variety of spiritual traditions.

That same small, weekly meditation circle from the early '70s contained others who made important contributions that helped integrate Eastern wisdom into the Western counterculture, particularly in New England. Their names are not as well known outside the wide circle of people they directly influenced, however. They included Ferris Urbanowski, the gifted, humble, charismatic meditation and childbirth teacher who worked closely with Jon Kabat Zinn to develop and expand his now world-famous program. Along with many other contributions she made to the lives of a great many people before passing away in 2019, she co-founded and fostered a Buddhist study and meditation circle in Vermont, which became a centering community for me and my second husband as we began slowly transplanting our lives to Vermont as we transitioned into retirement, beginning in 2012.

The opening of youthful minds to ideas from Eastern cultures in the late '60s opened another powerful door to cultural shift in 1971 when a meditation teacher named Satya Narayan Goenka led a ten-day retreat in Bodh Gaya, India, the birthplace of Buddhism. The retreat was held in a Burmese monastery where men slept on the roof and women in the corridors around the meditation hall. Participants later described a strong sense of lasting connection stemming from their common experience as young Americans who encountered each other after traveling far from home, both literally and figuratively. They described a thrilling sense of discovery in shared learning about a completely new way to conceive of life's meaning. Sharon Salzburg met Joseph Goldstein there, an auspicious moment for the mindfulness and meditation movements because they returned to the US and founded the Insight Meditation Society, now located in Barre, Massachusetts, which took root and grew to become one of the leading US retreat and research centers focused on Buddhist teachings.[3] One of the primary inspirations that decades later brought me and my second husband to numerous retreats at the Barre Center for Buddhist Studies over twenty years was the writing and teaching of former program director Mu Soeng, who had first served as a monk for eleven years at the Providence Zen Center founded by Seung Sahn.

The "hippie trail," which laid the foundation for these later developments, was a vaguely identifiable route defined by those traveling it, who passed information by word of mouth about where and how to travel. This vague route took young vagabonds to exotic destinations that changed their lives and also inspired spiritual teachers from those same places to travel to the US where they reached many other interested young people unable to make the overseas trip. As word spread, a flood of young people began to flow to India and Nepal in the early 1970s. US and European travelers began in Istanbul, Turkey, and landed ultimately in Goa, India, or Kathmandu, Nepal, depending on the season. Australians and New Zealanders started in Bali, Indonesia, crossing a similar route in the opposite direction.[4]

Mindfulness meditation is no longer the mysterious, exotic tradition it was when the hippie movement began spreading these practices across the US. Since then, they've become what could be called *an industry*. General Mills, Aetna, Target, and Goldman Sachs provide mindfulness training to employees. Mindfulness is taught in innumerable venues, from retreat centers to public schools to the military and even to prisons. Dan Harris wrote a number one *New York Times* best-seller called *10 Percent Happier* about mindfulness practice. The *Harvard Business Review* claimed that the mindfulness movement was close to taking on cult status in the business world in an article published in 2015. Psychoanalysts now widely use mindfulness techniques in their practices. If a group of young hippies hadn't traveled the hippie trail in the '60s, it's quite possible that none of that would have happened.

Many young *Americans* in the '60s and '70s were becoming disenchanted with the religious traditions of their families because those traditions required that they accept and structure their lives around a set of beliefs that clashed ever more starkly with the science they were learning in school and with their own experiences. Buddhist teachers taught a practice method, rather than a dogma or creed, something intended to be used to test the truth of its teachings against personal experience by each individual practitioner, a method that spoke directly to the spiritual dilemma facing young spiritual seekers and their yearning for greater *authenticity* in their spiritual practices. Testing religious dogma and belief in practical daily applications felt like a revolutionary approach to spiritual growth and harmonized with the widely accepted youth slogan of the time, "Question authority." Practitioners were not encouraged to believe at face value anything the Buddha taught but instead to put any form of Buddhist teaching into practice, actively using it to see for themselves whether the results panned out as expected. If the results didn't pan out, the practitioners were encouraged to use only the practices that worked for them, tossing aside the rest, at least for the time being.

The work of the American teachers who had traveled the hippie trail planted many seeds of a new spiritual crop, now known as American Buddhism. They produced many roots and branches because they didn't simply import a set of teachings. Instead, they adapted the teachings—as teachers of Buddhism have been doing for centuries, this time to US culture—while retaining the core practices: deeply noticing the experience of suffering caused by emotional reactivity and craving, noticing how that can end of its own accord when the story behind it is released, experiencing the point at which that suffering ends, and subsequently attending to an ethical path through life that supports and strengthens the ability to recognize and disengage from thoughts and habits that increase suffering for oneself and others.

It's important to note that the '60s and '70s were a time of relative peace and prosperity for the countries through which the hippie trail wound. Iran and Afghanistan both had cultural traditions that welcomed traveling strangers into homes, communities, and virtually anywhere they went. That open welcome and the overland route through Iran abruptly ended when Ayatollah Ruhollah Khomeini's Council of the Islamic Revolution came to power in early 1979. Russia invaded Afghanistan later that same year, effectively ending the overland route. The final blow came when Lebanon, a favorite hippie haven for purchasing marijuana, exploded into civil war. Kashmir and eventually Nepal also lost their former auras of safety.

Mass tourism began to replace adventurous journeys along the hippie trail as these changes unfolded. Goa, India, became a destination for package tours. By 1980, adventurous travel shifted its focal destination to Southeast Asia as war and genocide finally ended there, thanks in no small part to the worldwide peace movement to end the Vietnam War. It's possible to see the focus on a search for meaning that catalyzed youthful wandering in the '60s and '70s as the cultural hand that opened the door to world travel for today's international middle class. Backpackers and giant global adventure travel companies now support world wanderers who consider themselves authentic travelers, wanting to be changed by the foreign cultures where they immerse themselves rather than to go on sightseeing junkets, the same attitude held by those who traveled the hippie trail years ago.[5]

IN HER BOOK *We Are as Gods: Back to the Land in the 1970s on the Quest for a New America*, Kate Daloz describes how another swath of young people traveled within the US. They flowed out of middle-class suburbia to rural outposts in California, Vermont,

Tennessee, and New Mexico, among other places, in what came to be known as the back-to-the-land movement. Feeling a similarly deep objection to the lives they were conditioned to lead as did those traveling to Asia, these travelers settled in wild rural places to live in communes, co-operative houses, and handmade geodesic domes. "To a privileged generation exhausted by shouting NO to so many aspects of the American society they were raised to inherit, rural life represented a way to say yes."[6]

The refrain from the rock song "Born to be Wild," from the 1969 film *Easy Rider*, encapsulates the deep unconscious drive that swept young people into whatever exotic version of foreign or rural travel and living they could access. Although the rest of the lyrics never stuck, that refrain planted a taproot in my high school sophomore brain and continued to reverberate long after I became an adult. I was lucky in 1969 to have a mother who was equally eager to see the movie after reading its reviews. I imagine she saw the trip we made together to see that picture as a teaching and learning opportunity for both of us. It was also one of only a few opportunities I experienced of a one-on-one mother–daughter outing. Mom's long interest in social justice and civil rights, evidenced in the first job she took out of college (teaching art in an immigrant settlement house in Chicago), must also have been part of what motivated her to take me to see that film. As a fifteen-year-old, I wouldn't have been allowed admission without a parent. She also took me to see *The Graduate* in the same spirit. I remember both outings with deep gratitude as bonding experiences that gave me a new respect for my mother. Both times were precious opportunities to share popcorn, laughter, and conversation about life and society. Mom probably wouldn't have seen those movies without me, either, because Dad had no interest in such films, preferring the stress relief of Broadway musicals when he had time to take in a show.

A desire to cast off cultural conditioning and reunite somehow with the wild beauty of nature caught on in the hearts of many young people like me, in the 1970s, as we started making our way into the wider world. For those a few years older, the back-to-the-land movement reflected that same inner sense of themselves, motivating them to become self-sufficiently wild by creating unusual life shapes that didn't depend on what could be described as the institutionalized cultural grid. Back-to-the-land adherents literally removed themselves from dependence on corporately produced electric energy, fossil fuels, supermarkets, and department stores. Instead they chose to chop their own wood, cultivate their own food, and make their own furniture and clothes. All the hippie travelers sensed a need to change the conventional patterns of life that were destroying the environment and killing millions of people in Vietnam and elsewhere before it was too late.[7]

When I sought to go as far from suburban Princeton as possible in 1972, landing in the farm country of rural Minnesota to attend college, then following a continuing drive of the same kind to start life after graduation in Vermont, it wouldn't be much of a stretch to say that I was unconsciously following that same muse. Those who were five or ten years older than I had paved the way. Many were inspired, as I also came to be, by Scott and Helen Nearing's example, described in their book *Living the Good Life*, published in 1970.

The back-to-the-land movement was comprised almost entirely of privileged young people of European descent under the age of thirty, for whom a rebellious life choice was not as risky as it would have been for many others. The majority of these young rebels had been raised with a secure safety net suspended beneath their lives. Their rebellious choices were sometimes even financed by trust funds or monetary allowances from their families. Family support was mainly emotional for those from less wealthy backgrounds like mine. However, if things went terribly wrong, my parents and those like mine could still be counted on to bail out or take in their kids, at least until they got back on their feet. Even those who cut ties with their families altogether inherited the confidence of *white* privilege before that term gained common usage.[8]

The middle-class parents of these mainly *white* baby boomers had experienced the repercussions of the Great Depression and WWII while they were growing into adulthood, and they wanted to believe that affluence would continue indefinitely for their children. They buried any psychological trauma their childhood may have contained and projected onto their children their hope that the world had become safe and predictable now that those turbulent years had ended. The booming postwar economy from which middle-class *white* families benefited led many of them to be certain that their children would be able to attend college and enter professional careers. As a result, many postwar children in such neighborhoods were raised to believe that the world was a basically safe place, even as evidence in magazines and on television insinuated that it actually was not. Regular air raid drills were held in grade schools. Children, such as I was in the mid-1950s, filed into school hallways to kneel by the wall, covering our heads to practice protecting ourselves from the fallout from nuclear bombs. Photographs in *Life* magazine of civil rights protests where police used sticks, fire hoses, and dogs to beat back peaceful protesters, including children our own age, and other photos of Vietnamese children lying dead with their mothers in the jungle also informed our growing psyches. The middle-class parenting approach, used to redirect their children's attention away from such horrors, succeeded only in driving childhood fears underground and creating a vague sense that not only was society unsafe but adults couldn't admit that to themselves.

As a result, many left home in droves in their late teens and early twenties, the only way they could imagine to discover a more honest, life-affirming way to live and structure society. "Our work is guided by the sense that we may be the last generation in the experiment with living," [9] declared the 1962 Port Huron Statement of the college student group Students for a Democratic Society. That declaration was a major catalyst for a decade of student activism, first in response to the growing arsenal of atomic weapons on both sides of the Cold War and soon afterward in response to the horrors of the Vietnam War. Travelers on the hippie trail and in the back-to-the-land movement emerged from a pervasive sense that imminent death from either the A-bomb or the Vietnam War was what young people could realistically expect, coupled with confidence grown in the protected enclaves of their childhoods that had convinced them that they were entitled to the world they had been raised to believe possible. As psychologist Kenneth Keniston put it, "Never before have so many who had so much been so deeply disenchanted with their inheritance." [10]

Chapter Seven

Parting Delusion's Veil

There is a twenty-year-old woman who can't hold her anger inside. She argued loudly with her parents as a teenager but was unable to change her situation by shouting. This young woman was offered the opportunity to choose where to attend college. She chose the most academically rigorous college to accept her that was farthest away from home, so far that she wouldn't be able to return home during short school vacations like the long Thanksgiving weekend, so far that she would be forced to figure out who she really was from her own experience rather than from family rules about behavior. This young woman feels a strong need to escape her parents' protective ideas about who she is supposed to be.

When this young woman leaves home for college, her fire refuses to stay in the shadows, no matter how often she shoves it back down. It often surfaces as emotional pain in a big way unless she anesthetizes it with alcohol or disowns it in other ways. Nevertheless it follows her everywhere. This young woman discovers she can rid herself completely of the discomfort of emotional pain by smoking marijuana, a tool finally strong enough to silence the inner critic that has begun to speak far more strongly than her parents ever did. Marijuana has none of the down sides that drinking enough alcohol to get to that same place does, a practice that has already resulted in making her ill or obviously under the influence in public more often than she can admit, even to herself.

This young woman detests the constant battle within her own mind and emotions, between the indomitable critic and the needy wild girl who keeps getting in the way, undermining the confidence she needs to succeed in her studies and asking more of the young men she is learning to love than they can give. After transferring to art school, she is sorely tempted to jump from the fourth story window of her dorm building to kill that little girl inside, the one she blames for making her feel completely worthless, undeserving, and deeply confused. She chooses not to because she can't bear the thought of the deep pain such an act would open in the hearts of her sisters and parents.

The little girl inside this young woman does not want to be dashed on the stone sidewalk below. She goes into hiding deep, deep in the recesses of this young woman's mind, discovering a cave at the end of a long tunnel that leads down and out of the dark forest of confusion and pain into a place far beneath consciousness. That little wild girl crawls to the very back of that very deep cave and curls up with the intention never to surface again in the light of day.

WE CAN'T KNOW THE WHOLE of what is happening around us as it unfolds, and even when a more comprehensive view is possible through greater awareness, maturity, and distance, we can never see it all. We can see more, however, mainly by piecing together the stories of others who lived through the same era, fitting them into holes in personal perceptions of the same times. Any overlay of abstract concepts describing the why and how of experience only follows from reflection on patterns recognized through direct perception. Even then, finding the most useful and accurate data and patterns along with the words to describe perception continually shifts in an endless process. There are so many perspectives from which to view the same historical events, revealing different lines and shadows from different viewpoints.

Most of what I can say about personal experience comes from the situations burned into memory by their impact on my growing mind, combined with what I know about how they affected personal decisions as I responded to life. Combining those insights with what I have learned by reading the accounts of others who lived through the same times in other bodies and other places provides a more complete, though never all-encompassing, view.

By the time I began college at eighteen in the fall of 1972, the Vietnam War still required young men my age to be drafted to fight and die in Southeast Asia. The political campaign of George McGovern to unseat President Nixon after one term was well underway. I had by then gained a strong sense that President Nixon was extremely corrupt and dangerous. Four years earlier, as a naive high school freshman, I had argued with my father about who to support for the presidency, trying to keep an open mind and critically think about what I read in the news, despite Dad's visceral dislike of Nixon due to Nixon's past participation in the House Un-American Activities Committee (HUAAC) as one of Joseph McCarthy's henchmen. Dad had strong evidence of Nixon's nefariousness through Dad's personal experience in the way HUAAC poisoned the political environment, destroying any potential for Dad to realize the dream career that mysteriously dissolved just as he took his first step into it.

During his 1968 campaign, Nixon promised to end the Vietnam War—the most important political concern for anyone under thirty—and his Democratic rival, Hubert Humphrey, had been vice president under President Johnson, who had escalated that war. Many *Americans* were hoodwinked by Nixon's promise to end the war with a secret strategy, which won him the presidency. Luckily, I was too young at fourteen to vote in 1968, realizing a year later how mistaken I'd been to believe Nixon would actually keep his promise. Following his election, he did exactly the opposite, living up to his nickname, "Tricky Dicky." His secret plan involved escalating the fighting and expanding it beyond Vietnam into Cambodia, resulting in tens of thousands of additional deaths, including huge numbers of innocent Cambodian civilians.

By September 15, 1972, two of Nixon's closest associates had been indicted by a grand jury in connection with the Watergate burglary of Democratic National Committee headquarters the previous June. One of them, G. Gordon Liddy, was a former FBI agent, US Treasury official, and White House staff member serving as counsel to the Committee to Re-elect the President when he was indicted. E. Howard Hunt Jr. a close Nixon confidant, former White House consultant and former CIA agent, and four others formerly connected with the CIA were also indicted, in addition to a locksmith sympathetic to the Republican cause. The grand jury that investigated the Watergate scandal ultimately indicted sixty-nine members of the Nixon administration, most of whom had participated in the immense cover-up—designed to prevent knowledge of Nixon's direct involvement—of facts leading up to the robbery.[1] Forty-eight of them were convicted, which completely destroyed many young people's faith in the US government. By the time the grand jury hearings ended, nearly everyone under thirty who hadn't already opposed the war had lost faith in the patriotic purpose of what had become Nixon's war, even if they had volunteered to fight out of a sense of duty. Those who had done so had often gone into the armed services believing that the US was the wisest and most just country in the world, until they arrived in Vietnam and experienced what was really happening in-country.

While the drama of the Watergate scandal was playing out, I was immersed in college life. Many discoveries from that era were subliminally catalytic on an equally important personal level, informing something deeper than consciousness as I learned how to learn by identifying and asking good questions. These more elusive lessons profoundly affected the shape of living to come, lodging deep in memory, though lying dormant for years. Meditation as a way to gain peaceful transcendence, for example, was a concept that held my interest and curiosity early in college without my having any direct experience. It was a concept that stayed with me for years throughout various later times when I was desperate enough to try it as a last-ditch way to find inner calm. The concept of meditation grew as a valued tool each time I engaged it, times few and far between until well into my thirties.

Other discoveries engaged my experiential attention through physical sensation as I sought alternative ways to construct meaningful adult living and to learn things about a human body that I'd never considered as I stuck a toe in the vast pool of possibilities for structuring meaning differently from the ways I'd learned to in my family. In college there were the relatively tame but profound adventures of discovering and eating exotic vegetarian food with delicious tastes and spicy smells never encountered before. There were also hidden gifts to be found when engaging in political activism. At a time when the birth control pill was first made available on college campuses, young women like me were also passing around the book *Our Bodies Ourselves* by the Boston Women's Health Book Collective, educating each other about the wonder and operation of the female body in ways many of our mothers had never discovered and introducing the mysterious power and emotional turmoil of ecstatic sexual experience.

Another book being passed around and discussed on campus in 1972 promoted the concept that marijuana and LSD were less dangerous and addictive than the alcohol our parents drank at cocktail parties, a widely accepted social practice among families like mine. That idea led me to one fascinating and terrifying recreational drug experience with LSD, taken as a way to convince my boyfriend to stop taking it recreationally himself. That risky venture worked, though it also convinced me that the drug could easily destroy my brain because I awoke the day following a joyful afternoon and evening to find the trees still shimmering in electric green and myself still feeling the blood running through my veins as though every capillary was communicating instantaneously with my brain. With the aid of lots of water and nearly a full day of walking in the woods with my boyfriend, the trees eventually returned to their lovely, quiet, normal shade of green and my body felt like itself again. I never touched LSD again after that frightening day, and neither did my boyfriend who later became my first husband.

It was during those college years that I also discovered the elation of losing all self-consciousness while dancing to loud, energetic rock 'n' roll music in a crowd of other dancers. It held a power to break through the emotional pain of heartbreak, catalyzing complete abandonment of self-consciousness without any drugs at all. Listening closely to the music's rhythm and lyrics, allowing my body to move in any way it was inspired to, especially when dancing close to amplifiers, allowed the beat to become the movement in my bones, muscles, and ligaments, primed for such a response by years of learning modern dance and gymnastics. The body became the music, releasing all sense of a separate self in the process.

The peaceful release and mental regenerative power of long sessions swimming laps in the semi-dark college pool on winter evenings served the same purpose, as did learning about the deep relaxation that alternating saunas and cold showers can provide for a tense, exhausted mind and body. Another discovery was what raw emotional vulnerability felt like while attending a party featuring a naked group sauna, another experience I vowed never to try again. Luckily, no sexual abuse of any kind occurred. I left early with my roommate, convulsing in fits of embarrassed laughter after discovering how precious and sacred our bodies were to us, not meant to be so casually revealed to even the friendliest and safest of acquaintances.

The notion of biorhythms and how they apply to learning and effective mental work made another deep impression on my conscious mind at the end of freshman year following a group study session before a final exam in astronomy. I needed an A on the final exam in order to pass the course and, after enlisting help, became distraught when an all-night study session effectively gained me no new ground after 9:00 p.m. At about 2:00 a.m., I abandoned all hope of help from my two male classmates more gifted in memorizing answers from old tests than I and trudged back across the dark campus to my dorm to rest for a couple of hours.

I knew there was no chance of sleep because I had taken a small dose of speed on the advice of those two young men, who convinced me that staying awake all night with them to memorize the test material would empower me to pull down the A. After thrashing around in bed for a couple of hours, I bought a cup of black coffee from a vending machine and took a walk to clear my head, taking along the reams of notes I'd taken in class. Stopping to sit alone on a hill overlooking two ponds while I slowly drank the bitter liquid, I breathed in the coolness of the damp air, felt the earth beneath me, and noticed the gentle wind touching my face and lifting my hair while I dolefully pondered the mist-shrouded ponds in the dim predawn light, a view that perfectly reflected my muddled brain.

Still struggling to make sense of the material, I began flipping desperately through the notebook's pages using a flashlight when suddenly, with the first flash of daylight turning the sky from dim grey to clear blue at exactly 4:30 a.m., the first glimmer of dawn turned the sky a dim grey that gradually became clear blue, lifting the mist from the ponds and confusion from my brain. Somehow, I could now explain and remember how all my notes fit together. After that experience, I never again took any kind of stimulant other than coffee or studied beyond nine o'clock at night, opting instead when under pressure to go to bed early and rise at 4:00 a.m., make coffee, and begin work half an hour later. At that hour, I zoomed with ease through assignments that were impossible to navigate effectively at night. Devastating encounters with failure, confusion, and ultimately humility, which carried their own profound consequences, were also part of my young adult discoveries, along with the beginning of psychological education about the term *emotional boundaries* and how they are extremely different from one person to the next, often indiscernible until crossed and illiciting unexpected emotional reactions.

This spiral of memory brings back the taste and feel of those times and personal insights, although clearly articulating the unfurling pattern they created is by no means easy. Pulling out these threads from memory's weave also reveals glimmers beneath them of even older hues of the tapestry of culture deep in the psychic biome from which the '60s generation grew. Pulling on one of those threads might lead to a continuous unraveling—if anyone could actually follow it—all the way back through human existence. All that can be said with any real accuracy about that chain of being, as it relates to anyone's individual development, however, is like an abstract expressionist painting. The elements of the story are like the brushstrokes of an artist, suggesting a partially recognizable shape touched by light and shadow though inseparable from a color or pattern established by the action of painting itself.

IN COLLEGE I STRUGGLED to find a major that would inspire enough passion to maintain focused intensity and build the necessary confidence to face down the deep academic challenges that nearly derailed my studies at first. That struggle provided two revelations. First, my rational mind might not always perceive the best course to follow. Second, my deepest interest did not lie in expressing what I observed, thought, and felt using visual art, despite that kind of expression coming so easily to me, or perhaps because of it. Instead, I was surprised to discover that my deepest motivating curiosity resided in an area impossible to imagine before reaching a cliff edge of despair. The curiosity and drive to learn, which ultimately opened a successful path through college, graduate school, and career, lay not in visual art where I had consistently excelled without effort. It lay in seeking to understand how power is distributed and maintained through the social and political structures humanity creates, the various cultural means by which civilizations organize themselves around it, and what constitutes the basis of true power.

Only after confronting multiple areas of personal failure was I able to identify those diffuse intellectual motivations in any useful way, even though they had long resided at the root of many aspects of the cultural world that continuously held my curiosity. I also discovered that although I'd been able to adjust to many different life situations with little trouble and craved excitement and adventure, no matter how hard I worked, there was no path into comfort, or even tolerable discomfort, in the constant level of commotion and deep sense of claustrophobia I experienced while living in New York City during the single semester I spent there in art school, from September through December 1975.

Backtracking to August 1974, just prior to fall term of junior year at Carleton College in Northfield, Minnesota, I can begin to explain the trajectory of how these insights surfaced. That was the tail end of a summer spent in a collaborative, student-run acting troupe that stayed in Northfield for the summer called the Uninvited Company, which performed plays for the local community in the college theater on weekend evenings and also held a children's theater day camp during the week. All troupe members slept, cooked, and ate as a tightly knit community in one of the college's off-campus houses. We earned our room and board through the proceeds gained from parents of children attending our day camp and from selling tickets to several plays we produced, hocking the tickets on street corners in our eye-catching costumes in Northfield, a small farm community. I returned to New Jersey at the end of the summer unaware that I had contracted a bad case of mononucleosis while working and playing hard all summer. We of the Uninvited Company also brought home a real sense of pride in accomplishment, having paid the required rent for the house and fed ourselves through our own effort and imagination as an amateur acting troupe, doing well enough to also allow us each to walk away with a hundred dollars in our pockets.

For the first three weeks spent at home before returning to college, in August 1974, I lay prone and asleep for the vast majority of the time, having only enough energy to rise from bed each day to eat one meal before returning to sleep again. A diagnosis of mononucleosis from the family pediatrician confirmed Mom's fears after a week of this behavior. At the end of those three weeks of debilitating exhaustion, I was able to get out of bed and function relatively normally for most of two or three days during the week before the start of college. Feeling relief that recovery was finally happening led me and my parents to assume that I would continue to progress well enough to resume my studies, so I pulled myself together and flew back to school.

Although I appeared healthy, I lacked the physical energy necessary to do more than academically limp through first semester junior year. I was shocked at the end of the term to discover an inability to put words together to reasonably analyze copious research notes in order to write the final paper in my favorite art history course on a topic that fascinated me, a very strange situation for one who truly enjoyed writing. That situation left me confused and panicked. As a last resort I went to my professor, who upon hearing the details of my problem immediately asked whether I had been ill. When I told him my story, he explained that he had seen several cases of students suffering from severe illness like mine over the years and advised me to take a year off to recover. He said it often took that long before one's energy was physically back fully enough for the brain to meet the academic challenges of college.

Thankfully, Mom was able to hear the story I brought home at Christmas break, to her great credit. As a result, she chose to support my tearfully expressed insistence that this was not any kind of concocted excuse to leave school, as Dad seemed to think. In a rare, though calm and diplomatically articulated, confrontation to Dad's loud and adamantly expressed point of view, Mom insisted over his angry shouting that he trust what I was saying. The advice for me to leave school had come, after all, from a favorite academically strict art history professor at Carleton, which, in the eyes of a fine artist like Mom, may have given it added clout.

As a result, I spent a quiet winter at home. Healing began in earnest in the spring as I increasingly regained physical stamina by taking our family's Labrador retriever for long walks along the canal that extended from Trenton through Princeton to New

Brunswick, New Jersey. We eventually walked for miles every day for several weeks amid the bright green leaves and wild bird songs of the towpath along the stretch where drovers and their mules originally towed barges between Kingston and Rocky Hill, one of the wilder sections of the path and the most easily accessed from the bottom of the hill where my family lived.

Our dog, Tucker, loved these walks and seemed solicitous of me, trotting ahead and sniffing along the trail, then returning wagging her tail to see how I was doing before heading off again, rarely roaming out of sight. Sometimes I would throw a stick into the water for her and she would eagerly plunge in to bring it back. We created a special bond that way, which lasted until her death. Even after I moved away, returning only a couple of times a year, she would always greet me with great fanfare, and I was equally glad to see my old walking companion. When my stamina began to return in earnest, I took a job as cashier in the stationery department of the Princeton University bookstore, or what we townies called "the U store," a job I found on Dad's insistence that I at least earn some money if I wasn't going back to college. He still worried that I would never return, which to my core I knew was untrue, impossible though it was to convince him.

I spent several months at that job, enjoying the work that brought me into contact with lots of different kinds of people, including much older colleagues. I also made friends on my lunch breaks in the depressing staff lunch room with young people my own age who had opted after high school for work on the loading docks to support beginning careers as musicians or in the store's administrative offices to begin business careers as office clerks. When spring began to open into summer, my parents became motivated, while watching the realignment of my friendships away from their trusted social circles, to offer me an opportunity to spend nearly three months in Rome and Umbria, Italy. Becoming an au pair (live-in babysitter) for a family with two children under age three in a wealthy Italian family, led by one of Dad's favorite colleagues, seemed like a once-in-a-lifetime opportunity. I leapt without a moment's hesitation at this chance for solo international travel to an exotic city.

The stunningly surprising privilege of that summer in Italy was a life-changing opportunity that I would never have guessed could come from my usually overprotective parents. I imagine they believed that Dad's colleague and friend would be a good supervisor for their daughter who had apparently gone off the rails. By contrast, that parental brainstorm actually liberated me to spend three amazingly independent months exploring various parts of Italy, beginning in Rome, mostly out of sight of my father's colleague. At the start of this magical journey, I flew out of New York City on the eve of my twenty-first birthday. A window seat gave me a stunning view of the full moon in a clear sky over the open ocean—just as I crossed the culturally designated line into adulthood—and gave the full moon special significance for me from then on.

Soon after arriving, I was befriended by the Polish au pair whom I replaced. She spoke no English but was very outgoing and warm and spoke a little French, a language I also knew a little. We laughed and used many hand signs while spending a couple of overlapping weeks roaming the city together. The family's maid, Italia, usually shooed us out into the city to explore, unbeknownst to her employers. She explained that she truly enjoyed caring for the two children we had been hired to care for and her job of cleaning and cooking took no time in the small apartment where the family lived.

My new Polish friend introduced me to her friends in Rome, a motley collection of Italians and people of various Arabian descent. After she departed to travel a little before returning to Poland, I independently studied Italian with a vengeance and continued to be encouraged to explore by Italia, who had by then become a close friend and ally. I screwed up my courage and finally began to make many day trips alone into the city with a sketchbook under my arm, being sure to arrive home before the children's parents did. I made lots of sketches of wonderful Bernini fountains and visited as many of the historically significant cultural and artistic sights as I could, many of which I had learned about in art history class at Carleton and in ancient history class in high school. I imagined all of this exploring as preparation for an impending college transfer to Pratt Institute in the fall, where I would begin studying for a commercial art degree. Mom had supported this choice after I explained how it made no sense for me to attend Carleton to study art when there were some topflight art schools just forty-five minutes away by train in New York City, as opposed to a thousand miles and a plane ticket away in Northfield, Minnesota. Those schools, I argued, would lead me down a more certain path to a career than an art degree from a liberal arts college in the Midwest, while also saving the family lots of money. Mom had helped me put a portfolio together and gone to interviews with me at the Parsons School of Design and Pratt, where my grandmother had earned her art teaching certificate many years earlier. Dad went along with this plan, happy that I would at least be returning to school in some form, if not the place he preferred.

I kept a journal to prepare for art school while in Italy, where I discovered that I could be supremely happy exploring in a foreign country completely alone and learning Italian from my two-year-old charge while at the house and also from the young Italian men I encountered. They didn't speak English but were invariably polite and nearly always came to look over my shoulder as I sketched fountains, often offering to show me around the city after we struck up a conversation. The Italian adventures that resulted from those encounters and others in Umbria, Porto Santo Stefano, and finally in Florence in the company of an English au pair I met on the Santo Stefano beach are too numerous to recount here. Suffice it to say that I fell in love with Italy, Italians, and all that entailed and would have stayed forever except for the thought that if I did, an ocean would lie between me and my family.

Once I returned home, confident, healthy, and speaking fluent Italian to my parents' delight, I was eager to enter the new career path of commercial art that I had chosen to study at Pratt Institute. I soon discovered, however, to my great chagrin, that New York City was not a place where I could live or work for long. Despite making friends, working hard at my studies, and becoming fascinated by the work required by several courses, especially one focused on color, I soon became supremely unhappy. All the asphalt streets and steel and concrete buildings bordered by sidewalks sprinkled with only a few unhealthy trees, coupled with the constant din and confusion of sounds, sights, smells, and the hustle and bustle of the city left me nearly catatonic by early afternoon every single day. It was hard to focus or sleep in the din, which left me very depressed. I was devastated and at a complete loss over what to do next. New York City was different in nearly every way from human-scale Rome, which operated in a much more relaxed fashion among shorter buildings revealing an abundance of sky and liberally sprinkled with plenty of healthy trees and gardens.

In the midst of intense confusion and deep self-criticism near the end of that fall semester in New York, I sat alone in the high-rise concrete dorm room I shared with another girl in the Bedford-Stuyvesant section of Brooklyn, where Pratt is located. Ruminating on the endless loop of indecision concerning what I could possibly do to pull myself out of the sense of alienated, sad loneliness that by then dominated all waking hours, I reached for the journal I kept while babysitting and wandering around Italy the previous summer. Hoping to find something in my notes and drawings from that blissful time that could clarify a way forward through the swamp of contradicting fears, I made a surprising discovery.

Instead of the proliferation of sketches of fountains and scenery I expected to see when opening the journal, there was page after page of notes about Italian culture and the political and social organization of Italian society. In fact, I had to admit that there were likely *more* pages of notes in the journal than drawings, despite an imagined passion for visual art and a clear intention to use that summer to prepare for art school by sketching as a daily practice. Along with that discovery, I also realized how badly I missed reading and writing. That was an unwanted brainstorm because it pointed toward finding a way to transfer back to Carleton, which I was sure would leave my parents utterly exasperated. However, it was the clearest clue I had about why I felt so utterly stuck, and I had to change something because living in limbo felt very much like the two nearly catatonic weeks I'd spent in high school following my mother around, an utterly terrifying indication that such times could come again.

I can't double-check the contents of that journal today because it no longer exists. At a much later junction I transported a large pile of journals to a wooded campground, first by car, then by an overburdened children's wagon, and finally in the back of a pickup truck driven by a camper who offered to ferry me, my friend, and our abundance of journals to a campsite where we burned them, seeking to ritually rid ourselves of the negative voices they contained. Ritualizing the event cemented it in memory, helping to anchor a more positive approach to life thereafter. It took far longer than expected to accomplish the task, however, because the journals wouldn't burn unless we ripped the pages out one at a time and offered them up individually to the flames, requiring us to notice and release each gripe, one at a time, deepening our understanding of what we were letting go. During that campfire I resolved never again to write down any complaint about life when seeking a solution to an emotional challenge. Instead I would make notes only after I came to an insight that helped me to move forward. Now when rereading old journals, I can quickly find useful nuggets of inspiration, rather than the discouraging contours of repetitious internal wrestling matches.

Returning to the dorm room at Pratt in the fall of 1974, where I sat examining the journal from my Italian summer adventure, I finally decided to do what I could to return to Carleton and switch majors from art to political science and international relations, no matter what my parents' reaction might be.

Thankfully, my worried parents responded with encouragement, very enthusiastically on my father's part. When I subsequently called the college to ask if it was possible to return, a friendly, kind woman in the admissions office also welcomed my decision, telling me that as it happened, Carleton had just hired a new political science/international relations professor, about whom they were very excited. Upon my return, that professor became the academic mentor I needed, providing insight and inspiration and opening a window onto the workings of power in the world, which held my riveted attention for the remainder of my college days.

Once back on campus, academic engagement and achievement quickly took hold, allowing me to thrive at Carleton in ways I never had before. An emotional connection to the academic work had gone missing since freshman year, partly because fellow freshmen from prestigious boarding schools had been far ahead of me in their studies, and two misguided English professors quickly derailed my freshman dream of becoming a writer, resulting from the unrewarding way they responded to my passionate application to their subject.

Following my return for spring term, junior year, I gained more faith in my ability to write and analyze than I had ever had before, which also built more confidence to meet every other challenge, propelling me eventually into an internship in the college alumni office where I was paid to work as an assistant editor, doing layout, writing, and editing for the alumni newsletter. I also began to submit and be assigned stories to write for the weekly student newspaper. New faith in my capabilities provided the courage to open little by little to an almost wordless inner voice from a very deep place inside, most likely to surface on long walks in the woods or while cross-country skiing through snowy fields and wooded hills surrounding the college.

Ultimately, I made it to graduation a year late, just missing academic honors for a comprehensive paper in political science by a hair, I was told. That said, I was incredibly relieved to be finished with academia for a while, honors or no honors. I had absolutely no energy or desire to even think about graduate school, to the sorrow of my mentor, who said to my father at graduation, "I only wish I had had her for one more year." Knowing full well that he was implying I was making a big mistake by choosing not to go immediately to graduate school, I asked Dad in consternation, "What did he mean by that?! What's wrong with what I'm doing?!" Shrugging, Dad said, "I don't know, Jane. I don't see anything wrong with what you're doing." I saw in Dad's face, however, that he knew as well as I did what my mentor was implying, and although I know he was relieved to see me graduate, I could also see that Dad agreed with him, at least a little.

THREE WEEKS after returning home to New Jersey, I headed north to Vermont in the family's old Volkswagen Rabbit, donated to my life journey and packed to the gills with my belongings. It was the summer of 1977. I had five hundred dollars in my pocket, also donated by my parents to tide me over until I found a job. My parents may very well have imagined I would soon return. If that was the case, they never let on and I never looked back, except of course for visits home at least twice a year. I was determined to find my own way. Of course, having been raised in a family of privileged Scotch–Irish *American* roots, supported by the significant privilege that accompanies such families, I knew that if I ever ended up in the ditch, literally or figuratively, my parents would pull me out. It was clear to me then, and even more so now, that without that knowledge I would have needed far more courage to head in the countercultural direction I ultimately chose after leaving the family fold.

At first, having been enamored of the two reporters from the *Washington Post* who broke the Watergate story that ejected Nixon from the presidency and being like so many others of my generation, I hoped my writing skills and college journalism and internship credentials would be enough to secure a news reporting gig. Imagining it would be easier to land a writing position on one of the small local papers in Vermont instead of on a big city paper that would require a journalism degree, I headed north. My college boyfriend also lived in Vermont and wanted to stay there because he hoped to attend graduate school at the University of Vermont in Burlington. The two of us had created a secret plan near the end of senior year, which would first require me to get a job to support our living expenses while he worked at getting into graduate school. We also promised each other that we would eventually marry but not for at least the first year. Other parts of the plan included a chance for me to attend graduate school later, a desire to have and raise children together, and a dream of living happily ever after, if not in that particular order.

Chapter Eight

Nourishing Roots of Change

Living together as an unmarried couple to find out whether marriage to your chosen partner would work over the long term was a practice that flew in the face of conventional propriety in 1977 and one that had never before occurred in such large numbers before the baby boom generation arrived at maturity. A large part of what motivated the shift was the changing social role of women and confusion among young women like me concerning how to put life's pieces together: love, career, children, and shared responsibility. There was no road map. Many of us were aware of Gloria Steinem's and Betty Friedan's advice, for example, to avoid learning to type so that we wouldn't get stuck working as secretaries, still one of the few careers open to women entering the workforce in the '60s. Much later I watched many episodes of the television series *Mad Men*, finally having to stop in disgust, however, after realizing how true that stylized show was in its depiction of the culture of the fifties and most of the sixties, which also dictated the values guiding parenthood during that time. Much of that cultural paradigm still dominated US society when I graduated from college in 1977, although a large and growing cohort of baby boom women like me, the first beneficiaries of the federal Title IX law equalizing athletic opportunities for high school and college women, were having none of it. Instead, we tried to forge some kind of equal partnership with the men we worked with and the men we loved, though there were few honored examples in the world around us reflecting how that might work.

As time went by, I got many subtle messages from my parents that my career was not important once I got married, except as it was necessary to financially support my husband while he completed his graduate work. In their view, it seemed, a wife's primary role was to support her husband's career success. My dear father, in particular, was not interested in the voluntary activist work I was so excited about and that I came to consider the beginning of my true career. That work was far more important to me than the various low-paying jobs I could land in Vermont to support my husband and myself as he completed two graduate degrees. In my free time I combed bookstores for memoirs of women who had succeeded in striking a balance between raising a family and sustaining a career. What I found was very discouraging, particularly because most of the stories about how women had managed echoed my parents' sentiments and implicit warnings about the dangers of rocking the cultural boat. No clear path existed to develop the kinds of careers that women like me had been educated to pursue, at least not for women who also wanted children. There had never been any question that more than anything in the world I wanted to become a mother.

AFTER GRADUATING FROM COLLEGE and moving to Vermont, I lived with my college boyfriend for only a year prior to our marriage, which finally put my parents' minds at ease, ending their constant nagging about when that might occur. From the beginning, I worked at whatever job I could land in order to keep us housed and fed, most of which required skills that were not my strongest but could be mastered well enough to survive when using enough willpower. Volunteer work became the place where inspiration, imagination, and work blended and began to grow into the conceptual look and feel of a meaningful career. The first such opportunity helped us reduce our grocery bills as members of the Onion River Co-op where food could be purchased in bulk and organically grown vegetables could be bought at a discount if you volunteered to work on whatever was needed for several hours a week. I loved the smell of the place, highlighted by cumin. Doing whatever menial task was required, I felt connected to the growing movement to support local organic food production, which was closely aligned with the vegetarian eating practices my husband and I had also begun exploring to save money and stay healthy at the same time.

Another such experience was a brief stint as a volunteer for the primary campaign to elect independent presidential candidate John B. Anderson. As a college graduate with a degree in political science, I showed up after work in his Burlington, Vermont, state headquarters for a couple of hours during a few evenings, because I paid close attention to the intersection of Vermont politics and what was happening at the federal level, especially focusing on the activities of Senator James Jeffords and Bernard (Bernie) Sanders, who was elected mayor of Burlington for the first time the year my husband and I moved to Richmond, Vermont, shortly after marrying.

I first encountered Bernie on a drop-in volleyball field in a park on the banks of Lake Champlain during the summer of 1978 while supporting my husband and myself as a breakfast waitress at the Radisson hotel on the Burlington waterfront, which had a lovely view of the lake and the Adirondack mountains from its higher floors. As athletes and outdoor enthusiasts, my husband and I frequently played pick-up volleyball with other young people on mild summer evenings, games that took place on a big grassy field—all there was in the way of a waterfront park at the time. We had enjoyed a similar way to get some exercise and unwind in the college gym during the frigid Minnesota winter of senior year, finding a playful connection to each other through the game, as well as a sense of social connection.

Several times during those pick-up games in Burlington, I noticed a tall older man in the mix. He had wild, wavy brown hair streaked with grey that floated around his head, and he wore blocky black Buddy Holly glasses. He also seemed to feel right at home in the crowd, talking and connecting easily, though he looked to be about fifteen years older than most of us. He stuck out enough for me to ask another teammate, "Who is that guy?"

I'll never forget the response. "Oh, that's Bernie Sanders. He thinks he's a politician. He'll run for any office, even dog catcher, but he'll never get elected."

Bernie had represented the Liberty Union Party as a candidate for governor right before that party collapsed. Members of the state's Republican party thought of Liberty Union as a fringe movement that had no chance to ever gain a foothold in Vermont politics, which ultimately proved true. Vermont Republicans had dominated politics in the state for decades, giving it a reputation as a friendly though old-fashioned place, unless you were an ethnic minority of any kind. In that case, within its all-*white* rural farm-based economy, you would still be received politely but with a chill mirroring the state's winter weather, according to a number of stories I've heard from different sources over the years. I have no way of truly knowing about that experience, except from personal encounters with some who could be described as racist, a coterie of people that thankfully seems to have shrunk considerably over the years since then.

Since the early days of the state, Vermonters have been known to be fiercely independent in their views, basing the central premise of the conservatism that reigned in the late '70s not on ideology but on a common love of the land. However, there was a widely held assumption that to be a *true* Vermonter, rather than some kind of invasive weed blown in on the wind from the "flatlands," a term Vermonters used to refer to the rest of the country, you had to grow up in the state and claim several generations of Vermonters in your background.

Firsthand experience as one of those invasive weeds—and the early breadwinner for my first husband and myself in a place where my college degree was all but useless for landing a job—held a strong lesson in fiscal conservatism for me at the level of family survival. The value of a dollar psychologically rose ever higher as I scrimped and saved to pay the rent and put food on the table, simultaneously becoming very tired of waiting on tables and working at jobs for which I was extremely ill-suited, such as Avis Rent a Car at the Burlington airport. That 3:00–11:00 p.m. shift required paying attention to and memorizing a long list of computerized symbols with no visual relationship to their meaning, then creatively using them in high-stress situations to assist people in a big hurry to get someplace. Often the available rental cars weren't to their liking. All this occurred at a time of day when my capacity for recalling memorized details rapidly wanes (biorhythms raised their thorny heads again).

Despite my best efforts, which in the past had generally promoted me to somewhere near the head of the class, I endured the humiliation of being fired from that and another ill-suited position that immediately followed. Frustration over a lack of intellectual stimulation and this meaningless string of jobs played out in the background as I closely followed what was happening nationally and internationally in politics, largely out of the same fascination with the nature of social organization and political power that had captivated me in college. Only a couple of years later I found myself in the contradictory position of earning a living by working as an office assistant on the reelection campaign of Republican governor Richard Snelling while enthusiastically following Bernie Sanders' run for mayor of Burlington.

Unfortunately, I couldn't vote for Bernie while I lived in Richmond, but I could cheer him on from the sidelines. I had no allegiance to any political party, knowing some of the history of corruption that periodically arose in both. It seemed more important to elect a person of character and integrity, no matter which party they represented. A person of character and integrity would be capable of flexing at the right times, I reasoned, without compromising kindness and decency, using means that would reflect a goal of achieving the more perfect union *Americans* always hope for. That political perspective also kept my marriage relatively peaceful, though we often had challenging discussions about where to draw the line when choosing the means to achieve a more perfect union—our own, the state's, or the nation's. I generally enjoyed those debates, having grown up arguing about public policy and philosophy with my father, but it became ever more evident that my husband really didn't. Nevertheless, he and I both admired Sanders' down-to-earth ideas and cheered his election as mayor of Burlington in November 1980. Governor Snelling also won reelection that year to no one's surprise.

Another politics-related experience that caught my imagination had to do with ice cream. When my husband and I were still living in Burlington, the summer after we married, one of the few treats we could afford was an occasional ice cream cone. At first we sometimes walked up to a little sales window cut into the side of the agriculture department's building at the University of Vermont. There you could buy ice cream made by UVM students from the milk of Vermont cows. We thought it was the best ice cream we had ever tasted. It also gave us some precious time together while walking outside on the hill overlooking Lake Champlain, licking our cones, and dreaming about the future. The connection we felt as we walked together on beautiful evenings probably had something to do with how good that ice cream tasted in these rare breaks for togetherness during my husband's graduate studies.

One day, while driving home from a day spent hiking up Camel's Hump mountain—another rare, favorite summer activity—we noticed a couple of guys painting the side of an abandoned gas station. That piqued our interest because the place had been a downtown eyesore. We kept an eye on the changes they continued to make at that former gas station, watching it transform into an ice cream parlor, to our delight. The name that appeared, along with a whimsical picture of grazing cows, was "Ben and

Jerry's." Ben Cohen and Jerry Greenfield gave out free ice cream on the day they opened that first shop. We made sure to be in line for our free cones. The flavors had funny, funky, culturally humorous names that every baby boomer could relate to, like Cherry Garcia, a slight spelling tweak away from Jerry Garcia, the name of the lead singer of the Grateful Dead, a favorite rock group. Along with the original names for their ice creams that tasted as good as the names were funny, we loved the innovative use of an old gas station and became immediate fans. Their efforts also piqued my interest to follow the story of their developing company.

As Ben and Jerry's grew, moving before long to a larger shop closer to the heart of downtown, I discovered why their employees were so infectiously happy. Ben and Jerry not only designed uniquely colorful, cheerful ice cream shops that sold amazing ice cream, they also set up their business with a strict limit on the boundaries of its pay scale. No one in the company, including the owners who were still actively managing their store, could pull down a salary of more than seven times the salary of the lowest paid employee, a far cry from the usual corporate model. Employees were also given a stake in the company and Ben and Jerry actively engaged in social and environmental activism, using their ice cream business as a springboard to advocate for the political views they shared with the public-policy-minded hippies who had flocked to Vermont as part of the back-to-the-land movement. By doing so, they also educated those of us following their rise about a new concept that came to be known as socially responsible business practices.

A variety of encounters with grassroots efforts of various stripes were essential parts of my daily living for several years.

They subconsciously combined to feed a growing sense that it was more possible than conventional culture would like you to believe to be part of a solution to the social and environmental problems affecting the country. Through those examples, I could easily see how practical and effective it was to make everyday choices in ways that would contribute to just solutions to systemic cultural problems, in whatever small ways I could while shaping the one precious life that was mine, rather than blindly following conventional practices, which continued to increase the significant systemic problems so obvious to anyone studying them.

The garden project, which my husband and I began during this time to save money and stay healthy, using Frances Moore Lappé's book *Diet for a Small Planet* as a guide, sent down another root into my growing consciousness. My husband loved gardening for many reasons. Perhaps the strongest were that growing a garden was a way to provide food, get some outdoor exercise, and have some meaningful time together. Studying plants in depth while he earned a cell biology graduate degree also inspired his enthusiastic engagement, including his research into the best ways to make a go of it. During the summer of 1978, our community garden plot provided us all the food we needed beyond eggs, milk, flour, bread, beans, and rice, which we purchased using our membership benefits at the Onion River Co-op.

These experiences inspired and energized my search for creative ways to shape adult existence while supporting cultural change. They were also underscored subconsciously by my mother's constant plea as I was growing up to "set a good example." If these practices were adopted on a broad scale, I imagined how many of them could eventually shift society toward resilient life from the ground up, in partnership with more enlightened political leadership and public policies. From a mental health perspective, focusing on these practical daily choices also brought me a sense of purpose.

THE VOLUNTEER WORK and periodic outdoor activities shared with my husband continued to give life-support to inspiration as I worked at unfulfilling full-time jobs. Nevertheless, there were a few gems of early work experience that provided glimmers of hope. Several articles I wrote were published between 1977 and 1980, including one in the *Burlington Free Press*, the state's largest paper at the time. It was a freelance article written soon after arriving in Vermont, a year before I married my first husband, and it became the lead story on the front page of the paper's Living section under two large photographs I also produced. I was paid fifteen dollars for each picture and also for the story. The *Free Press* later bought several of my pen-and-ink drawings, paying fifteen dollars apiece for each of those as well. Clearly, this kind of freelance journalism did not pay the bills, but it encouraged me at first. Publication, especially in a prominent place for my first article, felt like a major milestone and fostered a sense of being on the verge of realizing my dream job. Although a second article accompanied by a sketch was rejected, hope for that dream lasted about six months, until the editor asked me to write an assigned article.

The editor wanted a short piece about what was selling well that year during the Christmas season. I was excited to be *asked* to write an article, but the topic left me cold. I persevered, however, calling around to various large, iconic Vermont stores, I discovered that long, full-bodied, red underwear was selling well in one of them. Thinking that might make a humorous beginning, I used it. The editor disagreed—in consternation and full-throated rejection. On seeing my draft, he decided to write the article himself, at which point I decided that I no longer wanted to write whatever tidbit he might throw my way and began to look elsewhere for writing gigs. In the meantime, I continued to wait on tables in order to buy my future husband's books, feed the two of us, and pay the rent and utilities.

A few more writing opportunities came along at much smaller publications, bringing bylines but no money. In the late fall of 1977, I also applied and was invited to interview for the position of assistant editor of a magazine based in Brattleboro, Vermont. After much intense emotional debate with my soon-to-be husband, however, I turned down the invitation, due to his insistence that there was no way I could possibly accept the position if it were offered. I would need to move at least an hour and a half south, he maintained, an impossibility with no middle ground if I was to continue supporting him in his graduate studies. After a very long walk in the cold, following that heated debate, I decided that if I really intended to marry this man, I would need to make more than one sacrifice for the good of the relationship, and although the conclusion left my heart sinking into my boots, I decided to let this ideal career opportunity vanish on the horizon.

Later I made a similarly fraught decision, turning down an offer of an interview for a part-time job in the public relations department at IBM. In another heated debate with my then husband, he insisted there was no other way for us to make ends meet (that didn't involve risks he was unwilling to take while in graduate school) other than for me to work full-time, no matter how menial the job, despite several plausible suggestions I made. Unfortunately, the only way to get a full-time position at IBM, the only big employer in the greater Burlington area at the time, was to first succeed in a related part-time position. As a result, I continued to wait on tables to keep us afloat. The best part of weekdays during that time was walking down the hill to work the breakfast shift at the Radisson hotel at five thirty in the morning, watching the sunrise over the lake, and drinking in its colors reflected in the water.

Finally, after persistently stopping in at the studio at least four times, I landed a job in the traffic department of WEZF, an easy listening local radio and TV station, an affiliate of one of the only three national TV networks at that time. I imagined that by taking that position, I could bide my time until an opportunity arose to apply for a position in their copywriting department. Unfortunately, once you knew how to do the extremely detailed, demanding job of effectively and efficiently scheduling commercials, the work of the traffic department—so named because of the flow of commercial advertising "traffic"—management was intent on keeping you there.

The job entailed working in a windowless room at one of three desks (my first desk job!). The department manager occupied one of the others. She was whip smart, had a high school education, smoked like a chimney, and was quite satisfied with the low wage she was paid for her high skill level. That attitude meant that the two college graduates working under her could never increase our salaries. The traffic department's work centered around putting a series of drawers full of punch cards into a very specific order by hand, according to a number for each type of commercial spot (the time period in which it was purchased to run) and its relationship to other spots in the same commercial break. Each commercial was identified by holes in the cards, made with a keypunch machine that sounded like a slightly quieter version of a jackhammer—a machine run exclusively by the three women in the windowless traffic department where the sound was a nearly constant backdrop to work in that smoke-filled environment. I was amazed that, despite the job's extremely poor fit for my skills, I was able to perform effectively enough to rise during the two years I worked there from assistant to the TV traffic manager to radio traffic manager when the other college graduate, coincidently a high school acquaintance, left for greener pastures. Despite dismal working conditions, the position provided me with a useful skill set over time: speedy visual scanning of long lists of details and the patience to stay focused and engaged with seemingly endless minutia without huge frustration.

The beginning of the end of my radio and TV career finally arrived one day when I broke out in a rash that covered my body with small itchy red spots accompanied by sporadic, painful esophageal spasms. The onset of these symptoms began subtly, soon after our two-person department was informed that we were to learn how to computerize the whole commercial scheduling mechanism and enter all punch card information into it while simultaneously scheduling the heaviest annual commercial load during the fall shopping season before Christmas. Even my boss was eventually motivated to complain to the station's CEO about our workload, something she had never done in her long tenure at the station. Eventually a management consultant was hired to review the situation, though unfortunately he came on board near the end of the process. The consultant revealed that we were both being asked to complete two full-time jobs in the time and at the wages of one, putting in sixteen-hour days and working almost as long on weekends, receiving no overtime pay. My work became all I had time for except eating and sleeping. My dreams were also filled with work, robbing me of the rest I so desperately needed. Ultimately I was able to quit, receiving full unemployment benefits because my doctor confirmed in writing that I would be unable to physically recover until I was removed from the stress of that position. He told me that the rash was caused by the high stress levels my body had consistently been enduring for five straight months.

The litany of what felt like continuous career failure, repeatedly pulling myself up from defeat to start again from scratch, dominated working life throughout most of the first seven years beyond college. The experience was painful, demoralizing, and destructive to my marriage. Making matters worse, my husband had his own struggles as his research and studies became increasingly challenging. A building tension between us also began to rise because, although he worked very hard and struggled in his own way to gain our combined forward motion in life, he was able to complete a master's degree in cell biology as well as a medical degree during that time, while I got a deep lesson in the value of a dollar, the challenges women faced in the work world, and what it felt like to repeatedly pull myself up by my bootstraps. Of course the school of hard knocks had a privileged cushion in the background for me, not available to most who must learn that way, painful as it still was. That hardscrabble education was invaluable and ultimately essential to the meaningful career that emerged much later, although it was not something I could add to my résumé to improve my professional prospects as were my husband's efforts.

Before he entered medical school I had begged my husband not to reapply. The long hours of separation we had already endured while he studied for his cell biology master's degree left precious few opportunities for emotional intimacy and shared activity. I knew that situation would likely never end if he became a doctor. I also knew that becoming a doctor was a very long-standing dream for him. He had told me the history of that dream in college. I married him anyway, believing he had moved on and that medical school was by then out of reach. When he had first applied, fresh out of college, the dean of admissions for the UVM's medical school had told him point-blank that there was "no way in hell" he would ever be accepted. His college grades just wouldn't make the cut, the dean had told him, despite his high score on the MCAT. Completing a master's degree with top grades at the same university changed the odds, however, and medical school beckoned once again. There was nothing I could say to dissuade him from reapplying.

At the heart of the matter for both of us was the love bond on which we both depended for a sense of security. Because I loved him, I wanted him to be able to realize his dream, and I wanted to be able to help him do it, even though my intuition warned me that his dream would likely squash my own. But who could really know the future, I told myself. Besides, we were a team, a partnership, and I had been able to get this far while doing things I never thought I could, so why not take one more risk? Ultimately, I reasoned, a doctor would eventually have the resources we would both need to raise children, my deepest longing.

We stumbled along well enough as I've described until I began working at what turned into a life-altering job at a start-up passive solar energy company in 1980, three and a half years after graduating from college. The experience was earthshaking. First, because I had found the job indirectly while using a new job-search tactic that I actually enjoyed—interviewing people working at jobs I might want to do someday, whether or not there was any prospect of working with them. That practice showed me that unconventional methods for job searching were much more encouraging and fun and also yielded more surprising results than anyone might expect. Second, and more importantly, my world was shaken into brilliant color after three years of black-and-white hand-to-mouth existence by an imaginative vision developed by a small group of intriguing people who were beginning to build an entrepreneurial solar energy company, and by my great good fortune to be given the opportunity to assist in the birth of the project. Third, I learned that an enthusiastic, optimistic imagination, coupled with a good command of the English language, gave me natural sales skills when selling products in which I deeply believed.

At a sales training seminar I attended with support from that entrepreneurial solar energy company, I also discovered that the most effective sales person does not fit the stereotypical picture that comes to mind, namely someone who says whatever it takes to hoodwink a customer into buying their product. Instead, caring about the needs of the customer, listening closely to what they tell you, and referring them to another vendor when that would better serve their needs had much greater long-term payback than exaggerated or false representation of products to gain immediate sales. As a result, I was able to shed my natural disdain for sales and see it as a means to connect suppliers of great products to customers who needed them, educating everyone who was curious along the way. There was mystery, nuance, imagination, and kindness in this approach, which ignited joy in me for selling wonderful products and later ideas.

Ultimately, working as the first staff member hired by the three primary partners, who were fueled by a shared inspirational vision of a wiser, more energy efficient world, I also learned what it meant to be part of an energetic, imaginative team of activists. That experience taught me that it was possible, with imagination and determination, to create work for myself and others rather than simply taking what corporate America dished out, and more importantly, I could earn a living wage while making a positive difference in the world.

That wonderful entrepreneurial company went under a couple of years later, thanks to one of President Ronald Reagan's first policy moves, which effectively destroyed the fast-growing prospects of the nascent solar energy industry. He ended the federal tax credits for solar products that had made them very popular following the energy crisis of 1973. Reagan's strategy to address the issue was to subsidize big oil companies instead. His aim was to ensure that multinational corporate oil companies, especially those with headquarters in the US, would be able to outcompete OPEC (the Organization of Petroleum Exporting Countries) whose oil embargo had created the 1973 energy crisis that led to long, snaking lines of cars waiting to buy gas and inflated home heating bills, among other financial problems. OPEC was the first coordinated international effort to reclaim national sovereignty over local natural resources in the Middle East and South America, resources that until then had been firmly under the control of the multinational corporations, headquartered in Western countries, which extracted them, especially the US. Founded in Baghdad in 1960 by Iran, Iraq, Kuwait, Saudi Arabia, and Venezuela, OPEC today includes thirteen members, adding Algeria, Angola, Equatorial Guinea, Gabon, Nigeria, the Republic of the Congo, Libya, and the United Arab Emirates to its original five.

The job I finally landed after the heartbreak of the solar greenhouse company's dissolution and a couple of other short, dispiriting work experiences taught me much more than I first imagined it could. It involved selling weight-loss programs on commission through a Nutrisystem franchise. I took the position thinking that at least the job would pay the bills using my sales skills. Instead, I quickly discovered that I actually enjoyed the work. The office mainly served women and had an all-female staff. The sales work primarily focused on educating women about the connection between nutrition, exercise, and health, subjects my husband and I had continued to study and practice together since first volunteering at the Onion River Co-op. I found that listening to the women who came to the Nutrisystem office for help and encouraging them to eat in healthier ways while taking better care of themselves inspired me to do the same. I was also able to pull in more income at that job than I'd ever earned before, despite working on commission for only six hours a day, a workday I could enthusiastically get behind. Earning more while working fewer hours was incredible, especially since free time had always been more valuable to me than money.

It's clear now that those seven years working to support my husband through his graduate studies was not wasted for either of us, as much as it often felt that way to me as they unfolded and for years afterward. The combined experiences of failing in my own eyes, turning down promising opportunities in favor of my husband's career goals, pulling myself out of the ditch where those experiences repeatedly left me—without falling back on anyone's help—and repeatedly readjusting my concept of where career energy needed to be spent in order to fulfill chosen marriage responsibilities reinforced a strong sense of basic confidence that I could do whatever needed to be done, no matter how hard any challenge might initially seem. There were other challenges during that time beyond the search for meaningful work, including a debilitating habit I increasingly used as an emotional crutch, which ultimately became an addiction.

Chapter Nine

Breath and Body Running Free

The insistent clanging of the alarm clock told me it was five thirty. Time to get up. Dragging my body from the warm, soft hug of bed, I stumbled into the bathroom. Splashing water on my face, I somehow resisted the strong urge to burrow back under the covers, moving instead into the day. As I threw on running clothes, a continuous inner mantra played, "No, you will not go back to bed. You must do this no matter how uncomfortable it feels." Hurrying downstairs, around the corner, through the dining alcove, then through the little strip of kitchen in the married student housing condo where we lived, and finally out through the tiny foyer, I closed the front door behind me with an airlock thud. Taking a deep breath of chilled morning air, I began to move my feet in a way I hadn't for years.

The first kick of my foot from sidewalk to dew-spangled grass on that long ago morning is still so clear that it could have happened a minute ago. The white and blue leather toe of the running shoe sent flying a multitude of sparkling rainbow-colored dew drops that were clinging to every bright green grass blade on the lawn. The low-angled, golden rays of the rising sun highlighted the unique beauty of colorful reflections in each glittering drop. The yellow, pink, and blue of the early morning sky graced the surface of every tiny liquid diamond, awakening my heart. Soft dampness permeated the air with the smell of late spring earth and bathed smoke-scarred lungs in a soothing balm. As my feet found a rhythm with my arms and breath, I became fully aware of my body waking into the morning. As I jogged, the cool air lifted my hair and caressed the skin on my legs, face, and arms. The birds trilled a welcome to the returning sun, expanding a happiness I hadn't felt for a long, long time. As I knocked those first dewdrops from the Vermont grass, my body remembered the feeling of moving this way, asking me how I could possibly have forgotten. Stunned with joy and hope that had lately been in such short supply, I remembered that this is how I had always moved as a child who could hardly sit still. It felt so good! Why had I ever stopped?!

Veering around the buildings and across the shared grassy lawn, I headed toward the old trees shading the highway and the edge of the long, broad field separating Fort Ethan Allen from the road. Turning left under the line of trees, perhaps thirty yards from where I'd started, I could already feel that, as natural as running was for my spirit, my body was deeply out of practice. My breathing deepened as I kept a steady jogging pace down the line of trees—not fast, just a slow jog. Although I focused on birdsong and the rustle of wind moving gently through new leaves, very quickly my breathing demanded center stage. It was hard to acknowledge, but I was already becoming winded before completing even a quarter of a mile. This breathlessness was the reason I had pushed myself out the door in the first place. I knew I needed to keep uppermost in my attention, somehow, a physical awareness of the disaster I had made of my lungs, hoping that a daily visceral reminder at the crack of dawn would help me to reverse a deeply ingrained impulsive habit. Allowing the ever-more-frequent impulse to rid myself of emotional pain instead of feeling it had, after seven years, led to an insidious daily pattern of self-destruction that was beginning to take control of my body and mental ability to effectively engage with life.

Running was a conscious healing choice, not inspired by love of its rhythmic motion, though it became so over time. Taking up running was a choice made in desperation, realizing I'd never be able to give up the emotional dependency I'd developed without some kind of uncomfortable reminder of just how much tar I'd been caking on my lungs by inhaling so deeply so often and holding it in for so long. As a natural dancer and athlete, I knew I would lose my ability to access the consistent recreational joy those activities brought, when I occasionally paid them some attention, if I didn't save the precious natural air bags of my lungs that allowed free movement as often and in as many ways, for as long as I liked.

I had known for months that I needed to give up the habit of turning to marijuana every time life seemed emotionally impossible to manage, a pattern that had gradually created a downward spiral. The very thing that lifted me out of pain and loneliness also left me in a listless deep grey hole when I came back to sober reality. I knew it was essential to find some other way to climb back to sanity when life felt so utterly grey that the only thing that seemed to make sense was to have "just a little hair of the dog that bit you," a dangerous practice that only delayed yet a further fall into deeper grey. No matter how I had scolded myself, however, I hadn't been able to hear my own strong admonitions against it until the day I began to run.

The habitual choice to escape reality by smoking marijuana, first only occasionally on weekends in college, arose for many reasons. At the root of them all was a truth I had still to discover. Beginning in puberty, I had learned to abandon my deepest sense of where to look for and nourish joy because I came to believe that the activities that most inspired me to engage enthusiastically with life lacked any kind of value beyond recreation, which was only something to do when work was finished, work being more valuable unless you were a child. Through such subliminal conditioning, received along with abundant love from my family, I came to understand that my internal drives to dance, drum, invent imaginative stories, or achieve self-directed goals of athletic achievement were motivations that led only to frivolous daydreams on which it would be impossible to build a life of any significance. Coming to that conclusion broke my heart.

Choosing to run was the first unwitting step toward listening to what my heart had to say about the matter and the first foray away from bending to the conditioning that had buried natural reservoirs of inspiration and hope deep underground in a way I still failed to grasp. However, I could immediately feel the truth of this critical food for my starving soul, along with its effects on every bodily cell, as I tried to run that first quarter mile. Giving up before I reached that distance while hacking, coughing, and gasping for air, I walked, hands on my hips and head hung low, back down the line of trees toward home. However, that first explosion of the innate joy of movement had pierced the smoky shroud around my heart. The run had been long enough that I could feel the way my body loved the oxygen running provided. I felt it just enough to create a continuous memory of beauty and joy that began to counter the urge to reach for a joint when that yearning threatened to overwhelm everything else once again.

Running became a strong anchor in the storm of recovery from what was, at the very least, an emotional addiction (the prevailing opinion at the time was that marijuana was not physically addictive), opening a door that I never again allowed to close, no matter how searing the pain of the world. The loving encouragement of my young husband was also essential in those initial weeks of newfound intention. His help was requested and provided without reserve. At least once he talked me out of throwing in the towel by walking me around outside for hours until the urge to get high subsided.

My husband and I had first connected when I returned to Carleton after my year away. We began smoking pot for periodic recreational release and heightened enjoyment of the generous-hearted group of friends we socialized with at school—when we weren't buried in books—or sometimes as part of the skiing, hiking, and camping adventures that united our hearts throughout what became a fourteen-year relationship. With my recovery process, however, smoking pot would never again be a healthy option. Not for me. The supposed impossibility that marijuana is a physically addictive substance was a major part of the reason I had allowed myself to take the first toke in the spring of 1974. How could it really be any worse than the alcohol my parents were by then using to relax daily at cocktail time? My grandfather had initiated daily evening cocktail time a year or so earlier when he came to live with my family in Princeton for half the year following the death of his wife, my step-grandmother. He spent the other six months with my uncle in Chicago. The vast majority of baby boomers I knew believed that using marijuana was a good deal safer than drinking, and for many it was.

I began to realize the myth of that story for me, however, when I went down on hands and knees in the apartment where we lived while my husband attended medical school and combed the rug with my fingers, searching desperately for marijuana seeds and stems and scraping the tarry residue off the inside of the bong so I could smoke the dregs because we were out of pot. I felt an overpowering drive to get high. I also knew deep down that this was not how I wanted to live. This was not who I was. In that moment I also realized that I had to find something to do when the urge to get high hijacked consciousness, something that would unequivocally remind me about the ever deeper hole I was digging by living high, which was how I was functioning by then. My habit was so pervasive that I was starting to forget things. My short-term memory was weakening even though I was under thirty. I had seen brilliant people ruin their brains in college using LSD, another "nonaddictive substance" that had been touted as a shortcut to enlightenment when in reality there is no such thing. I was determined not to be the chump who succeeded in ruining my brain with marijuana!

With my husband's help in those first weeks, when it was physically impossible to run as much as necessary to fully replace the smoking habit, I began to heal. While running as the sun rose, before driving to work in Burlington, a sense of being more fully alive rose with the movement and stayed with me a little longer each day in a kind of natural technicolor, similar to what I saw in the trees and gardens past which I ran as spring, then summer, flowers emerged and bloomed. Sometimes I ran a short way again at the end of the day. Every run engaged my conscious will to push beyond what seemed physically possible, even when I'd already covered the same distance twice. After a day or three of running one distance, I added another few yards, followed by running that new distance until it felt manageable—although never until it felt easy—adding another few yards as soon as the old distance was consistently reached without too much mental effort. Instinct told me that if I pushed too hard to reach any particular distance, my mind would rebel, derailing the whole process. Patience and respectful inner listening were essential skills this process began to root in my consciousness in entirely new ways.

The mental game was as important to the healing process as the physical one. Once a certain distance had been covered at least twice, I had faith that my body could do it again, laying down memories that allowed me to keep going near the end of each run as my body pleaded to stop before whatever point was that day's goal. After working up to running the whole loop around the front field, my husband and I circled it in the car to measure the distance. I had run a whole mile! That, in itself, buoyed my spirits. After a few more months I worked up to running four loops around that field, then gradually added a second field to the daily run. By the time snow began to fly in late November, I was running five miles a day. Having gotten that far, winter didn't slow me down much.

My husband and I were skiers, having cemented our relationship during weekly downhill skiing trips organized by Carleton College, during which we traveled by bus an hour to a ravine that dipped deep into the flat Minnesota landscape. Over the course of these trips he gradually became my skiing coach as well as my boyfriend, gently guiding me in the finer points of style and technique from his long experience on ski racing teams in college and before that for his Vermont high school. As a skier from New Jersey and a physical daredevil, I had limited experience but could make it smoothly down any intermediate slope by the time we met. I'd skied for a few days each winter during two ski trips organized by my high school. I had caught on quickly and could negotiate wide, gradual downhill runs, trying small jumps and spins for fun, which frequently left me face down in the snow but never injured. My technique was not at all consistent enough to safely handle the sharp turns needed to negotiate steep, expert mogul fields, however.

As the winter weeks progressed in college, my boyfriend and I also spent time together cross-country skiing in the woods and fields around the school, something I had quickly learned to do under the guidance of another friend during the winter of freshman year. By the time we became husband and wife and he entered medical school, we still skied as often as we could, but his immersion in his studies meant that was not often. When he would finally get home after an extremely long day, he was exhausted and in no mood to talk, much less do anything other than study or drink beer while watching TV. Weekends weren't much different. The rhythms of my breathing and my running legs soon became my favorite companions as a result. They reconnected me with living experience and my natural way of being that had been mentally relegated to childhood, and I rediscovered that way of being in a whole new way as longer and longer distances became easier to run.

As this running practice deepened, I knew that no matter what emotional storm arose I always had movement, breath, and the company of trees, birds, and nature to see me through. When ice and snow made running treacherous, I walked or sometimes cross-country skied alone around the loop of the field. I kept moving forward in one way or another every day, spending plenty of time outdoors, especially when emotions surfaced that threatened to block productive engagement with life. Smoking pot was out of the question and the more I replaced it with outdoor movement, the more certain that choice became. I later learned that this practice was actually reconfiguring my brain, growing new synapses connected with vigorous outdoor movement in times of trouble, while neglecting and in the process shriveling the old ones connected with the habitual pattern of smoking pot. With time and practice those old synapses withered into distant memories, making it easy for me to redirect my attention, when tempted, onto how far I had come and to generate a clear awareness of the dangerous repercussions that relapse, even once, would likely set into motion.

By the time March rolled around, I had resumed daily running, although usually on the pavement due to snow. I had also set my sights on running the Vermont Island Marathon come summer as I gradually built stamina to push past the four-mile mark long enough to get into *the zone*, the point when endorphins kicked in for me. (This race is now called the Champlain Islands Marathon, held in the fall, following a different route.) It had become clear that I could count on those endorphins to transform the running experience from a steady, consciously structured discipline of breath and legs into a flowing, effortless, thought-free movement. At that point the run consistently became an experience of living and being in union with the natural beauty through which I ran, dissipating any sense of separation. The experience brought a new kind of peace, contentment, and quiet joy that I'd never had before. I couldn't get enough of it. Thoughts disappeared into the rhythm of legs and breathing. There was no to-do list, no imagination, no ego—just movement, breath, sun, trees, wind, birds, and sky. I discovered that the run could be sustained longer by counting breaths at the beginning, exhaling for one or two beats longer than inhaling. Releasing every last ounce of air before filling my lungs again set up a continuous pattern in which thoughts disappeared and attention refocused on the breath's rhythm. Past four miles, the rhythm took over and counting fell away. Moving unity is the best way I can articulate the experience, the unity of my body and breathing with the road, wind, trees, birds, and fields, providing a deep sense of freedom. I never wanted to stop.

A couple of months before the July marathon, I had progressed to consistently running seven miles a day, always allowing at least one rest day each week. The pattern of running seemingly endless loops around the fort became monotonous, even with the help of endorphins. Adding even more distance by running still more loops had no appeal, so I took to running the dirt roads abutting Fort Ethan Allen at the time, discovering a beautiful, undeveloped ten-mile loop past woods and farm fields. That became my daily run during the last month or so of conditioning. During the last couple of weeks, I ran the ten miles, then dipped into the condo, gulped a couple of Tylenol, and ran it again, doing that once each week, the minimum needed before tackling a marathon according to the running magazines I used as research guides. I was ready!

On race day I lined up with the mass of runners at the starting line on Grand Isle and began to jog at my usual slow, steady pace. As I ran in the bright, humid eighty-degree sunshine, the tight pack of marathon participants began to thin. Many moved ahead and many fell behind. I found myself running next to an old man who wanted to chat and give me advice as we jogged along, which for me was anathema to the joy of the experience, so even though he advised the slow pace we both were keeping, which I knew was the best approach, I thanked him and moved out a little faster in order to lose him and access the rhythmic silence that made running a joy. I was so full of energy and excitement that running slowly was almost impossible anyway. I eventually made it across the finish line, a feat now held in my memory with gratitude as one of my finest achievements because of the fundamental changes (which still ripple out today) that it ignited on so many levels. In four hours and forty-five minutes I ran 26.2 miles, which didn't put me in dead last, surprisingly. Instead I finished somewhere in the middle of the pack.

A significant amount of pride accompanies the memory of achieving the finish line in the Vermont Island Marathon in the summer of 1983, especially since I'm not naturally built as a long-distance runner, the long, lean kind. Short and compact, I have the build of a gymnast, my high school sport of choice. Pride in completing the race also came from learning, shortly after collapsing on the grass beyond the finish line, that approximately half of the initial pack of runners had dropped out of the race by the halfway mark due to the day's oppressive heat and humidity, which had us all sweating rivers. We also drank gallons of water, provided by volunteers along the way, some of it laced with electrolytes, which sounded like a good idea. However, I later discovered that those electrolytes were likely part of the reason I wound up with my head over a toilet bowl, emptying my stomach shortly after the end of the run.

And yes, I ran full tilt across the finish line with a number of people still behind me. A few enthusiastic spectators, including my husband, lined the road to cheer us on. When I rounded the last corner at a fast walk and realized the end was in sight, I dug down deep to run the last half mile up the gradual hill to a few much-appreciated cheers, a huge hug from my husband, and immense relief at making it to the end with dignity. After walking for a short time to settle my breathing a little, I dove onto an empty space on the grass, unable to consider another step. After a couple of minutes though, my stomach began to protest and I dragged myself, still breathing hard, into the restroom. The old man who had suggested I slow down early in the race had crossed the finish line about half an hour before me.

None of the articles I'd read to prepare—a minimal number admittedly—said much if anything about the possible side effects of such a long run. There was one short-term benefit that was amazingly great for a twenty-nine-year-old woman concerned about her looks, as I was deeply conditioned to be. Every single shred of fat on my body disappeared and stayed gone for more than a week after the marathon. That meant that the sculpted shape of every muscle in my legs became readily apparent. I also felt ebulliently alive, totally soaked—like every bodily cell was—in oxygen and feeling as though my whole body had been washed for days in fresh spring air.

Despite the lasting healing and long-term psychological benefits reaped from that run, the grueling end of the marathon was enough to convince me that once was enough to run such a distance for the likes of me. A hint of that conclusion revealed itself during my two twenty-mile practice runs a couple of weeks earlier. Even then, ten miles felt like my personal limit, but by sticking it out through the required training and completing the full marathon well enough to run the last half mile across the finish line, I realized a goal that seemed utterly impossible until it was achieved. That realization was the most valuable lesson of all.

Training for and running the marathon also turned my lungs around, which was no small thing, and cured me of my oppressive desire to smoke, even though tempting fingers of memory turned my head whenever I smelled a faint whiff of that sweet smoke on the breeze. However, I no longer craved it. Instead, whenever emotional energy built up that could be labeled anger, frustration, sorrow, or loneliness—depending on the inner story—I would tie up my running shoes and head onto the nearest tree-lined track to clock a few miles and breathe free with the trees. That same remedy is now achieved in long-distance walking, hiking, biking, and swimming when there's no longer enough snow for cross-country skiing, my current sport of choice.

The keys to contented living are so simple and available yet so internal and constant that they're usually taken for granted. The breath and the body hold these keys to the kingdom of peace. Western culture is so focused on thinking and speaking that even now, when yoga, meditation, and jogging have left the fringes of popular culture where they began in the '60s, those two keys to healthful living are only rarely explored to the full capacity of the healing they can provide. That's true because we're all thrown into this swirling, confusing dance of living and have to find our own unique way to survive within the cultural structures our predecessors created, organizing and managing the chaotic surprise of living in whatever way we can imagine to support community bonds within whatever cultural mix surrounds us.

Running the marathon at twenty-nine was my first step back into a way of perceiving truth in a far more mysterious way than our rational minds can comprehend, a way that is so much more rewarding, though therein lie monsters too. From what I've had the privilege to experience, however, far more terrifying and soul-killing monsters lie on the purely rational, outwardly focused path through life that is sold to the *American* public in particular and the world in general through the amazing technological innovations brought into being over the last sixty years. Unfortunately, US culture generally uses those rationally created innovations to take the mind's focus out of the living moment and out of nature that produces it. Those innovations then suck so many into a mechanistic mind-space that makes them oblivious to the ways in which nature, including their own bodies, is dying as a result of unconscious addiction to technology's wonders. Technology has no comparison to the magnificence and wonder of nature. It is terribly unfortunate, to put it mildly, that such innovations have vastly improved some aspects of life while sucking life completely out of so many others.

Running the marathon did not immediately bring me some earthshaking conscious insight into its personal impact. However, it left deep tracks of a powerful new kind of awareness and unshakeable knowledge that there is always another choice in any circumstance, even when it feels impossible to choose anything but what the emotions are screaming to do. Choosing to take an internal step back at such times, no matter how impossible it may seem, to observe and feel the pain bubbling up, ask for help, and remember the consequences of impulsive responses opens a door to choosing more wisely in challenging moments, forging, step by step, a consistently available new route out of inner turmoil. Discovering that, in itself, and building on it can save your life.

IN THE LATE '70S, when I married and began to financially support my husband through graduate school while struggling to find meaningful work that could feed, house, and clothe the two of us, it looked from the outside as though hippies were drifting back, as predicted, to the middle-class lifestyle they'd abandoned in the '60s. It was true that most of the young people labeled as hippies had become very different people with very different views from the people they were when they headed out of bucolic suburban homes to go "back to the land," but not in the way generally reported at the time by mainstream media. Many had gained a deeper understanding and appreciation for the depth of social and environmental change needed to truly shift US culture to become more just and life-affirming. What looked like giving up to conventional cultural adherents was actually a serious process of digging in and getting to the real work of building a kinder, more inclusive culture for many former hippies. That was clearly evident to me while watching the growth of Ben and Jerry's ice cream company and participating in the growth of the Onion River Co-op and the solar greenhouse company that had provided me with such a rewarding work experience. Quietly and persistently, in multiple arenas of action, a growing contingent of baby boomers was reimagining and re-creating numerous aspects of the Western cultural model at the grassroots level of local communities, inventing and building new ways to do business and grow nonprofit organizations and creating networks to link them, all based in whole or in part on the hippie ideal of being the change you wanted to see.

The eruption of the huge waves of protest in the '60s, alongside the social and educational changes inspired by innumerable scientific discoveries of that same era, created an immense cultural dissonance in the years that followed, revealing stark differences in political and sociological perspectives concerning what changes were needed and how soon they should take place. This controversy is still playing out today in disturbing ways. The ongoing cultural dissonance can be better understood when considering that the festering wounds of racism, classism, misogyny, and homophobia, to name some of the most pervasive prejudices, began to be widely exposed in the '70s. They began to be revealed as systemically embedded aspects of institutional structures that lie at the core of Western cultural conventions. Today nearly equal numbers of people want to push that realization back under the cultural rug as the numbers who want to reimagine culture in order to heal the life consequences of prejudice. As these fault lines began to emerge while I was beginning to form a family with my husband, a measure of chaos began to shake the heart of Western civilization's organizing principles, which has only increased in intensity since then.

WHEN ORGANIC LIFE IS THREATENED by chaotic storms of all kinds, resilience is determined by the ability of an organism to adapt and flex within whatever natural conditions present themselves, like the way in which healthy trees survive icy winter blizzards, bending in all directions before returning to peaceful, upright stillness when the wind dies down. From where I sit, the same applies to the social contracts we make with one another to structure societies in ways that support human resilience and the survival of life on Earth. Despite the fear caused by the increasing howling that can today be heard from many powerfully dissonant voices within democracies throughout Western culture, true resilience will only arise when that traumatized howling can calmly be heard and wisely addressed by enough people to allow all the howlers to find ways to feel safe and included within a new commonly held cultural context.

History has shown that suppressing hurt and angry voices under an orderly dictatorship—or any kind of repressive authoritarian structure—allowing only some voices to fully express themselves, and measuring the value of what they say by how loyal their words are to the dominant perspective only creates an increasingly brittle, life-threatening social structure. Such civilizational models smother and forcibly control the dissent and chaos created by the trauma inflicted on individuals, thus preventing systemic crises in the short term while simultaneously preventing the natural growth of resilient hope capable of moving society beyond reactively expressed human fear and pain in the long term. That resilience can only be accessed once emotional experiences have been acknowledged and peacefully released, changing society's common understanding of itself while gradually changing the commonly held social contract in the process.

A story that is still only beginning to be told by the baby boom generation as its elders begin to reflect on their era—one that will continue to be written by historians from future generations—is the momentous shift in power structures that the explosion of the '60s inaugurated and the hard, quiet work that a vast array of baby boomers entered into following their loud protesting as young people. When protests gave way to family building and child-rearing, many began also to build networks of local civic organizations to address social problems, and those organizations continue to expand laterally across the globe, rooted deeply in local communities and connected through all types of media that were not even dreamed of when these groups first began to form.

This network of organizations answers to no government or corporation when operating successfully. It answers instead to the people it serves by virtue of heartfelt commitment along with a now legally codified responsibility for such organizations, in most countries, to put whatever financial growth they attain into direct program benefits for their constituents. This network also works to find ways to mediate between business and government in favor of those it serves. The vast web these organizations created gained a new name, though its reach and power are still only vaguely understood. The third sector, or the nonprofit sector of Western economies, partners with business and government, the two other essential legs of the three-legged stool required by modern, vibrant, creative, though messy democracies to thrive.

Chapter Ten

Reframing Perception

All the hard life lessons I'd learned as a young adult gave me the strength to climb out of the emotional/psychological hole opening under my feet when we both realized, one year after my husband's medical residency had been completed, that our values and life goals had become deeply irreconcilable. Our shared struggles to reach a middle-class lifestyle had destroyed our relationship. Our conditioned adherence to the cultural practices that informed and supported our upbringing played a large part in both the endurance and destruction of our marriage, which increasingly sidelined our individual emotional needs as we went along. As a result, despite the deep love and delight we shared for two beautiful daughters, born during my husband's internship and residency, along with our continuing concern for each other's well-being, an unshakable pain engulfed our union, ultimately bringing a mutually agreed upon choice to divorce and opening the door to the heartbreaking challenge of single parenthood.

THERE IS A THIRTY-FIVE-YEAR OLD WOMAN who lies crying on the bed, rolling from side to side. She has pain in her middle. That pain keeps her rolling in the same way she did as a baby. It feels like a knife permanently stuck into her breastbone. She is afraid.

She can't make the hurting stop. She desperately wants it to stop. She wants him to come back and hold her, but he doesn't. He is angry with her for being afraid.

This woman looks younger than she is. Often people think she is ten years younger. When she is happy she easily dances, paints, and runs with the energy and abandon of a child. She often feels like a little girl in a grown woman's body playing a charade, though she knows that isn't true. She doesn't like that feeling. She despises herself for having so little self-esteem. She yells at that little girl inside and tells her to be quiet and go away. Having replaced her dependence on drugs with long-distance running, this woman knows she can be strong when she must, but with two tiny girls to care for, she can't just drop everything and run whenever she needs to. She must simply endure the pain and keep smiling and attending to her daughters' needs and desires while bringing as little of her deep sadness into their lives as she can possibly manage.

WHEN THE CONDITIONED EXPECTATION that life would unfold along the lines characterized by my parents' example was utterly shattered, exploding daily reality into the undreamed-of possibility of living through and beyond divorce, I began a process I've come to think of as collecting the bones of the wild, essential self and seeking ways to sing them back to life. Clarissa Pinkola Estés eloquently illuminates the archetype of the Wild Woman in her 1992 book, *Women Who Run with the Wolves*, in which she describes a collector of bones of ancient wisdom who lies within the beating heart of every woman. Her book delineates the ways in which the living root of women's natural power was driven underground as the culture of *power over*, rather than *power with*, came to dominate civilization from the dawn of agriculture on. In Estés' telling, the wild woman lives on in mythical stories capable of empowering women's psychic connection to the liminal world, linking human DNA to the continuous interdependence of living earth.

Finding a way back into the embrace of fully connected living within natural systems and leaving behind the harshly limiting boundaries—between humanity and nature—indelibly embedded in the Western cultural narrative became the psychic "shero's" journey I began during the divorce. In 1992, the year the divorce was finalized, I read *Women Who Run with the Wolves*, which gave me a firm lifeline to grab onto, breaking my precipitous fall into what seemed an endlessly dark, bottomless pit of despair.

HAVING EMERGED AND TRAVELED FAR BEYOND that terrifying pit of confusion and grief that began with divorce, I now see the whole experience as the greatest gift I could ever have received. I also know that I would never have gained that insight without the inner protection of the enchanted childhood my parents were able to provide, along with the ever-ready hands of my sisters and several dear friends who appeared just as they were most needed, pulling me from blind despair back onto a perch where light revealed hand- and footholds up the side of that emotional ravine, especially in the earliest days of the journey. Without their help, I would likely never have reached the sunny plain of contentment that allows me to write these words. Mostly women's voices kept me going during the long climb that ultimately landed these feet firmly on the opposite rim of the chasm that opened in front of me as my husband walked out the door of our shared home for the last time.

I'll never forget a late-night phone call with my sister nearest in age after he left, who listened without interruption to my tale of despair.

"If you didn't have two small children, what would you do?" she asked.

I quickly answered, "Go to graduate school to study public policy," following the plan my husband and I had made together.

She responded, "Then do that." When asked how she imagined that was possible, she said, "You'll find a way."

That conversation inspired the courage I needed to put one foot in front of the other and grope my way along a steep but manageable path out of the pit. Later, my youngest sister's voice kept me going when my self-esteem was once again flagging in the midst of the early years of my consulting business. She said, "I really admire you. I could never do what you're doing." When I protested that her career path was so much stronger and more significant than mine, she countered, "Not really, because you're creating your own job from scratch. I wouldn't know how to begin to do that, much less succeed the way you are."

There were so many other voices too, particularly in regular meetings of several circles of women where we literally sat in a circle and used a communication process designed to bring out the wisdom that inevitably emerged from the circle's mysteriously unified center. A talking stick or stone, which each speaker took from the center to designate her turn to speak, signaled us to give her our undivided attention and provide no verbal response to the words she spoke while she held it. Everyone in these circles was committed to listening closely to each other without preparing what we would say as each person spoke. We allowed the inspiration to claim the talking stick to rise naturally from within a period of silence following each contribution, giving each speaker's words time to mysteriously meld in our minds, ultimately yielding insights much deeper than the sum of the circle's parts by the end of the meeting.

The whole circle felt like one mind, from which messages surfaced in various individual minds whose unique experiences held elements of particular insight useful to the whole. Those messages would never have emerged without the unity of the circle, formed by the equal commitment and shared responsibility for the quality of the process on the part of the women sitting on its rim. This healing form of communication was one I learned and instigated in various settings as a result of reading *Calling the Circle: The First and Future Culture* by Christina Baldwin, in 1995, the year following publication of its first edition. A mysterious, nearly visceral connection rose in this circling process, creating deep bonds between many who sat in those circles. It's inspiring to remember that even as they have evolved and divided, as all living things do, a couple of those circles that originated in the '90s are still active today.

Using Christina Baldwin's circling process to contain challenging discussions of all kinds also helped to maintain a continuously connected circle rim for the three lives that grew and shaped each other over the eighteen intense years of the essential home ground that my daughters and I came to know as the "Girls' Club." Various men and boys were invited in and included from time to time, for varying lengths of relationship, but it was deeply understood that we were a female family unit in a chosen structure of care and honesty beginning that first day my husband chose to leave the marriage and family household for good.

Because the girls were so young—three and five at the time—I wanted to immediately find a way to tell some kind of positive side to the story playing out before their eyes. First and foremost I explained that they were not losing their father, that he loved them dearly and they would always have him in their lives, just not in the same house. From there I improvised, using a consciously chosen enthusiasm to bond with them and shift the focus away from the pain of loss, at least for a little while, onto the potential gifts this new family form could provide us. I pointed out that we now had an opportunity to create something new, a girls' club, which we could shape together in just the way the three of us wanted—with no boys allowed!

Bravely and loudly they immediately got on board with the idea and we moved on from there. As their mother, I was the circle guardian, doing everything possible to keep the center steady through all the emotional ups and downs that were inevitably involved. My daughters didn't have the same kind of bubble of protection as they grew that I had enjoyed, one I had originally assumed I would always be able to provide. Instead, our daughters needed to face some emotional challenges far more difficult than any I had had to face as a child. However, as a mother fiercely committed to the healthy growth of these young, growing spirits and their abilities to navigate life's unexpected shifts and challenges, I taught them every new insight and tool of emotional resilience I gained along the way, as soon as I learned it, if possible, or as soon as it was age-appropriate, if not.

I made it my business to set an example of strength through the way I used emotional expression, forgiveness without forgetting, cultivation of open vulnerability, and demonstrations of courage in the face of fear, as well as I could, teaching also the positive value of tears and the central importance of love as a practice, not merely an emotion. Cultivating my daughters' strengths as they grew and learning every new development I could lay my hands on about the most emotionally intelligent way to raise children, especially daughters, I did everything I could to listen deeply and carefully to what might be behind overtly expressed or carefully repressed emotion, anger in particular, as my primary parenting strategies.

All these years later, I am deeply thankful that the wisdom at the center of that mysterious circling practice worked. The circle held and deepened through the years as we taught and learned from each other. It has now expanded into an extended family circle, which includes three exceptional men and three amazing grandchildren who are teaching me the art of grandmothering in the same way my children taught me the art of mothering. Whatever ability I have to fully embody my roles of mother and grandmother are forever beholden to the little girl I used to be who adamantly declared from about age five that she would never grow up. The opportunity to fully enter the joyful world of childhood with yet another generation, guided by the wisdom gained while growing into the person I am today, is one of the greatest gifts life has ever provided.

Uncovering ancient stories of women's particular innate ability to open to the liminal connection between daily reality and intuitive knowing was the first part of my journey out of the chasm of despair. Singing those stories back into living experience by holding them ever more consciously and firmly at the center of the Girls' Club circle was the second, and discovering how to shed the psychic limitations of the culturally conditioned self, reconnecting with an increasingly embodied natural life-force in partnership with the wisdom and knowledge gained through experience, was the third, into which I hope to continue to grow as long as I live.

The bones of ancient stories from matrilineal cultures, in which women's power was held and honored in collaborative equality with men's, lie in many disparate places. They have unique power, which doesn't just benefit women. However, it is women's stories that have historically been silenced within colonial cultures of all kinds, right alongside native stories of every continent. The shared wisdom of women and men who are able to approach daily reality from the unified rim of Gaia's circle of life creates stories with the capacity to entrain consciousness toward the production of naturally life-sustaining communities wherever they congregate.

As such, these are the stories that most need revival to heal the shared planetary psyche and open minds to the powerfully creative aspects of everything formerly labeled *feminine* and too often reviled and repressed within Western culture in both male and female psyches. Reenchanting our perception of the world to inspire awe at its very existence can only be encountered when thinking and doing slow down enough to allow the wisdom of the heart and the body to emerge in a way rarely found in Western cultural traditions.

THE CONTINUOUS HEARTACHE that became the emotional tone under every other feeling as I maneuvered through the long divorce process was the first catalyst that drove me to seek psychotherapy.

That process triggered an intense search for meaning that revealed an inner story buried under layers of conditioning that had suppressed it. Before that all began, however, those layers would have looked a lot like water, had I been a fish, something so pervasive that its presence was nearly impossible to see. Through wise and compassionate reflection within a number of different kinds of professional therapeutic relationships, the story's premise and cause became clear enough to begin to let the whole narrative go, gradually replacing it with a more hope-filled tale about inner strength that I eventually learned to own.

When, as a young adult, I first entered the psychological woods of what I imagined would be adventurous encounters with the world beyond my family as I left for college, heading out in what appeared to be a kind of hero's journey of self-discovery, I approached the challenging, mysterious tangle it presented with my normal enthusiasm. That approach had generally energized and empowered me to find the path home from actual tree-filled woods as a child, even if I became a bit lost and afraid at some point. Getting lost only added to the excitement of the adventure as a child but never prevented a return home in time for dinner, usually with a lively story to add to family conversation. Why would this adventure of making my way in the world as an independent adult be any different, I had reasoned, especially since I was taking a path of self-discovery with clear contours laid out by family tradition?

Uncovering the hidden story of that younger self *did* involve eventually finding a path out of the psychological woods in time for a metaphorical dinner with my parents. In fact, as is often true, the story of the journey down that path contains many beautiful, sun-dappled glades and woodland flowers alongside thorny, frightening patches. However, the lovely glades began to dominate the retelling only after the wiser, more mature voice of the grown woman I became gained the trust and took the hand of her younger self, finding her in the deep metaphorical cave hidden under the thickest part of the psychological tangle.

Chapter Eleven

Growing Community

When looking back at life, trying to discern whether one's actions have made a dent to help shape something more positive and beautiful than what went before, it's easy to notice failures and imperfect attempts, well-intentioned as they may have been. Or in reverse, to notice and exaggerate the importance of what little effect one had on the mammoth quandaries and intransigent structures inevitably bumped up against when trying to foster justice, peace, joy, and compassion in human society. In the end, the best any of us can do is to live as close to the integrity of our values as possible, always holding open the door to learning through listening to others and engaging in self-reflection before responding in words or actions. If one is lucky enough to have children and an environment conducive to raising them in an atmosphere of love and encouragement, living in this way may alter the course of a family trajectory in a profound way, superseding the importance of career accomplishment. As such, I resonate strongly with Robert Kennedy's words from the "Ripple of Hope" speech he gave to South African student activists seeking to dismantle the racial oppression of apartheid in 1966:

It is from numberless diverse acts of courage . . . that human history is . . . shaped. Each time a man stands up for an ideal, or acts to improve the lot of others, or strikes out against injustice, he sends forth a tiny ripple of hope, and crossing each other from a million different centers of energy and daring those ripples build a current which can sweep down the mightiest walls of oppression and resistance.[1]

I am proud to have been part of the waves of change that rolled over this world as many baby boomers began to see through the delusions under which Western culture had lived for so long, setting about lifelong efforts to realign their lives to support social and environmental justice. We learned and stumbled as we went, but through millions of small, daily choices, striving to be the change we wanted to see, we strengthened and brought into being new social structures that continue to grow compassion and resilience.

LIKE ME, most of us who were working on the front lines of the solar energy and environmental movements in the 1980s and '90s in order to build networks to connect entrepreneurial businesses, local governments, and nonprofit organizations were not fully aware of what exactly we were creating. Along the way we brought new approaches to meaningful work and created new kinds of businesses, civic organizations, and social arrangements. Much of this cultural change began for each individual the way it did in my case, as a volunteer activity embedded in the youthful surge of change that rose in the '70s. Subsequently, for me, over nearly forty years of consistently working in and learning about start-up businesses and grassroots nonprofit organizational development in various paid and unpaid capacities, my understanding of how they could most effectively meet the moment for those most in need evolved into a successful consulting career by the time the new millennium rolled around.

That synopsis of my career path puts into personal context a very wide-angled overview of the massive shift that was only beginning as baby boomers approached their thirties and forties. Many continued to be intent on finding ways to nourish life in creative, altruistic ways, as I did, feeding a shared vision, as well as the better world it imagined, with every choice available in the realms of work, family, and every other aspect of life open to choice while striving to survive and thrive. Altruism has always been a sacred, community-building value, probably since the beginning of the human family. In the United States, nonprofit organizations first sprouted as institutionalized forms of altruism, a very positive human urge embedded right alongside many negative ones brought by immigrant European colonizers to this country. Those altruistic institutions included churches, universities, and hospitals, European social structures that many early colonizers considered critically important components of civilized society. The structures of altruistic organizations, however, when coupled with the rebellious *American* ideals of rugged individualism, self-governance, and equal representation under the law, eventually morphed into new, distinctly local forms. Because the government of the young country, recently established as independent by the American Revolution, had an extremely limited resource base, powerful incentives existed to provide local versions of necessary social and health services that depended not on government support, but on volunteers, private donations, and fees to carry out their missions. Following colonial times, every new era contributed a new set of ideas, principles, and practices to feed the growth of these caring, community-based institutions, building them over time into the uniquely effective powerhouse of the modern economy that they are today. Due to their loose, informal affiliations with each other, which define the fluid, multifaceted character of this massive network, it still flies largely below the radar of academic economists.

The Progressive Era of the late nineteenth through early twentieth centuries was a particularly significant one for civic organizations in which new ideas about how to structure these altruistic institutions gained powerful voices that accompanied an increase in political reform and social activism paralleling booming industrial growth. Policies such as the end of child labor, voting rights for women, and prohibition of alcohol were written into federal law as a result. This was also the time of the "robber barons," when captains of industry accumulated vast quantities of wealth, spurring some of them to reflect on how society's conditions had facilitated their success. Andrew Carnegie's *The Gospel of Wealth*, published in 1889, promoted the concept of a debt owed to society for great financial success. He encouraged repaying that debt by donating financially to altruistic causes, a philosophy that eventually resulted in the still powerful philanthropic foundation known as the Carnegie Corporation of New York, or simply, the Carnegie Corporation.

In discussions with several people in my work as a development consultant, including a female vice president of the Carnegie Corporation's division that funds emerging social justice organizations, I sought a major grant for a group fostering civic education and political engagement among low-income people of color. That organization possessed a board of directors and staff drawn from the constituencies it served and had reached a transition point with the potential to tip its work from statewide to national expansion. Those conditions triggered the interest of the Carnegie Corporation's vice president with whom I spoke. Nothing in nonprofit development is ever certain, however, like anything else in life. In that case, although a good many of the necessary pieces were in place, fortune tipped in another direction. Still, the experience left me with great respect for the Carnegie Corporation and hope for other groups similar to the one I represented.

The recent history of the nonprofit sector's development is rarely thought of in conjunction with the cultural changes the baby boom generation brought to Western culture. The full impact of those changes can't be understood, however, without acknowledging what was also taking place as the first wave of young adults from my generation began to enter the workforce as the civil rights and anti–Vietnam War movements grew in size. In other arenas private citizens started to organize brand-new types of nonprofit organizations designed to tackle specific public policy issues, learning from the intersectional growth of the organizations behind those two movements. The federal government also became increasingly involved in social and cultural welfare programs under the leadership of Democratic presidents John F. Kennedy and Lyndon B. Johnson. Those years were the times when I was first becoming aware of politics as a rising adolescent, and the man who would eventually become my second husband was completing his bachelor's degree in political science.

The 1969 Tax Reform Act created a whole new set of professional opportunities for young people by providing new incentives for widespread philanthropic giving, writing Section 501(c)(3) into the federal tax code. That move transformed the potential tax status of every organization that did not accept public funds, did not engage in political activity, and did not join forces with those that did into a private foundation. When organizational leaders found that they could legally designate their agencies' tax status as charitable organizations and provide tax exemptions to donors, applications for 501(c)(3) nonprofit status increased by leaps and bounds. The nonprofit sector expanded rapidly, providing many more opportunities to find meaningful white-collar jobs in social service and public policy fields just as the front edge of the huge wave of baby boomers began looking for work.[2]

There was also a dramatic shift in the relationship between the government and the nonprofit sector during the 1960s, particularly during President Johnson's War on Poverty. With that policy initiative, the federal government began implementing social policy as well as legally codifying it. Several restructured funding arrangements fed the growth of this social role for the federal government. One of the most significant was providing ongoing financial support to local nonprofit service agencies in the form of federal grants to state and local governments. These grants could then be redirected to collaborative partnerships between local governments and grassroots nonprofit organizations in order to more effectively address pressing local problems. Such groups were better equipped to do that work because they were organized by and beholden to the people most affected. This new funding mechanism led to the creation of thousands of new nonprofit agencies that had no relationship to conventional fund-raising networks like the Community Chest, a traditional funder and formerly the only way a charitable organization, other than a church, could gain financial support.[3]

In 1976, the year before I graduated from college with a bachelor's degree in political science, there was another momentous shift in the power of the nonprofit sector at local, state, and national levels. Congress passed a bill allowing 501(c)(3) nonprofit agencies to legally spend up to one million dollars per year on government lobbying efforts. This gave activist groups a much greater voice in public policymaking than they had ever had before. By 1981, I was working to build the strength of the nascent solar energy industry in Vermont by helping to lead voluntary nonprofit organizing efforts. The entrepreneurial solar greenhouse company that had so inspired me had gone under by that time, thanks to then president Ronald Reagan's energy policies ending solar tax credits. However, nonprofit organizations continued to sprout. The continuing growth of the third sector began to significantly influence the workings of the economy's two other sectors, government and business.[4]

Restructuring relationships between the nonprofit sector and the government was a controversial policy from the get-go. Many nonprofit leaders of existing organizations were apprehensive about what funding from the government would do to the nature of their organizations, fearing a shift that would pull focus away from directly responding to the needs of their constituents through their nimble, independent organizational structures and redirect that focus toward preserving the new governmental revenue stream. On the other hand, government policy makers worried about their ability to hold nonprofits accountable for the way they spent government funds, particularly in light of the increasing number of groups and the many services being transferred from government agencies into their hands. Many political conservatives were especially concerned about the expanding reach of the federal government through collaborative arrangements with these nonprofit agencies.

Ronald Reagan's campaign for the presidency had addressed this concern in 1980. His platform promised to shrink the size of the federal government. Early in his administration, Reagan had followed through, winning passage of legislation that substantially cut federal funding for social programs, transferring funding responsibility to state governments while simultaneously cutting federal funding to states, hobbling their ability to carry out the work.[5] Reagan's effort to shrink the federal government while continuing to feed the growth of giant corporations, especially oil companies, did so under the mantra that they were the best "job creators." He predicted that the benefits accorded to these corporate giants would "trickle down" in a waterfall of prosperity to benefit everyone, a mirage believed by so many people that he is still remembered as one of the most popular presidents in US history. He was actually a very slick salesman for big business.

Nonprofit organizations beholden to their local constituents in a virtuous cycle of service were forced to cut their programs, sometimes severely, as a result of Reagan's policies, truncating opportunities for local communities to work together in traditionally democratic ways to help themselves. However, they were better able to survive than related small businesses due to their committed volunteers. Small renewable energy companies disappeared at an alarming rate, however, just as they were putting down roots and beginning to bloom and just as these visionary companies began ramping up multiple methods to head off climate change, so evident to many people even in 1981. It was devastating to watch how fast the number of small renewable energy companies declined in the course of one year. At two consecutive solar sales conventions I attended in a warehouse on a Boston pier, with Northeast winter cold just ahead, fully half of the young companies that exhibited in 1980 had disappeared by 1981. Consequently, over a much longer time than would otherwise have been necessary, the renewable energy industry struggled to innovate and evolve, ultimately succeeding, despite an extremely unbalanced economic playing field. Most renewable energy companies that survived the Reagan years were forced to use a more centralized corporate structure instead of the dynamic, locally based small business model the federal tax credits had made possible. Many community-based nonprofit organizations were similarly able to eventually restructure and compensate for lost funds by tapping into other federal funding sources like Medicaid or refinancing their operations. Many others found ways to increase their percentage of private donations and earned income as alternative methods to sustain their budgets, increasing their need for private fundraising capacity in the process. That shift created an opening for the career I later developed. Expanded use of vouchers, tax credits, and bond issues to fund nonprofit social and health agencies reflected the need for a growing diversity of government funding sources to sustain necessary community services provided only by local nonprofit organizations.[6]

A 1982 SURVEY of nonprofit human service organizations in sixteen communities in the US showed that fully *65 percent* had been created since 1960, notably during the late '70s and early '80s. The same growth spurt was happening simultaneously across multiple continents. Civic engagement in locally focused self-help projects was blossoming everywhere, mainly under the radar of business and government leaders. In the Philippines, twenty-one thousand nonprofit organizations had formed by1994. Nearly one hundred thousand Christian Base Communities were built from local action groups across the Brazilian countryside. An estimated 30 percent of Kenya's capital development from the 1970s to the 1990s came from the Harambee movement, facilitating the beginning of multiple local development projects carried out by nonprofit groups rooted in the communities they served. Similar developments were occurring in Eastern Europe and the former Soviet Union. Well before the fall of the Berlin Wall in 1989, important changes had also begun taking place at the grass roots of Eastern European society. Nonprofit organizations were the primary sources of inspiration and energy driving those changes. One could say, in fact, that a kind of second society was being formed, comprising thousands, even millions, of networks of people in local communities across the globe working to provide each other with mutual aid to enhance local resilience.[7]

However large this huge group of nonprofit organizations was becoming, it could not accurately be described as an organized global movement in the conventional sense. As commonly understood, organized political or social movements have leaders who guide their development based on clear ideological principles. People can recognize such movements and choose whether or not to join them.

Scholars and strategists can identify and study their documented views and ideals. Such movements also have followers. However, this movement, which Paul Hawken identified and described in his 2007 book *Blessed Unrest*, did not fit the standard model of a social movement. It was and remains dispersed and interrelated but not officially linked. This massive movement has no manifesto or doctrine and no overriding top-down authority. It continues to take shape and grow in schoolrooms, farms, jungles, villages, companies, deserts, fisheries, slums, and even fancy New York hotels. Its most distinctive feature is that it emerged everywhere simultaneously, on a global scale of humanitarian civic engagement, rising first from the grassroots of local communities.[8]

IN 1986, the year before my second daughter was born in Minneapolis, Minnesota, during the time I was co-chairing the Minnesota Renewable Energy Society, the Earned Income Tax Credit became law. Programs the legislation made possible became major income sources for nonprofit agencies focused on creating a more just diversity of available housing, especially in cities. Welfare reform was enacted in 1996, two years after I graduated from Tufts University with a master's degree in Urban and Environmental Policy. It greatly increased demand for nonprofit services of all kinds, from job training to child care to multiple varieties of family support.[9] Not long afterward, the Internet exploded into all aspects of cultural life to begin a shapeshifting process that would, in a civilizational blink of an eye, utterly alter every conventional communications network just before the world transitioned into a new millennium and create the wholly undreamed-of boons and challenges that would completely reshape the way politics, business, travel, and entertainment would be perceived after the year 2000.

In 1991, the year after I began negotiating my divorce, I entered graduate school. That was also the year when the World Wide Web became available for public use. That opportunity forced a cultural adaptation to a technology that had never before been seen. For the nonprofit world, it gradually became a fertile avenue of growth. Once that shift was institutionalized, online giving exploded, generating 2.1 billion dollars in donations for nonprofit organizations in 2012 alone, for example. Social media platforms like Twitter and Facebook gained large followings, beginning in 2006. Social media fundraising campaigns followed, such as the ALS Ice Bucket Challenge and the #BlackLivesMatter hashtag, which both started online and transformed initiatives born at the grassroots into giant social movements at lightning speed.[10]

In 1993, while I was still in graduate school, Bill Clinton became president and Congress gave a big boost to the growth of the nonprofit sector by passing the National and Community Service Trust Act. With a mission to improve lives, strengthen communities, and foster civic engagement through service and volunteering, the Corporation for National and Community Service was established, which came to be known as the "Corporation." This new agency further developed federally funded youth–service models initiated in the early '60s by President John F. Kennedy. The Peace Corps, serving internationally, and its sister organization Volunteers in Service to America (VISTA), serving in the US, opened opportunities to gain meaningful work experience for volunteers, providing them with various combinations of stipends and room and board in exchange for service to underprivileged communities. Both programs were relatively modest in scope as they began their work. Along with the launch of the Corporation and its flagship program, AmeriCorps, the federal government under President Clinton established service learning as an educational priority. These combined strategies created a much more extensive role for nonprofit organizations to address social needs in local communities. Nonprofit goals also grew as a result of new federal grants and financial support contracts with the federal government, enabling them to provide the essential social and health services not otherwise available in many low-income communities.[11]

Throughout President Clinton's two terms in office, ending in 2001, the Corporation struggled to maintain its budget and was frequently in danger of outright elimination. This was partly the result of its drive to institutionalize the federal government's relationship with the nonprofit sector. Nevertheless, the Corporation and AmeriCorps have funded thousands of paid positions in social service work, at home and abroad, including one for my older daughter after she graduated from college. Volunteers received stipends and work experience that expanded their professional skill sets and leadership capacities in exchange for community service. Those programs also expanded the staffing capacity of innumerable community service agencies that served an extensive range of missions at the local level, from social welfare to environmental education and advocacy to early childhood education. AmeriCorps also inspired other new hybrid models of social-entrepreneurship and community service in the process.[12]

The financial crisis of 2008 was in full economic destruction mode just before Barack Obama was inaugurated president in 2009, the year my younger daughter graduated from college. At that time, I was working to strategically support executive directors of hyperlocal nonprofit organizations to keep the funding they depended on from private foundations, which were also struggling with the repercussions of the financial crisis. Many of the policy and management issues these small organizations faced were not caused by the financial crisis alone, however. They also reflected the evolution of government–nonprofit relationships. The dramatic growth in government contracts for nonprofit agencies, enabling those agencies to provide essential community health and social services not available through government agencies, vastly increased the number of such groups. As a result, raising operational funding became increasingly difficult, inspiring nonprofits ultimately to seek greater participation in the public policymaking processes. Coalitions of such groups grew in support of shared goals and mutual support to surmount the fundraising difficulties they all faced.

THE START OF THE CAREER that developed for me in a step-by-step process over the course of these institutional changes was triggered by many things. One experience that always comes to mind, however, when asked what started me on this path, occurred while I was still waiting on tables in Burlington, supporting my first husband through graduate school. I clearly remember trying to imagine, as I hiked Camel's Hump one day with my husband in the late '70s, what might spark enough inspiration to jumpstart a more meaningful career path. As we clambered over the steep, rocky path we loved so much, it soon became impossible to ignore the insidious damage to the leaves of many trees, especially near the top. We realized that this must be the result of the acid rain we had been hearing about that was affecting Vermont's forests. Polluted water was falling from the sky onto the leaves and entering the soil that fed the trees after unfiltered smoke particles were carried by the wind all the way from midwestern utility smokestacks. Those smokestacks had been specifically constructed to spew smoke so high into the atmosphere that it would bypass local communities in places where the utilities operated—Chicago, Illinois, and Milwaukee, Wisconsin, for example. As a result, the smoke traveled the eastern-moving weather patterns to be dumped in the rain that fell on hundreds of thousands of trees in the forests of New England. I got energized as I looked at the trees and remembered those facts, saying, "I've got to find a way to do something about that!"

That spark of inspiration stayed with me. It spurred my engagement with the long process of discovering and shaping a meaningful career, starting with the position earlier described at the start-up solar greenhouse company and continuing to grow as I was elected or appointed to volunteer leadership and organizing positions in local and statewide initiatives to address public policy concerns. Helping to lead networking support for start-up renewable energy companies in Vermont during the Reagan years was the first of these, followed by the same work in Minnesota after my husband and I moved to Minneapolis for his medical internship and residency.

As co-chair of the Solar Association of Vermont and vice chair of the Minnesota Renewable Energy Society after that, I worked to counter the devastation wreaked on small renewable energy businesses by Reagan's energy policies. Later, my active involvement in local and statewide initiatives—one that convinced the town in which I lived to institute locally based curbside recycling and another that expanded coastal environmental protections in Massachusetts—continued to grow my organizing experience and understanding of nonprofit agencies while I studied for a master's degree in Urban and Environmental Policy from Tufts University.

That official credential came into my hands at the end of 1994, two years after my divorce was finalized, validating expertise in the kind of work required by the career I'd been learning by doing through years of voluntary service wherever my former husband and I had lived. Six years later, that degree, along with widespread personal access to the Internet in my home office, brought me paid work with board and staff members of multiple local, state, and regional nonprofit organizations. I called that sole proprietor consultancy Creative Initiatives. It became part of the first wave of a growing cadre of workers known now as "the gig economy." Through that work and the sole proprietor shiatsu practice that preceded it, which grew from a two-year certificate program in Five Element Chinese Medicine, I was able to remain at home and stay deeply connected to my daughters' lives.

Being available to them whenever they needed—while simultaneously striving to augment the meager child support I received from my ex-husband—had always felt essential to me. His child support payments were necessarily limited by the huge financial burden he carried, including massive student loan debt and a giant annual medical malpractice insurance bill. He was also supporting a second family following our divorce and had committed to largely fund the college education of our two daughters later on. Although our relationship had mostly disintegrated, I recognized in his continuing support, in the face of his own financial challenges, confirmation that underneath the pain we both felt a fine thread of our original connection and continuing care for each other lived on.

Chapter Twelve

The Mystery of Spirit

Throughout human history, people have cultivated spiritual connections, conceived of and accessed in a multitude of ways, that inspire storytelling about life's meaning based on what they encounter. Many people have engaged spiritual practices in search of greater awareness by using prayer in various forms, from trance dance to contemplative meditation. Others have sought mental shifts to access spiritual experience by consuming psychoactive substances. Still others have participated in communal practices at holy sites believed to possess rarified spiritual energy. These many methods to engage a deeper, wider quality of awareness all involve physical practices that bridge the expanse of human imagination, from sitting quietly for extended periods to walking on hot coals or whirling endlessly in circles of dervish dancing. However, there has never been a time like the present when so much is known about such a wide diversity of spiritual practices and the particular qualities of insight each can provide.[1]

Today it's possible, for people financially able to educate themselves through travel, to directly experience myriad ways to approach the psychological question everyone eventually encounters—What is the meaning of life?—within the cultural settings that produced them. Becoming seekers of that question's answer was a newly available possibility for the wide swath of mainly suburban young people in the baby boom generation who came of age just as airline travel became widely accessible. Those who could put the motivation for their search into words compared it to a sense of waking up, compelling them to leave conventional lifestyles behind, travel to distant lands and take up alternative living practices, whether in their home country or abroad. Because so many had the same inspiration at the same time, this deeply felt individual experience morphed into a cultural process that revealed itself to be another kind of social movement—a consciousness movement, as it began to be called in the 1980s. The consciousness movement had been exploding into Western youth culture since the late '60s, but a true definition of what was happening went far beyond individual motivations. Thinking of it in those terms became far too limiting for those seeking to describe the scope of cultural change that the movement inspired.[2]

Out of shared hope and concern for the future of humanity, the consciousness movement continues to grow on a global scale today. Anyone committed to it can see the trend. A connection to hope is generated and sustained through actions people are inspired to take, which in turn inspires others to act. Those actions bring hope in the same way to ever-widening circles of creative action. The practices that together make up the whole of this moving, evolving process support those engaged with it to safely move beyond the traditional protectiveness of inherited religious practices, often defined by strict boundaries of dogma and belief governed by institutionalized hierarchies.

Hatred strong enough to produce violence often arises when the dualism of evil–versus–good is fostered by the leaders of belief systems which identify "the others"—those who do not follow the same practices, whatever they may be. Those "others" are considered ignorant at best or heretical at worst, requiring some form of reeducation or punishment by true believers, which has consistently resulted in various levels of violent conflict between differently believing people everywhere.

The consciousness movement, by contrast, reinforced a different, broader path to spiritual development. Whether conscious of the contours of the movement or not, participants found hope and inspiration in the variety of spiritual practices it offered to replace the despair that had prompted so many of these young people to abandon their families' conventional religious practices in the '60s and '70s. What could be called a cultural awakening was ignited as increasing numbers turned to this new approach to spiritual expression. It truly became noticeable in the combined efforts of a multiplicity of organizations, movements, and resulting cultural trends that linked to each other across the globe. The human potential movement and the tendency of increasing numbers of people to identify themselves as spiritual but not religious are only two of the aspects that characterized a larger shift in worldview. Through ever-widening cultural exchanges, as more and more people began to travel internationally, it has since become easier to reject traditional religious practice in favor of personally eclectic spiritual understanding and practice without enduring the pain of social ostracizing—or worse—as in earlier eras.[3]

Some of the practices that contributed to the consciousness movement have been used for centuries in Buddhist, Hindu, Taoist, and Indigenous traditions. Meditation, many forms of physical prayer, bodywork, yoga, various martial arts, nature-based and herbal medicine, the laying on of hands, thera-peutic touch, and acupuncture are some of the spiritual practices that individuals combine in various ways. A focus on supporting the development and flourishing of the individual and humanity in general, as well as all life forms, lies at the core of the choice to engage these modalities, cultivating what Albert Schweitzer called a reverence for life.

WITHIN MY LIFETIME, scientists have begun to piece together their understanding of a much broader plane of interacting natural sys-tems, broader than has ever been accepted before in such Western institutional disciplines. The scientific study of ecology, for exam-ple, only began to be recognized as a serious scientific discipline in the decades of my adulthood. Wider awareness of the mysteries of the universe, organic chemistry, and the human genome began to reveal a fascinating and disorienting truth—that we are not static beings but moving, changing, flowing whorls of momentary ener-getic being within the greater fabric of Earth and the universe. Some people can see through the veil of the linear narrative most commonly perceived as reality. A few rare souls can perceive with openness to even greater depths of experience that foster a wider, more inclusive, compassionate view. Those gifted few define the edge of the possible, and even the utterly improbable, for those living with a consciousness beyond the common reaches of other people in their times. Certainly Jesus of Nazareth and Siddhartha Gautama were two of these extraordinary people. Many others pushed the common boundaries of perception and experience in other times in more limited ways, such as Henry David Thoreau, Margaret Fuller, Mahatma Gandhi, Emily Dickinson, Kahlil

Gibran, Sojourner Truth, Dr. Martin Luther King Jr., Thich Naht Hanh, and innumerable others.

No matter who these insightful beings were, however, as humans they inherently possessed various blind spots associated with their embodiment in the times and places in which they lived. It was their singular ability to express the experience of heartfelt resonance with timeless wisdom, however, that raised them to pinnacles of historical memory. Their ideas continue to reverberate in the river of words passed from one generation to the next in ways that inspire and enliven other minds to open to truth, compassion, and the increasingly enlightened relationship to the living matrix of Earth, fostering the will to act to preserve and sustain the mysterious life-force at its core, that which makes living possible in all forms. Those actions over time are what constitute the evolution of the cultural structures of society, and also, as Kahlil Gibran has pointed out, their words and insights look different when cast in different lights by different listeners.

One can choose to count the darkness only or the light, but the wisest among us—those who can speak with quiet, encouraging calm at the boundaries of perception—have honed the ability to take in both dark and light. They can hold that perception gently before choosing words to describe what it allows them to understand, communicating to others in a way that inspires many to learn from them and embody new understanding as time unfolds. The result of this process can be observed in daily life. For instance, a hundred years ago, when the grandparents I knew and loved as a child were young, laws for protecting the environment, ending Jim Crow segregation, instituting workers' rights to form unions, determining a federal minimum wage, and providing old-age insurance and government-subsidized healthcare in the United States were widely considered impractical, utopian dreams or dangerous socialist plots. There was also violent resistance and confrontation in the streets in response to advocacy for the concept of women gaining the right to vote.

Now, just two generations further on, most of us take these formerly heretical ideas for granted. They are understood widely as common-sense-legislated boundaries defining the democratic government under which we live. The radical ideas of one generation often become the common sense of the next. When that happens, credit for the changes rightfully belongs to individual activists and the socially rising movements of resonating minds that find the path, inspired by carefully chosen words, a path that ultimately brings those radical ideas from marginal cultural visions into mainstream acceptance. Unfortunately, most Americans don't know the history behind our country's social structures. Only a superficial brush of those ideas is taught in most high schools, and only rarely can you find it in reports from mainstream media outlets or online educational networks because what constitutes the accepted version of history is determined by the dominant institutions of any culture, which erase the stories that do not serve them. In fact, the story we know as history is always under siege.[4]

CIVILIZATIONS GROW OUT OF a confluence of need and belief in order to collaboratively generate peaceful coexistence with enough protection and food to raise children and safely care for those who are weak, sick, and otherwise vulnerable. A foundation of shared understanding about how living works is essential for peaceful consensus about acceptable forms of interpersonal interaction.

Each time new information poses serious challenges to a civilization's underlying belief system, political battles are bound to play out in the public square, rising out of the emotional well connecting shared belief to the drive for personal survival. Backlash is destined to arise in opposition to any attempt to widely institute new knowledge within any culture and always voiced loudest by those whose personal sense of power is rooted in the system being challenged. Such people generally attempt to block movement toward change at a rate nearly equivalent in strength to the size of the change being advocated. This is true because those whose perceived needs are fully met within the behavioral paradigm of the old belief system defend it as though their lives depend upon it, which they do, at least in cultural terms. For them, those terms shape the outer image of living, which has come to be seen as essential to personal survival, and at least on a psychological level, it often is.

Defense of old ways is by no means a bad thing because not all new social concepts are wise or beneficial. Whatever truly is, however, will eventually move forward through those who resonate from personal experience with the heart of the new concept, although the full implications of any such change may take longer than a generation to have a significant impact. History has repeatedly shown that when such existential challenges are severe enough to threaten a foundational shift at the deepest level of a belief system, the ugliest, most violent side of the threatened system will inevitably rear its head. The power of such backlash is sometimes enough to slow the rising shift but not to stop it when that shift is rooted in deeper understanding that proves to be more life-sustaining than what it replaces.

The world of ideas in which we are all inextricably immersed has become inseparable from the global communication and ideological exchange made available to nearly everyone, of every possible perspective, via the Internet and other modern technologies. That web of ideas, both nourishing and destructive, is raising the current shift in consciousness to a tipping point, and starkly revealing horrendous underbellies all over the world in a monstrous backlash against cultural change, catalyzed by rapidly spreading scientific discoveries and spiritual practices that are deepening and expanding awareness of the evolutionary potential of human consciousness.

Mounting cultural pressure toward a tipping point in the evolution of human consciousness is reflected daily in so many arenas, not the least of which are weather patterns. It's not hard to see how weather patterns are connected to the increasing speed of commercial production and constant human activity, if one can stop long enough to look around. The speed that prevents that observation is encouraged and rewarded in economic arenas, even as it magnifies the effects of pollution and destruction of essential biodiversity. Those effects, too often ignored, can be traced back to the very limited time available to any of us, caught up in one way or another in the commonly accepted mindset of global culture in order to survive, generally precluding time for deep reflection. However, it has become increasingly hard to ignore the new intensity of weather patterns moving across the globe. It's not a big leap to imagine them demanding, ever more insistently, that human beings take responsibility to change our thought patterns, which continue to foster that intensity, in order to effectively use the readily available tools at our fingertips to not only stop but reverse the ravages of climate change.

The clear and present danger of climate change is now widely understood in scientific circles to have been wrought by the institutional thought patterns and resulting physical and social structures of Western civilization. The ever-more-intense changes now making themselves known are speaking in the language of lashing winds, the growing size and frequency of mega storms, mega fires, massive immigration shifts of both people and animals, and new disease pandemics—a language impossible to ignore once experienced. Those winds of change are calling into question the whole concept of the hierarchy of being and value that underlies the conceptual framework on which modern civilization has been constructed.

Academics working within their own hierarchies of value have often unwittingly reinforced such structures as a result of the way they have examined and taught their subjects within institutionalized higher education. Scientifically breaking down complex tapestries of living interdependence into simpler parts— as one might do to understand a machine, examining in greater detail the way each piece works within its own system—can easily leave out critical interlacing phenomena that characterize and differentiate living beings from machines, making it impossible to see what's happening at the macro level.

Dissecting reality in this way—pulling it apart into separate specialized silos of inquiry—has fostered great strides in human understanding of everything from entomology to particle physics. Those siloed processes are extremely valuable and should not be abandoned, just as Newton's laws describing one level of reality were not discarded simply because they didn't apply to other levels of understanding discovered later. Even though undiscovered, however, a wider level of reality always exists. We now know a whole lot more about levels of reality that were beyond human conception in Newton's time. The quantum level, for example, functions within a completely different set of physical laws from those governing the common, everyday reality we all take for granted and that was so well described using Newton's laws.

As IS TRUE with all major cultural shifts, the one now rising is emerging from the grass roots, the most basic, local level where the most disturbing effects are experienced most acutely. The grass roots of culture are where thought, belief, and the human body connect with the rest of nature. They grow at the most local, personal levels where human life is simplest. This time, those grass roots are also globally connected through a complex network of electronic communication continuously spawning new offshoots, similar to recently discovered networks of fungi connecting vast communication systems of tree roots beneath the soil. That electronic human network has evolved far beyond any point of imaginable return.

The impending cultural shift does not negate the power, efficiency, and benefits of the concept of hierarchy. The beneficial aspects of hierarchical social structures could efficiently, yet compassionately, implement new human wisdom if those within it so chose, instituting the value of collaborative power as they did so—"power with" rather than "power over." The cultural tipping point currently pushing humanity to reexamine itself and its place in living Earth systems is rising out of a place of mutual care and compassion, fostered increasingly out of the death and destruction being wrought by mammoth hurricanes, fires, and floods. It is not rising from the heart of whatever violent confrontation is the focus of the news media on any particular day. The heartfelt call for change continues to move and unite those on the ground, through what has often been called the movement of movements by those within it. That call is fostered within the laterally empowered and empowering Third Sector, inspired by altruism and rising to the challenges of each local moment, unbowed by the din of pushback.

When enough of humanity comes to terms with the implications of recent scientific discoveries, there is potential for a new understanding of human consciousness to completely reconstruct the organizational model of human social being. Sharing and lateral empowerment in innumerable spheres are already changing the way we communicate and interact physically, mentally, and emotionally. These ways of being are not alien, nor are they new. They have been at the heart of religious traditions and moral philosophies for centuries, though they have made their way into the shape of commonly embodied human cultures at a very slow pace, partly due to the natural mind-over-matter hierarchical thinking and organization that has often enshrouded them within institutionalized hierarchical religious structures. For a more compassionate, laterally empowered cultural structure to begin to more fully emerge, not only must old beliefs change about institutional structures at the intellectual level, the emotions conditioned by them must change as well.

Broader understanding of the connection between emotional awareness, consciously directed thought, and wisely embodied action has grown by leaps and bounds over the course of my adult life. Although far from fully realized, understanding is spreading globally about the need to integrate reflective thought and wise, embodied action in order to sustain life on Earth, and that movement shows no sign of slowing no matter how many gauntlets are raised in its path. The new global belief structure, revealing itself in growing pockets across the planet, honors the unique life-giving mystery of all existence, from the microbe to the cosmos. It recognizes various levels of development within consciousness as well as within physical being of every kind. Humility, compassion, and generosity increasingly challenge arrogance and greed in public discussions, however underreported that shift may be. The wisdom of this way of living is rising from humanity's combined need to survive, just as every other way of publicly being human has risen before. Listening to and cultivating consciously expanded awareness is becoming increasingly valued in hearts worldwide. Understanding and integrating the mysterious connection between thought, emotion, psyche, body, and environmental habitat continues to create a widening arc, bringing the human species to this vulnerable moment of powerful opportunity.

Chapter Thirteen

Walking the Dragon's Path

Psychological growth that initiates the ability to become more consciously aware is never easy. Becoming truly strong mentally, emotionally, or physically always includes confronting limitations and pushing boundaries, boundaries and limitations often only vaguely understood and beyond individual control, intricately intertwined as they are with whatever conditions brought them into being. I know this deep in my bones from navigating single parenthood. That situation thrust me into an unexpected journey of psychological exploration, seeking meaning in places I would otherwise never have looked.

Finding little deep, healing emotional comfort in conventional Western religious practices, I took my own heart's counsel to move in whatever direction inspired curiosity, hope, possibility, and potential for kind human connection and new avenues to sustain inspiration, courage, and mental and emotional stamina, even as my daughters and I continued to attend the Unitarian church wherever the Girls' Club lived. Whatever new life shape I could commit to needed to have room for curiosity, wonder, beauty, and love to thrive. It also needed to be one from which I could draw energy to move creatively and confidently into the world in my role as a single parent and also find a nourishing way to live as a single woman—two spheres of being that over-lapped but were not identical. As a result, the first several years after our marriage dissolved enfolded an unexpected journey of self-discovery, including two years spent in the painful process of hammering out a divorce agreement while in graduate school as a stay-at-home mom to two tiny daughters.

Much of what I learned during that time was delivered through sporadic periods of psychotherapy mixed with numerous evening and weekend workshops at local and regional retreat centers. Those workshops were led by respected teachers from various unconventional approaches to spiritual practice, at least from a Western cultural perspective. They opened windows into ways to heal the heart's connection to life that were new and fascinating to me, even though they had been used by millions of people around the world for centuries. Those explorations can best be characterized by offering one in detail. It's a tale written from daily recordings made during the culminating trip of a yearlong study of Incan shamanism. What began as an introductory evening workshop opened into a series of quarterly weekend workshops at the Providence Zen Center in Rhode Island. They in turn culminated in a hike on the Inca Trail in Peru during the summer of 1995. My daughters experienced a different kind of adventure. Nine and six at the time, they had the educational opportunity to stay for one week with each set of grandparents, providing a generous taste of both the loving extended family they could depend on and the very different cultural contexts of two separate families that had built the foundations of their parents' childhoods.

THE INCA TRAIL IS VEILED IN MYSTERY and legend as it winds its way through the Peruvian Andes, spanning sixty-five miles from Cuzco to the ancient ruins of Machu Picchu, the sacred city of light for a people hidden in the mists of time. Answers to a vast array of questions linger among the stones on the shrouded path to the story that lies behind Machu Picchu and other sacred sites of the Inca, answers many believe will never be found. In an effort to experience whatever truth might possibly be revealed through direct encounter, however, a motley group of twelve travelers joined a long line leading to the Aero Peru ticket counter in Miami to receive boarding passes and check duffel bags in the early summer of 1995. The group was a mixture of women and men spanning the age range of midlife and sporting everything from a long white ponytail and drooping mustache to flowing long or tightly curled short locks on tall and skinny, short and round, or athletic bodies, some with sun wizened, dark brown, or pale freckled faces and some still harboring the last vestiges of youth.

Taking a leap back in time to that evening, the leader of the group is revealed as a tall medical anthropologist with a PhD in psychology from a widely respected university, having spent years living with, studying, and documenting the stories of indigenous shamans in Peru. He sports a boyish grin and a *Raiders of the Lost Ark*—styled hat, someone easily noticed and followed like the Pied Piper. My hiking partner and I join the line behind him and after more than an hour of snaking through different parts of the airport, climb aboard a cramped old-model plane to begin a mythical journey.

We are travelers eager to explore another way to conceive of living meaning, each one with a personal reason for making the trip that is linked to deep concern over the direction of Western culture. All have entered into a four-day hike to Machu Picchu, followed by camping visits to other sacred Incan sites, and have chosen to set aside traditional Western concepts of meaning for two weeks. We are all intent on engaging imagination, hoping to discover ancient wisdom while walking the Inca Trail in ways that honor the traditions of Incan descendants living today. Each hiker also holds a healthy dollop of scientific doubt to keep consciousness grounded in modern reality, though all are eager to enter with respectful curiosity into ritual practices specific to the Inca. Our guide has offered this experience as a means to learn of the wisdom passed down over generations among the Q'ero people living traditional lives high in the mountains. He tells us that their shamans sense the importance of this time and, due to the growing threat to the fragile balance of life posed by industrial society, are now willing to spread their long preserved knowledge beyond their own communities.

The sun begins to set behind the airborne plane as our group flies toward the deep darkness of approaching night. A spectacular blend of magenta, orange, and yellow inflames the cloud caps and their underbellies, melting into turquoise on tourmaline where sky meets water. With faces pressed to the window we see the colors gradually fade behind us. As the sun drops into the sea that stretches away in all directions, the plane is completely enveloped by night's impenetrable blackness.

On the ground again in Peru, our party emerges from the stuffy flight where smoking was freely permitted, to stand nearly comatose in an endless wait for luggage at midnight, followed by a bumpy bus ride through miles of barrios. In the wee hours of morning we pass row upon row of shacks cobbled together from adobe, abandoned shipping crates, and corrugated metal, decorated here and there with loud large advertising posters. Landing eventually in stark institutional hotel rooms somewhere in Lima, we collapse into exhausted sleep.

LOOKING OUT OF MODERN BUS WINDOWS as we retrace our route to the airport following breakfast the next morning, we watch a constant stream of bicycles, cars, and old-model buses, which trail people who cling in groups to every door, balancing precariously on the buses' running boards. The buses belch smoke and are enveloped in a gloomy haze amidst a swarm of other vehicles around our bus in which we sit in modern comfort. Sidewalks are dotted with regularly spaced piles of garbage that mar the landscape of modern adobe rooftops on multistory buildings. Most of these buildings sport bent, rusting iron rods protruding toward the sky from lower floors, giving the impression of a whole city in delayed construction. Our guide explains that this prickly rebar adornment represents hope for the buildings' occupants. The families living beneath have a plan to someday add an additional story above their apartment to house their children's families. We begin to wonder whether Lima's condition reflects internalized oppression by generations of natives forced to succumb to Spanish conquistadors.

Arriving in Cuzco, by contrast, we find a thriving city with flowers flowing from window boxes of cheerfully painted, well-kept adobe homes and shops lining steep, hilly streets reminiscent of San Francisco. Not one piece of rebar can be seen. Our guide tells us that 60 percent of native Peruvians were never really conquered by the Spanish. Cuzco's beauty seems to confirm that claim. The steep mountainous terrain, coupled with the heat and moisture of Peru's deep rainforests, is said to have provided long-term hiding places for many natives to evade the brutal intrusion and subjugation of colonizers who rarely ventured into such places for long. However, the successful colonizing invaders captured and slaughtered hundreds of Inca at Machu Picchu in the conquistadors' most heinous raid, which has long been trumpeted throughout Western colonial culture, spreading a myth that the Inca were annihilated in the same way a similar myth was spread across North America, claiming that natives were effectively wiped out during the Westward expansion of the United States.

A brightly colored, cheerful mural on Cuzco's airport wall welcomes visitors, we modern versions of the pilgrims the mural proclaims have been coming here for ten thousand years to honor this mountain city on its plateau ten thousand feet above sea level. Before transferring to another comfortable touring bus, we get a lesson in managing the steep shift in altitude. Cuzco sits more than twice as high as the tallest peak in New Hampshire's White Mountains, where my hiking partner and I spent several weekends summiting increasingly rigorous peaks in preparation for this trip. So at a rest stop during a walking tour where we learn a smattering of Cuzco's history, we taste the coca tea we're encouraged to drink, and we find it gently calming for sea-level hearts already working overtime for oxygen before taking one step on a hiking trail. Coca tea, made from the leaves of the same plant used to distill cocaine, has none of that drug's effects. The coca leaves are chewed like gum by people who live in these high mountains to calm their stomachs and prevent headaches, symptoms of altitude sickness that strike all who quickly move up and down many thousands of feet. We're advised to alternately drink plenty of water along with this tea during our four-day hike because we will climb to at least fifteen thousand feet, higher than any of us has ever ascended before. After the tea has been consumed and our hearts have slowed their pace to normal, we resume walking to continue acclimatizing.

Cuzco is an architecturally fascinating city. The foundations of its older buildings are in a class by themselves, made of massive stones carefully chosen for their places in each construction, then carved to fit like gloves next to their neighbors, using no adhesive material between them. These boulder foundations, along with the aqueducts still bringing mountain water to the city, are remnants of Incan architecture built thousands of years ago. They show fewer signs of wear than the modern foundations on buildings around them. Our guide explains that the people of Cuzco were able to escape the worst of the conquistadors' violence because the altitude was very uncomfortable for seagoing men. He tells us that the Inca built Cuzco in the shape of a jaguar, a sacred symbol of power, atop what are believed to be ley lines—energy lines in the earth beneath certain geographically specific places, like the veins in our bodies. Here they are said to radiate out in a full circle from the center of the city where the navel of its jaguar shape is located. Along each line, sacred sites were built. Like most civilizations that build empires, the Inca believed Cuzco, their capital city, to be the center of human culture.

After a delicious lunch of grilled mountain trout and garlic soup, we board another bus, this one headed to Ollantaytambo where our hike will begin the next day. We aren't starting in Cuzco, where the Inca trailhead is found, because the purpose of the hike is to walk the ceremonial portion of the trail. The first twenty-nine miles hold no sacred sites, so they will be bypassed. Before setting off, however, we visit the trailhead, which is framed by two giant boulders said to have the capacity to balance the male and female energy of every pilgrim. When hands are placed on them, they are believed to have the capacity to center and ground pilgrims in the present moment for the duration of their pilgrimage. We place our hands on the great boulders, first on one, then the other, meditating on the connection with the rock for several minutes as instructed. As we do so, the beginning of the story that will carry us throughout this trip is introduced with the statement that the Q'ero—direct descendants of the Inca—continue to sustain their ancient culture high in the Andes, herding llamas at seventeen thousand feet. They grow and harvest tiny potatoes and drink llama milk as the foundation of their diet.

Our guide spent ten years among the Q'ero and also among the shamans of the Peruvian rainforests and plains, gaining their trust, learning their ways, and recording their stories. His academic mentor was a Q'ero descendant who bridged the gap between cultures to also become an anthropologist in the Western academic tradition while retaining the knowledge he gained in shamanic studies under Q'ero elders. Unfortunately, researchers who use cultural immersion techniques as part of their research toolbox are often ignored by those exploring native cultures using conventional Western academic methods who insist on observation from outside, a method often deemed more scientific and thus more valuable.

Western institutional research anthropologists often frame their theories from within their own cultural perspectives, using what they think of as scientific observation and losing a depth of cultural understanding only gained by consulting respectfully with those whose ancestors have lived as natives for centuries. Those who have been initiated into such native cultures pass essential folk rituals and stories down through generations in carefully prescribed ways, communicating significant elements that defy words and rational analysis as means to understand them, all of which requires immersive experience for clear insight into the meaning and cultural value of those rituals and stories. We hikers are here to listen to these stories and experience the associated rituals with open minds, learning from a perspective closer to the source of native wisdom practices. Rituals and symbolism directly related to Incan tradition—as well as traditions shared throughout the mythology of the Americas, learned by our guide in his cross-cultural research—will also be included. These rituals and symbols are drawn from indigenous cultures populating the full spine of mountain ranges that extend from the Rockies through the Andes.

The native peoples of North and South America originally came across a land bridge from northern Asia to Alaska. Over centuries, these nomads traveled down the mountain ridge that morphs from the Rockies into the Andes at national borders, some putting down roots in various places along the way, founding both Mayan and Incan civilizations long before any civilization began far across the Atlantic Ocean, in what was first known as Phoenicia, where Western culture emerged.

Departing the trailhead for the path to Machu Picchu and reboarding the tour bus, we fall back into civilization's ways. The air-conditioned bus winds its way along the Urubamba River valley between snowcapped peaks towering thousands of feet above Cuzco. The red-brown earth of the mountainsides below their snow caps is dotted with eucalyptus trees brought to Peru by the Spanish, along with low-growing shrubs, patches of golden grasses, and little else in this dry time between winter and spring in the Southern Hemisphere. Passing through a village with barely room between its buildings for the bus, we receive blank stares from serious faces as brown as the mountains where these people live. Stoically, they stand aside against village walls to wait for the bus to pass. Children run pointing, laughing, and shouting ahead of us, but their elders never crack a smile or say a word. Their worn clothes and sandaled feet support thin, wiry bodies. Men wear traditional red ponchos with unique woven patterns identifying their home villages. Women's long dark skirts contrast with the colorfully patterned shawls tied around their shoulders, in the folds of which many of them carry produce or babies. The women's faces are shaded by black bowler hats, framed by two ebony braids of hair, or their hair is pulled back into one long rope falling to their waists. Legend tells of a European salesman from the nineteenth century who ventured high into the Andes to sell bowler hats. The story describes how people living in villages like this were so impressed by a rare stranger able to make the long, arduous climb that they enthusiastically bought all the hats he could sell. This windfall encouraged the salesman to return year after year. As a result, those hats became standard garb for high mountain villagers and remains so today in many places.

After stopping at two spectacular overlooks where we behave as any tourists would, snapping pictures and gazing in awe, the bus winds through the last mountain pass and downhill to the night's hotel in Ollantaytambo at nine thousand feet. This hotel is the only Western-style building anywhere in town and the only building with the modern luxury of a satellite telephone, unavailable in others where dirt floors invite chickens and guinea pigs to run in and out at will.

After a siesta and a delicious dinner of wild mountain trout, we gather in a circle of chairs in the hotel courtyard under a sparkling blanket of stars to share stories of why we have come. We discover that the group includes a lawyer, an aroma therapist, a nurse, a bank manager, a writer, a graduate student, two computer software engineers, two builders, a commercial artist, a photographer, and a retired postal delivery clerk. All the stories we tell that evening meld into one that could apply to any of us. Each feels gripped by an internal call to honor humanity's sacred ties to native people and their connection to nature, particularly in this time of widespread despair over increasing environmental destruction led by the culture on which everyone in this group depends. A major life transition also lies on the horizon for each of us.

WAKING EARLY, we repack our luggage, leaving behind what isn't needed during the next four days of hiking. Whatever is not absolutely necessary will be kept on the bus until we board again at Machu Picchu. This process will ease the burden of native porters who will carry our duffel bags, tents, cooking equipment, and food over thirty-six miles of the hike. After completing this task, we shoulder day-packs loaded with sunscreen, a change of clothes, some snacks, and two liter-sized bottles—one filled with water, the other with cold coca tea—then put on hats to block the intense sun and head to the trailhead to meet the hearty souls who will carry our camping gear.

The porters are a group of native men between the ages of twenty-five and fifty with lifelong experience in trekking at this altitude. Wearing the rough sandals they live and run in every day (though we are outfitted in sturdy hiking boots), they laugh among themselves while preparing duffel bags and backpacks with ropes, preferring to tie several of them to their backs rather than use padded straps. Some sit cross-legged or squatting, relaxed under bright, multicolored ponchos woven in varying designs, chewing coca leaves and watching us with open expressions as we snap their pictures and apply suntan lotion. None of them speaks English.

Originally there were four Inca trails entering Machu Picchu from each compass direction. The path we will hike is the only one usably intact as we set out. Once all is prepared, the porters head out and provide an awe-inspiring sight as they begin to run up the trail, grouped together about a foot apart, and quickly disappear like a colorful centipede, despite the weight of their heavy, unwieldy loads. Soon afterward we follow them, walking a mostly flat route that hugs the Urubamba riverbank beneath a towering snowcapped peak, each of us moving at our own pace. The mountain is called Waqaywillka by the natives, renamed Veronica by Western colonizers. Waqaywillka is believed to hold the spiritual energy of the sacred valley of the Urubamba, standing as guardian to twelve power peaks surrounding Cuzco. Such mountains, which in native tradition guard every valley in Peru, are known as Apus.

Apus are especially revered for the meltwater they provide in the spring. The water flows from the mountains' apexes into the valleys, fertilizing crops and fostering life of every wild kind along the way, including the fabled black jaguars living in these mountains. A power beyond human control is invested in the towering mighty sense of these giant peaks and their ability to foster life with the gently melting flow of water. Equally revered and respected is their ability to extinguish life with floods and landslides. The mountains represent the mysterious power of the foundational nature of Earth. They are considered living beings, not gods, though very powerful in their effects on human, plant, and animal life, all deeply understood by the people here to be integral parts of the living balance that supports the mountains' strength.

Hearing this story, I recall a fellow graduate student at Tufts who grew up in Lima. After graduating from college, he went into the jungle surrounding the mouth of the Amazon to work with native people to save the Peruvian rainforest. He showed me a large collection of wonderful photographs of the place and described the work he had done to support communities living deep in the forest, work that was his stepping stone into graduate school. He also told me that he would never again be able to enjoy Western comforts because of the way he had come to experience the living beauty and wonder of that place, which became an essential part of him. It now feels far more like home, he said, than anywhere in civilization ever did. He could hardly wait to return to the jungle and the work of defending the lungs of the world. I have continuously donated money to the Rainforest Action Network as a result of that conversation.

Each day, beginning today, we will hike one segment of thirty-six miles of the ceremonial Inca Trail, stopping to do rituals at three temples along the way. On the fourth day we will enter the sacred Incan city of Machu Picchu. Traditional Incan spiritual practice, according to our guide, is based on a spiraling concept that moves through four challenges and gifts associated with the directions of the compass, which are each associated with a symbolic animal one can imagine embodying when that archetypal energy is needed. Spiritual growth in this tradition spirals out in what can be conceived of as a medicine wheel, around which practitioners continuously travel until the day they die. As we begin our hike, we enter that spiraling journey, aiming to complete its first circuit in our arrival at Machu Picchu.

The medicine wheel work we address during this first hiking day is the work of the south, where each round of the spiraling journey always begins. The work of the south, like that of each direction, is psycho/spiritual in nature and needs to be fully embodied in physical practice to activate the intuitive mind, uniting its wisdom through physically experienced action in cooperation with rational knowing, deepening creative psychological perception and wise response to whatever presents itself in living experience. The archetypal being of the work of the south is symbolized by a great snake named Sachamama, who can shed the past by shedding her skin. The process of confronting, opening to, and healing psychological wounds is conducted in this tradition as an act of power and love rather than one of recovery, as conceived in modern Western psychotherapy.

The ceremony associated with the work of the south invites the powers of heaven and Earth to bear witness to the psychological transformation associated with physical acts connecting the body to both the spiritual and Earth planes of existence. This practice is different from the Western psychological approach, not only due to ceremonial ritual. It also bears witness to the person each pilgrim is becoming as opposed to witnessing what has been endured before arrival at this moment. Attention is directed toward immediate experience and actions believed to have the power to influence the way future processes of becoming reach back to this moment, pulling spiritual development forward. In the native traditions of the Americas, we learn that time is not linear but circular, with elements of past, present, and future contained in every moment.

Medicine people of the Incan tradition work with four levels of consciousness within which psycho–spiritual healing takes place. The final, rather than the first, level is the physical somatic level. In Western practices, physical symptoms are generally seen as the first signs of diseases needing treatment. Shamans see the physical realm as where disharmony is ultimately observable in the condition of the body after an imbalance has long gone unaddressed at deeper levels. In such cases, the imbalance finally bubbles up to the surface of the body. A simple example is how blocking an important emotion while making a life-changing decision may result in a headache or illness. That correlation is understood in Incan tradition as the body's way of calling attention to a need for deeper understanding and internal rebalancing of disharmonies in the daily living patterns of the afflicted person, disharmonies that ultimately resulted in physical illness.

Under the somatic is the symbolic level where messages can be transmitted from the conscious to the unconscious through acts of ritual, or in reverse, through dreams and visions. Under the symbolic level is the mythic, which can be known but not told, and finally the energetic or essential level where the deep shift in balance we recognize as true healing must first occur, according to ancient native traditions. Clearly, Incan shamanic healing is conceived very differently from Western approaches to curing disease. In this shamanic approach, many may be cured of disease when they heal, though sometimes healing involves accepting where the balance of living has taken the patient, which may mean making peace with death rather than returning to living. Both results are accepted as perfectly healthy at their appropriate time and on no particular timetable and are understood not as statistically predictable life expectancy, as in the West, but as a unique length of living that rises from the interactions between the particular physical attributes of each being, their natural environment, and their living experiences.

In modern Western psychology, all healing processes are considered intrapsychic, understood as confined within one person's body and experience, working from its literal or physical level inward to its energetic core expression, our guide explains. In Incan shamanic tradition, instead, healing the mind or body is initiated first at the energetic level, where all living things are inseparably one, and uses physical ritual to bring healing up to the level of conscious daily living only when the process is complete. In this approach, all being is united within each individual in what can be described as an extra-psychic process. All living being is understood as the ground of that process, and nothing observed on Earth is understood as nonliving. Living reality for each human process is understood to unfold while tightly interwoven with every other Earth process. When using physical ritual to engage that ground of being for healing, one is believed to be able to call in energetic forces outside the individual psyche to "stalk consciousness." By calling on the spirit of the serpent, Sachamama, for example, the idea is to engage a mythic archetypal energy in living form from within the unity of all being, rather than to use an imaginary symbol. Our guide explains that the serpent spirit energy is archetypal and known by dozens of names in dozens of native cultures, and it possesses the ability to continually affect one's living once it is called. The ability to have a dialogue with nature as a way to initiate archetypal engagements is the mainstay of Incan shamanic healing practice.

Those of us from the now globally dominant Western culture are used to traditional intrapsychic healing processes specific to the bodies with which we identify. However, believing that we have to come to peace only within ourselves—conceiving of each person as separate and only physically interrelated—we deny any greater capacity to affect the process from within the naturally occurring universe. In the Incan tradition, psychological healing practices seek to realign the human psyche with all the forces of creation, which together permeate every aspect of reality.

WINDING THROUGH the first stretch of hiking trail, we pass small mud and thatch huts, beside which wide-eyed children stare at us from the dust where they sit in the shade of eucalyptus trees. The sparkling white majesty of the mighty peak, Waqaywillka, presides over one of the few fertile valleys we've seen on this trip. It stretches an emerald tapestry of living fertility from the base of the mountain to the river and across to the base of the mountain on the other side. Thinking of internalized fear and limitation from past personal experiences as I walk, I begin to consciously engage a process of meditatively shedding them by choosing, again and again, to suspend disbelief as doubt inevitably rises in order to experience this way of relating to life for at least the duration of these two weeks in Peru. Picking my way along the stone-strewn path, very aware of the rough ground beneath my boots, I open my mind wide, leaving only one small, healthy nugget of doubt in order to engage imagination creatively in this experience of the most physically challenging hike of my life.

At lunchtime we stop by a briskly flowing stream. Several of us who arrive ahead of the others dunk ourselves into the icy water, hiking clothes and all, seeking relief from the hot, dry air. Although we will need heavy sweaters and down vests tonight, daytime temperatures have already risen above eighty degrees Fahrenheit. Thankfully the air is dry, though it lacks even the slightest hint of breeze to mitigate the baking sun. As we sit by a stream and wait for the rest of our hiking party, we watch a local farmer cross the little bridge over the stream while herding a group of burros laden with goods for market. Later, a group of Brazilian hikers greets us cheerfully as they pass while we sit eating the cold chicken, salad, bread, fruit, and chocolate prepared for lunch by the camp cook and drinking coca tea to wash it all down.

Following a forty-five-minute rest, we're off again, headed up a slightly steeper incline beside a jagged rock face. Some in the group have just reached the lunch spot as my hiking partner and I depart. The camp cook and logistics manager will make sure they reach the evening's campsite before supper. By two-thirty, we reach a plateau overlooking the ancient city of Quriwayrachina, on which the temple of the hummingbird presides. The plateau is perched over a terraced valley that once contained an ancient city. It is breathtaking still in its precisely ordered construction carved into the base of the mountain. Quriwayrachina originally served as a checkpoint, we've been told. Elders sat in judgment of the spiritual readiness of pilgrims to journey up the Inca Trail, turning back those not yet spiritually prepared for its challenges.

After a short time wandering through and admiring the temple, my partner and I head over the plateau's edge and up a stream to our campsite where the porters have already pitched every one of the group's small tents. They sit laughing and chewing coca leaves on the hillside, having reached this destination hours earlier despite the heavy packs they carried at a run the whole way. Making our way past a cow, pigs, and chickens owned by the family who opened their backyard to our camp, we change clothes, rest in our tent, and explore a little more before gathering with the larger hiking party in the central group tent for the first evening of tea, hot chocolate, and our guide's stories of Q'ero tradition.

Cold shadows call for down vests as we sip cocoa. We learn that this first hiking day was designed to be an easy warm-up to make sure we were capable of the three more strenuous days to come. Although it was moderately tiring, my partner and I experienced nothing more rigorous than the hikes we had regularly walked in the White Mountains to prepare. As part of the discussion over tea, we learn that one in our hiking group will need to abort the journey here because she is already having serious knee pain. She tearfully admits that it is best for her to instead go tomorrow by train with one of our guide's local assistants to wait for us at Machu Picchu. We all enthusiastically assure her that we will carry her with us in spirit as the rest of us continue on. Though all of us feel sympathetic toward our hurting hiking partner, we understand from what we've been learning that in Incan tradition her knee pain would be considered a clear indication of a deeper lack of readiness for the spiritual journey she would face on the trail.

After dinner, we all set out across Quriwayrachina's terraces with only flashlights and starlight to guide us along a path to the temple of the hummingbird. Brisk, cool air and a sense of mystery heighten our attention as we enter the spiraling walls of the roofless ruin. Opening our minds to reverence for all those who came before, we space ourselves evenly around the walls of the circular space at the heart of the building, an unusual and significant shape in Incan architecture, we're told. Regularly spaced niches, six feet high, contain carefully carved holes on each side at the level of human hands. According to natives, these niches originally housed tamed condors that lived in the temple. A rope was tied across each opening to prevent the huge birds' exit unless participating in ceremony. Following any ceremony's completion, the shaman would release the condors to fly to the upper reaches of the spirit world with gifts and prayers for the ancestors, the sun, and the Great Spirit, symbolized by the sky.

We hear a story about why the hummingbird is the temple's namesake. Incan legends tell of a race between a powerful, sharp-eyed condor and a tiny, speedy hummingbird. The hummingbird challenged the condor to a race to the upper reaches of heaven, identified by a bank of clouds passing overhead. The condor laughed, answering that there would be no contest because of the difference in endurance levels between the two birds. "You can surely fly quickly," he said, "but I can fly much farther than you will ever be able to." The hummingbird insisted, however, so the condor agreed. The two birds started at exactly the same moment, which was only fair, and of course the hummingbird sped ahead immediately in its darting burst of wing speed, fast enough to hide momentarily behind a leaf in the topmost branches of a nearby tree. Being so small and fleet, it vanished before the condor's keen eyesight could identify the tiny bird's path while the huge bird worked laboriously to lift its wings and body above the ground, intent on the goal of the cloud bank ahead and sure of its power and endurance.

As the condor flew past, the hummingbird darted out from its perch and alit on the big bird's shoulder. As all hummingbirds are, the tiny bird was nearly weightless and the condor felt nothing. The hummingbird rode silently and courageously into the sky until the two were just short of the cloud bank, at which point the hummingbird suddenly darted ahead, shocking the condor who only saw it fly by to win the race. This story is offered by our guide as evidence of why the hummingbird's wily wisdom is so deeply valued by the Inca. The condor is venerated as well, of course, for its strength and its wide and deep vision when soaring high in the sky. This story illustrates that, although strength and vision are essential for reaching challenging goals, it is often a sharp, wily kind of wisdom that will find a way to use those tools to allow even the most vulnerable to achieve those goals. It is said that the condor was impressed by the hummingbird's cunning, and the two became inseparable friends from that day forward. Of course the condor also allowed the hummingbird to ride its shoulder back to earth.

Each of us choosing a niche in which to stand, we begin a ceremony within the ancient ruin. Our guide shakes a large gourd rattle at the star-spangled sky and calls on the nature spirits of this land to enter into ceremony with us. A bat dives across the gathering as he begins, which feels like an answer to his request. Next we move, one by one, in a silent spiral from our niche toward the center of the circle where our guide taps his "mesa," a collection of power objects, on each of the chakras along our spines. The mesa is composed mostly of stones collected from places associated with significant spiritual experiences, then encased in a native blanket and sanctified by Q'ero shamans. The chakras are the same in this tradition as those identified by Hindu yogis. This practice is believed to open the body's energetic field to the flow of Earth energy, empowering each of us to return to a sense of being Earth's children in the same way we were as youngsters, returning to a sense that we are not separate from Earth's all-pervasive love. This healing ceremony is intended to reignite a birthright ability to reciprocally communicate with rocks, trees, and animals.

Our guide describes how Western culture is precariously balanced on a myth that contains its own destruction. The Judeo-Christian creation story of the expulsion of Adam and Eve from the Garden of Eden sets up a polarization between humanity and nature, he explains, which gives our culture the unenviable task of living in a hostile natural world from which the bonds of nurturance have been severed for eternity. His cross-cultural research has revealed that no other root cosmology believes that humans were thrown out of the original sacred garden. Correspondingly, he says, no other culture has approached the level of destruction of habitat wrought by Western practices.

Native American creation stories that were carried throughout the regions connected by the mountainous spine extending from the Rockies through the Andes, say that God/the Great Spirit left the finishing touches of creation to humanity, a responsibility that remains in a legacy of love, trust, and cooperation between the people of the earth and the Great Spirit. Our guide adds that Australian aboriginal culture also tells us that we are integrally connected through song lines circling the earth, which sing us as much as we sing them, characterizing the earth and humanity as inseparably one. Religious Hindu and Buddhist cultures connect humanity inextricably with the earth's wheel of birth, death, and rebirth through belief in reincarnation, which includes humanity, Earth, and its creatures in one unified, evolving system.

Our ritual at the temple of the hummingbird aims to reconnect the umbilical cord between each of us and the earth, symbolically and psychologically reentering the sacred Garden as integral beings meant to bloom there in harmony with the rest of the natural world. I feel very good and peaceful about the ceremony because I have long gone to the woods, the ocean, and the mountains for healing, telling the trees and water my stories in silent communion, rewarded with a sense of being able to take their healing energy back with me afterward. A tree hugger since I could climb, I've always kept this communication very quiet, held in my heart just above unconsciousness for fear it would disappear, speaking of it only to people sure to understand.

Following the ritual, we silently search for stones to carry to the cairn at the end of tomorrow's trail. The stones symbolize our individual journeys from the south to the west. Another stone will be gathered and carried to the following point during the work of the west. In Incan tradition, the carrying of stones from point to point creates seiches, or energy waves, which will connect our individual energy with power points of Earth energy along the trail. This process is believed to create an energetic pathway to allow continuation of the transformative work we begin here as we carry on with daily living long after this hike has been completed. As we walk, we will draw the energy lines we're creating into Machu Picchu. We're told that, as a result of this process, we could continue to walk the Inca Trail in our energy fields for several months, if not longer, transforming our lives in ways we will only understand later when looking back.

Ending the ceremony by blowing our breath into coca leaves we each hold out to the mountains, the Apus, the living spiritual guardians of the land, we throw the leaves to the night wind to carry them where they will. Our guide thanks the nature spirits for being with us and just as he finishes, another bat dips in flight to pass through the sanctuary. In shamanic tradition, we are told, the presence of an animal at key points in a ceremony is a clear sign of universal energy in alignment with ceremonial process. We walk in meditative silence back through the darkness to our tents to get some rest for the big day ahead.

AWAKENING WITH THE FIRST RAYS OF SUN, I push the frosty tent flap aside and gasp at the sight of the shimmering ruins of Quriwayrachina bathed in the first golden glow of daylight and illuminated bright pink against the blue-black mountains behind. All else is in shadow. I later learn that this site was chosen for the temple's construction for just that purpose, enabling all who walked the mountains early in the day to see a shining temple high in the towering peaks as they began tending animals and gathering water. Building temples on such sites was one of the powerful wisdom traditions of the Inca, which helped them retain peaceful dominion over people far and wide through an intricate understanding of the movement of the sun, moon, and stars. That knowledge allowed them to make use of architectural design to harmonize with nature, creating magical moments when temples would suddenly be lit in amazing brilliance that few in their kingdom could understand, inspiring awe, fear, and reverence in those who saw these spectacles and folded them into tales defining meaning in their world.

After tea and a hearty breakfast of hot quinoa cereal, we are comfortable once again in summer clothing and eager to mount the steepest leg of the trail. We have each exchanged the pebble we collected last night with another person in our hiking party in order to carry a partner's struggles with the past up the trail for them, imagining they have been transferred into the stone by the way it was held and attended to. We will leave all these pebbles at the top of Warmi Wanusqa, "the pass of the eternal woman," as our guide describes the name's meaning. This evening we will camp just below its elevation of nearly fifteen thousand feet above sea level, the highest point of our intended journey. In this symbolic way, we will create energetic bonds with each other in the Incan tradition as we hike the rocky incline. When I look back as we ascend, the thatched homestead beside our camp quickly shrinks to the size of a toy.

The practice during this first day of serious mountain hiking is to envision a kind of spiritual umbilical cord emanating constantly from the earth as we walk and to open to the idea that the mountain will help us ascend by providing energy through that cord to the center of our bodies. Surprisingly, imagining this to be true does make it feel easier to maintain a steady pace while climbing the continuously uphill path. I experience the difference as a shift of mind, from the brain giving commands to move one leg, then the other, to an open focus on the heartfelt experience of joy pumping out to the body from the energy of walking. That energy can easily be imagined as coming from the earth by the large, playful part of me that still enjoys reimagining living experience by creating stories, in the same way we did as a group of childhood playmates in Basking Ridge. As I put one foot in front of the other, breathing rhythmically and deeply thanks to years of long-distance running, I focus on the idea that as I walk I am returning to the earth as my oldest and dearest friend and life-giving guardian, reuniting personal experience with the whole grand web of living being.

Reaching the lunch spot in the shade of a tree beside another welcomed icy stream—smaller than yesterday's as it's higher on the mountain—our energy bubbles up enough for us to exchange laughter and take pictures during this break from meditative climbing. After lunch we enter the edge of the high jungle, however, and our individual climbing speeds separate us by long stretches. Mentally we also climb within individual narratives of separate inner worlds. The separation produces no anxiety for me because there is only one, well-maintained path up and over these mountains, providing no opportunity to get lost.

After perhaps an hour of steady climbing, with an incline similar to a very long forty-five-degree staircase without risers, my thighs begin to scream, and they protest even louder when I sit to rest and drink coca tea in hope of relief. The air up here is much thinner than any I've ever hiked in before, as the back of my head also reminds me with its throbbing. Just as I finish replacing my water bottle and shouldering my pack, despairing of ever reaching the top, a royal blue hummingbird the size of my hand appears hovering over the path ahead. Distracted from physical pain by its stunning beauty and size, I creep slowly forward to get a better look. The bird moves a little higher and farther ahead, still hovering directly over the path, and stops in a new place as I pause as well in order to keep from scaring it away. This pattern of the bird's movement followed by mine repeats itself about five times over the space of about five minutes before I realize I have effortlessly climbed another fifty feet or so.

From that point on, I consciously shift perception away from my throbbing head and screaming legs to focus instead on the wonder of the natural world around me and to feel renewed energy for the climb in a joyous sense of connection initiated by the hummingbird. Although helped by the elation experienced during that final stretch, I am still surprised to find myself the second hiker to reach the campsite. The man ahead of me and I congratulate each other and await the arrival of the rest of the crew. Tonight's campsite is perched on a broad ledge between two sets of peaks. From the Urubamba River valley, thousands of feet below us, rise towering, snowcapped mountains, the peaks of which appear to be near to our eye level and almost even with Waqaywillka's snowcap, although it rises still higher above them. As the other hikers trickle into camp, no one has trouble sitting for better than two hours, contemplating the vista and sharing stories of our individual climbs, as we eat snacks, rest, and wait for everyone to arrive and have their own chance to rest before tea time.

At three fifteen, forty-five minutes before tea time and the stories our guide will tell us about Incan history and ritual as we relax and reconnect, I feel strangely restless. Although the thought frightens me, I have a compelling urge to climb one of the mountains beside our camp. I have imagined that the highest point on the trail will be atop at least one of the lower peaks we've been hiking through, eventually providing more of a panoramic vista than we've yet seen—something akin to what I'm used to after climbing to the top of mountains in New Hampshire or Vermont. However, I have learned that the highest point we'll reach will come tomorrow morning at a pass *between* two mountains, not far above where we are now. I know I will be extremely disappointed if we reach the end of this journey without a view from the top of at least one of these mountains near the apex of our hike.

Scanning the nearest mountain, I see no path to the summit, only a lot of long, dry grass and scrubby bushes. With encouragement from my hiking partner to give it a shot anyway, I start climbing, imagining it will take me no more than forty-five minutes to climb up and back, getting me back in time for tea so that I won't be missed. Clambering up the steep incline, I focus as I've done all day on the energy of the earth pulling me upward. Attending only to the climb and where to put my foot or hand next, I feel as if the mountain is urging me on, offering up her grassy hair as a whispering companion to show me the way. Each time I become confused about where to move next, I stop to silently ask the mountain to show me the path and follow the intuitive message that rises to my attention during each pause.

Nearing the top, I realize that this mountain is actually much taller than it appeared from camp. Looking back I see that the twelve-foot-square main gathering and eating tent below has shrunk to about a quarter of an inch across. Adrenaline begins to pump, though still the yearning persists as though the mountain is calling me and cradling me as I climb. Soon guided away from the peak's summit—partly by rational choice as I notice the extreme difficulty of the terrain straight ahead—though still using the intuitive process that got me this far, I begin to traverse to the left. Climbing across the mountain a short distance from the original climb's trajectory, I round a bend to discover a perfect seat astride a great rock jutting out from the mountainside just below an insurmountable outcropping of stone.

A panoramic view just short of 360 degrees delivers the thrill and sense of accomplishment I sought through this climb. A spectacular, multilayered bowl of stony snowcapped crags, lit by the golden rays of late afternoon sun, surrounds the encampment far below my dangling feet. Exhilarated, I realize that risking this climb has given me back the fearless part of myself I long ago buried and denied in endless attempts to gain acceptance and approval with varying success. Meditating on the surging energy that unites me with the mountain before starting down, I search my pockets for a reciprocal gift of thanks to give the Apu for showing me the way, honoring that Incan tradition. Emptying them of a small pile of cracker crumbs, all I have with me other than my clothes, I know from what our guide has said that, when given with full-hearted gratitude, even that small offering is thanks enough to feed some part of this living mountain. On reaching camp below, I find I have missed tea time and everyone is relieved at my return, although thankfully I receive no reprimand for my independent foray.

That night I dream of an old native woman who climbs down from below the large outcropping rock beneath which I sat after climbing up in the evening. I awaken as she pulls the tent flap aside to enter. She approaches to squat beside my head, so close that I can see the wrinkles on her face and the gleam in her eye in the dim light. I feel surprise but no fear at finding her there. Leaning down to whisper in my ear, she gives me advice about how best to live and how to hike the remainder of the Inca Trail. After imparting her wisdom, she turns without another word, quickly lifting the tent flap and returning the way she came, clambering up the mountain to disappear into an opening beneath the great stone. In the dream, I awaken and encounter our guide walking contemplatively through the campsite. He tells me that the old woman is the spirit of the mountain.

When I truly awaken shortly after dawn, I leave the tent to greet the new day awash in a peaceful joy I have rarely known. When I encounter our guide walking contemplatively through the campsite with his morning tea, he confirms that his judgment in the dream is the same as he would give me now in daylight. He tells me that in missing tea the evening before, I missed the story behind Warmi Wanusqa, the pass of the eternal woman—the highest point of the hike—which we will cross this morning. He suggests that it was the spirit of Warmi Wanusqa herself who came to me last night, a dream interpretation I still savor.

MY HIKING PARTNER AND I have fared well so far on this journey, in terms of energy and health, allowing us to stay near the front of the line of hikers as we each climb at our own pace. However, nine members of the group have had some form of "Montezuma's revenge," the intestinal disruption we all feared before we began. The shamanic explanation for these uncomfortable symptoms is that they result from processing subconscious psychological issues through the body. In this way of thinking, the symptoms occur due to a lack of readiness to accept into consciousness the deep psychological meaning at their root. Western medicine says instead that the people who get sick in this way are more susceptible to the altitude and the viruses in the salads we've been eating for lunch. It occurs to me that both explanations have merit. I'm very thankful to have elected to have all the recommended inoculations before the trip, all of which were suggested but not required. That seems pertinent because I'm one of the few who got them and one of the few who has not succumbed to any form of diarrhea, something that has even affected my partner to some degree, who didn't think the shots necessary.

We reach the high pass of Warmi Wanusqa by mid-morning. I look back to see that the pass is significantly lower than the spot on the peak where I sat last evening, reinforcing my gratitude for that solo experience. Nevertheless, the view is stunning on both sides of this high point. The hair-raising trek ahead is also clear as the path plunges deep into the valley beyond, rising afterward to a second pass nearly as high as this one. Although the distance is impossible to judge by simply eyeballing it, that pass appears to be several miles away. We learn that our lunch spot is several miles beyond the second pass, leading everyone to think that our guide's encouraging words about an easier day today were a ruse because of the length of this hike. However, there is little choice but to continue and, although we're all tired even as we begin, our spirits remain high.

At the pass of Warmi Wanusqa, we each deposit the stone carried from Quriwayrachina onto a large cairn, pick up another from the ground, and begin the work of the spirit of the west. Today we will search within our psyches for the luminous warrior who has no enemies in this world or the next, the warrior who steps beyond anger, violence, and fear. The animal associated with the west is the black jaguar that can see in the dark. When we have done this psychic work well, this tradition tells us, we will be able to choose our own destiny rather than remain at the mercy of the consequences stemming from our reactive responses to life's experiences. Upon reaching the next temple, we will leave behind the death mapped out for us by our culture and genes, freeing us to follow our heart's calling instead. In this way we will be enabled to start down the path to a destiny of a very different kind.

As we walk, we are advised to imagine the company of the rare black jaguar, the mythical though real animal that can walk invisibly through the darkness of the rainforest with uncompromised vision. The jaguar is the symbol of courage, the spiritual work of the west, just as the snake, which sheds its skin, is the symbol of transformation, the spiritual work of the south that we completed yesterday. Though work in all these realms never ceases, each section of the path contains spiritual elements, we're told, which can be ignited to continue unfurling when directly engaged.

We snake our way down the open path from the pass of the eternal woman into the dry bottom lands of the valley, dipping from fifteen to ten thousand feet above sea level, and cool our faces in the "River of Joy," a small, cold stream trickling through the valley's lowest point. There we encounter two thatch-roofed adobe houses and two children with bare feet and dirty faces who come out to stare at us and say, "Hola." Their brown eyes are large, round, and sparkling. I wonder what it would be like to grow up in a place of so much natural wonder yet so little material comfort as I hand them each a couple of pieces of hard candy, a treat we all brought for just such occasions.

There are no trees on this part of the trail, only low scrub bushes accompanied by patches of dry brown grass. My hiking partner and I hear a rattlesnake near a rocky outcrop but luckily avoid its attention. The hike up the other side of the valley is just as steep as yesterday's. Encouraging myself with the words of an assistant guide who told us as he passed that there will be little uphill after this, I concentrate on the rhythm of my steps and let the mountain pull me, nourishing inspiration on the spectacle of the mountains surrounding us whenever my legs begin to scream again. In the searing heat, I'm thankful for the two liters of liquid in my pack. Although they're heavy now, they will undoubtedly be empty by day's end. Arriving ahead of the others at an ancient circling stone wall on a cliff—the ruins of another temple called Runkuraqay—I have time to rest quietly alone. I sit on the wall and look back across the valley. From where I sit, the pass of the eternal woman is etched in bright golden brown against the deep blue sky. The pencil-thin line of the trail winds down to the right, dotted here and there with specks of white that must be hikers who started after we did.

My hiking partner appears around the boulder below the temple as I finish the last of a snack of oranges, crackers, and chocolate squares. I'm glad we've waited for each other as we walked, gaining appreciation of key experiences together. There's a heightened sense of the moment when shared with a good friend, an energetic synthesis that makes it come alive in a more expansive way. Our guide has explained a similar energetic synthesis that allows the porters to move efficiently along the trail as they travel closely together and stay in exact step with each other while jogging with our equipment on their backs. Each place where the man ahead has just removed his foot is filled the next instant by the man behind, creating a kind of moving human train and a group energy source available to each of them. We've been told by our guide that as the porters ascend, they move through space as though through water, leaving a wake of energy behind and also projecting it ahead like a building wave. We all do this without knowing it, we've been told. When two or more people hike together in close proximity, they can connect energy filaments, helping both the person in front, who gets a feeling of being pushed, and the person behind, who feels pulled ahead by their companion.

As we hiked the White Mountains in preparation for this adventure, my hiking partner and I experimented with this possibility and confirmed a clear, physical feeling of increased energy when we hiked close together. If one of us stepped to the side while hiking behind the oblivious one in front, breaking the invisible energy line, the downshift in energy was palpable to the one ahead, confirmed each time as they invariably looked back to see what had happened only shortly after their partner stepped silently aside.

As our guide joins us, we learn that this third day of hiking will not be limited to the work of the west. Upon reaching the mountain ruin of the temple called Cajamarca—also designated as our lunch spot—we will leave the focused practice of engaging our courage to walk invisibly in the darkness of the unknown and begin the work of the north where the spirits of the ancestors are symbolically present. We will then complete the medicine wheel journey on a shorter hike tomorrow, culminating in arrival at Machu Picchu. The object of walking the path in the spirit of the north is to move beyond engagement with power, even the power of knowledge. Moving beyond power means letting go of any sense of controlling experience and releasing instead into a synchronous relationship with living, which in Incan lore involves stepping outside of time as we know it and into the mystery of sacred time—circular rather than linear—which includes in every instant everything that linear time separates into times past, present, or future.

The native shamans of the Americas, we've been told, speak of two kinds of time: one that flies like an arrow, or monochronic time, and one that turns like a wheel, or polychronic time. When we live within the concept of monochronic time, as we do in Western culture, our development is completely bound up in the concept of cause and effect, with one act leading in a linear way to another, forever. That mental construct limits personal growth, our guide has told us, by forging successive links in a living causal chain and defining who a person is solely in terms of past events leading ultimately to the present. We've been learning that no aboriginal/native culture functions that way. Instead, when emotional or physical disturbance presents itself to someone in such a culture, they are understood to be out of balance with all of nature, past and future, in some way. In order to heal, they must find the tools to return to a proper relationship with heaven and earth, past and future. The path to such a recovery involves a rite of passage, sometimes a ceremony.

We've been told that as we engage the spirit of the north today after lunch, we will be stepping out of our normal sense of causality and may find ourselves in a situation with a cause two months in the future. On the other hand, we may perhaps find ourselves merging with or influencing events that have happened in the past, or both at the same time. As such, there will be the possibility to define ourselves in terms of who we are becoming, offering an opportunity to step out of the personal psychological struggle of seeking spiritual growth from within the mental construct of Western civilization.

Three essential teachings of the work of the north include invisibility, mastery of time, and mastery of an ability to keep a secret from oneself. The first, invisibility, involves becoming transparent by using various means to blend in with whatever life forms surround us—particularly cultural forms—allowing ourselves to be seen because there's nothing left to hide. Successfully coming to the work of the north for a shaman means no longer requiring power because power is only a tool needed to protect something that needs to stay hidden. The second teaching, mastery of time, allows one to move into a synchronous relationship with living by aligning vision and intent. By doing so, the universe is activated to move in harmonious ways to support action toward that vision. This process is found in every sacred tradition, our guide has explained, although it's usually thought of as engaged by a messiah figure of some sort. On the medicine wheel, however, anyone willing to do the work with integrity has the power to engage the process. The third element for mastering the work of the north is to gain the mysterious ability to keep a secret from oneself by developing a capacity to mentally separate chosen actions in the present from intuitive insights about what the future may hold and preserving the authenticity and synchronic power of each such act in the moment when it occurs.

As we head out again from our snack and rest spot, putting one foot in front of the other along the rocky path toward Cajamarca, or the "Temple of the Sun," we begin to realize just how long today's hike may be. A rumor that passed earlier through the group sounds prescient now—although the hike won't be as steep as yesterday, it will be the longest one, and we haven't been told what exactly that means. Feeling an already aching tiredness in my legs and back, I realize the balance of the day will be a test of endurance and courage for all of us, regardless of what part of the medicine wheel our imaginations will be trying to engage as we walk.

My hiking partner and I are the first to reach the lunch spot at two thirty, not a good sign since it's probably only halfway to tonight's campsite. Cajamarca is an amazing roofless ruin atop a flight of steep stone steps that could well serve a four-story building. None of us would willingly climb these steps at this point in the hike, except to reach the lunch that awaits at the top. When the city surrounding this spot was alive with Inca, Cajamarca was a monastery that provided a resting place for pilgrims. The remains of its structure are perched atop a peak nosing out into the valley with precipitous cliffs dropping off to the valley's floor on three sides. After exploring the nooks, crannies, and magnificent views from this temple, we meditate in the sun, contemplate what it means to walk with courage and see clearly in the darkness, and wonder what vibrations may bubble up into experience from the energetic and mythic realms we have sought to activate during this whole hiking adventure. The camp cook arrives maybe fifteen minutes behind us along with a group of our fellow hikers. When the food is ready, we eat in silence, all of us feeling very tired. When we've finished, my partner and I leave our stones from Warmi Wanusqa on the highest point we can find and each pick up another. Making the most of this rest stop, we allow several groups of fellow hikers to set off ahead of us, and we continue to sit silently, opening our hearts and minds to the ancient energy of this place and reveling in the chance to rest a little longer before beginning the last leg of today's journey.

When we finally set out again at four o'clock, my partner and I imagine we must already be well on our way to hiking fifteen miles, making the stretch beyond Cajamarca into a lesson in faith. We decide to walk together for the rest of the day, knowing how tired we both are and the dangers that could present themselves if we walk at different paces and leave each other alone on the trail at various points. As we set off, we visualize sending energy back down the trail in the direction we've come to support those from the larger hiking party who have still not reached the lunch spot. Not long after setting off, we pass through a welcomed coolness of high rainforest, which brings with it a meditative peacefulness and strong sense of a long line of ancient travelers lining the path, pulling us along by some sort of energetic signature still vibrating in the earth. Whether or not that sense is a vague hallucination caused by our bodies' exhaustion and the thinness of the air or a psychological need for aid in this final stretch of the day, we viscerally feel the energy of their presence.

Passing through a particularly bright spot as we emerge from the forest, Sallqantay, the mountain Apu of this region, explodes into view, its rocky apex mostly snow covered, although the heat of the day where we walk continues unabated. My hiking partner suddenly experiences a momentary blackout. To our great relief, he quickly recovers after briefly pausing to rest against a boulder. A long drink of coca tea revives him enough to press on. We both hope the end of the day's trek is just around the bend.

Many bends later we finally see tents ahead, but our hearts sink as we realize they aren't ours. Asking a wandering camper whether he has seen our porters, we are directed up yet one more slope. Our group planned to camp just over the next ridge, he says. When we are once again immersed in rainforest and pausing to drink the last drops from our water bottles, my partner tells me a sharp alteration in his body chemistry has plagued him ever since he blacked out earlier. He's been internally battling an unaccountable rage, along with utter physical exhaustion, leaving him unsure whether he can continue. Because there is no way I can carry him and somehow we must keep climbing, I suggest using the only tool available—hiking close together with me in front. Perhaps that way I can leave enough energy in my wake to provide the boost he needs to get over this ridge into camp. With no other option and feeling desperate, he accepts. We begin to move in tandem up the ridge, his foot placed exactly where mine just left, one step after another for at least another mile, until we reach camp just before sunset.

The cold sets in quickly after the last solar rays sink into the valley, especially given our sweaty clothes and achingly tired bodies. After changing into dry winterwear, we bring sleeping bags into the main tent for further warmth while sitting in a subdued vigil with four others, all too exhausted to speak and waiting patiently in a daze as the rest of the group slowly trickles in. Soon after we arrive, my partner takes our guide aside and they leave the tent.

Later he tells me he needed to describe his feelings of unfocused rage in search of an explanation. He then relates how, after hearing the story, our guide took him to a spot with a particularly good view of Sallqantay, now a huge looming presence hovering over this campsite's ledge. Instructing him to send the anger down through his body into the earth, the guide told him to breathe in the essence of this powerful mountain, which had called to him through the blackout experience. When he returned to the group, I was amazed to see him emotionally transformed and was relieved to find that his rage had nothing to do with repressing something I inadvertently did or said during our hike.

By eight in the evening, the majority of our hiking group has arrived and we lie in a human ring of snoozing bodies waiting for dinner. At nine we hear that three of the final group have just been spotted. My hiking partner and I go out to meet them. One of them has needed physical support since the second pass, a very long way back. Several porters were sent to carry her into camp if needed. Thankfully she was able to make it on foot with the help of her two strong male companions, one of whom collapses into my partner's arms while the exhausted woman collapses into mine, everyone nearly in tears. We learn that the final member of the party yet to reach camp had to end his hike deep in the first valley beyond Warmi Wanusqa due to a terrible case of dysentery. The family living there kindly offered him shelter and care until he could be evacuated by helicopter. We return to the main tent where the others are gathered and gratefully eat our meal now that we are all present, everyone unusually silent and quick to collapse into tents afterward without a drop of energy for anything but sleep.

WE AWAKEN TO A SHEET OF GOLDEN CIRRUS CLOUDS skimming across the sky above the black peaks level with our plateau. As we drag our aching bodies into another day, the monolith of Sallqantay is rose colored in the morning light. It looks the part of the spiritual entity it's traditionally believed to be, towering high above the other mountains with its broad, rocky, snowcapped edifice dominating everything in sight. This will be the last day of our hike. We cheer as we hear that it's literally all downhill from here, and better still, today we enter Machu Picchu.

As we prepare to hike, I feel like Dorothy from *The Wizard of Oz* as she comes out of the woods to glimpse the Emerald City. The excitement of reaching our destination pumps unimagined energy reserves into everyone. We eat hot quinoa cereal one more time and gather a monetary offering for the porters, whom we will not see again. They will inevitably reach Machu Picchu long before we do, their job finished, and depart for their homes in the mountains.

It is customary to give the porters a hefty tip. They sit expectantly in one bright red–yellow–brown–blue mass on the side of the mountain a short distance from our cook tent. They clap and cheer after our gift is bestowed, and we return their praise with our own clapping and cheering for the indispensable part they played in what for us has been an amazing odyssey. Although they have intentionally kept utterly to themselves in camp throughout the trip, they have been an inspirational presence in their communal cooperation down to their preferred practice of sleeping in the open while huddled together under a continuous blanket of ponchos, a mass of humanity efficiently sharing bodily warmth. That is their way. They have our deepest respect.

Starting down the trail, I feel invited to dance by the big flat rocks making up this part of the path. Holding back at first, I soon give in to excitement and imitate the porters' technique of leaping from rock to rock. Huge surges of joy ripple through my body. I am ten years old again. At lunchtime my partner and I stop at the temple ruins of Wiñay Wayna, where we eat sandwiches and experience the ceremonial cleansing our guide has suggested, dunking ourselves in the wonderfully icy water of fountains flowing continuously from the mountain into semi-enclosed stone pools behind ancient rock walls. Pilgrims are said to be able to enter Machu Picchu as pure as children after washing in these fountains. That purification initiates the work of the east. Drying off afterward in a sunny field of long grass, I have rarely felt so exhilarated.

Collecting our packs again, my hiking partner and I head out fully refreshed and pondering the work of the east. The challenge of this last quadrant of the medicine wheel is to walk through life with beauty and impeccability, bringing to each encounter a purpose, investing each act with meaning symbolized by the eagle and the condor. Both fly near the Hanaq Pacha, the upper spirit world, seeing clearly far and wide and simultaneously deep into the undergrowth far below. Mayan tradition describes a corresponding archetypal figure, often called Quetzalcoatl in Mexican legends and described by our guide as a feathered serpent that has completed the journey through the medicine wheel to acquire wings.

The work of the east is to clarify visions of the future. Our guide has explained that there are medicine people still living in the Andes, shamans whose sole work is to sit in counsel, meditation, and ceremony, envisioning what's possible for the planet.

Their practice is to create holes in time for people to step through, spaces between dimensions through which those who are prepared can reintegrate themselves with a transplanetary community beyond time. The work of the east for us is to nurture the seeds we have planted in our hearts throughout this journey. We've been told they will reveal their potential in our lives to the extent we make room for them. As they grow in our awareness, their connection to this extra-psychic process will continue to unfold. Engaging the work of the east raises possibilities above probabilities in importance. It is said that such engagement also provides the opportunity to develop bodies that age differently.

The primary thing informing our bodies in the past, our guide has explained, has been our physically inherited genetic code, which transforms and evolves very slowly except during times of accelerated evolution. The last time there was an acceleration of that kind was one hundred thousand years ago when the human brain doubled in size and our species acquired a neocortex. All the prophecies of native peoples of the Americas speak of such a time reoccurring at some point in the next fifty years, our guide says, when an evolutionary window of opportunity will open again, allowing humanity to make a quantum leap into who we are becoming as a species. The seeds we are nurturing as we focus on the work of the east are seeds of luminous being that may connect our spiritual development to these mythical extra-psychic processes.

Machu Picchu was called the city of light by the Inca and is understood as a place to nourish such seeds: Buddha nature, if one follows a Buddhist path; the inner Christ for those on the Christian path; or for the Inca, the god/king/priest or goddess/queen/priestess of Andean cosmology for those on the shamanic path. To the degree in which each person is able to embody the seeds' potential, the seeds will transform from the inside out in ways that can't logically be comprehended, our guide has explained. The sources informing the process exist outside ordinary understanding. I wonder if there will be any noticeable effects of this hike over time or if we will even be able to see and acknowledge them if there are after we reenter modern *American* culture. Only time will tell.

When I stop to rest on a rock overlooking the Urubamba River, now a thin snaking line seen through a blanket of trees covering thousands of plunging feet of mountainside, memories of last night's camping glide by. That peaceful reverie and some cold tea revive me as I wait for my hiking partner. Together again, we admire the beauty of a plant seeming to grow out of nothing on the branch of a tree. I am so full of joy I feel I could fly. Machu Picchu, atop a nine-thousand-foot peak, rises from the river valley surrounded by higher peaks, upon one of which we now sit. We're not yet in view of the city, though we've been descending all morning from camp at twelve thousand feet. We know from photographs that there's a rise in the trail at the edge of the bowl framing the ruins, although it's hard to know which rise it will be. We keep hoping it's the next one.

Hiking at an easy pace, taking turns leading and following, pulling and pushing each other's energy filaments, we alternate between walking in meditative silence and shared laughter over memories of the hike's first three days. Finally we clamber up what we pray is the last uphill stretch, aiming for a spot we saw from just below where people were pausing to take pictures. Energy is still bubbling, though my legs and breath say I've never before asked so much of them for so long. We push on until we stand stunned by the view. A small temple has been constructed just over the brink of this ridge, probably built for the same reason we stop—to make a space to contemplate entrance into the city below. We can see the last stretch of snaking trail curling down the mountainside. The Urubamba River winds through the depths of the valley around the base of an independent peak that rises just beyond the ruins from the plateau that holds them. Machu Picchu is a breathtaking vision, covering the apex of the central plateau, which stands alone and surrounded by valley amid higher peaks. Standing transfixed, we take in the valley, the surrounding peaks, and the wondrous ruin, something I never believed I'd see in all its glory, even as I'd daydreamed of doing so since sixth grade while studying South American history.

There are no trees on this side of the mountain to block the view—or a fall. Seeing the long, steep slope ahead, I suddenly have no desire to contemplate the path. If I do, I might not be able to move forward at all. A dizzying feeling takes firm hold of my mind. We must move, however, if we are to reach our destination, walking straight down the steep trail for about fifty yards, relying only on ancient stone steps less than a foot wide. I descend like a toddler might, using both hands and feet to stay close to the earth with my heart in my mouth. Finally I can rise to my feet again to follow the path across the slope, as it weaves back and forth in a gradual descent, calming my pounding heart. As we round the last hairpin turn, we see our friend who had to leave the hike at the temple of the hummingbird. She waits to greet us as we enter, holding a basket of fruit. How wonderful to be welcomed into Machu Picchu by a friend and a hug. I can hardly believe we have actually arrived. Bone-tired, we sit in the shaded interior of the ancient guardhouse just above the ruins, listen to her description of the layout, and gaze in awe at this amazing city.

We absorb the information in a daze and later wander like sleepwalkers among tourists. As the sun begins to hang low in the sky, we slowly make our way down another path to the appointed meeting place, looking forward to the promise of a hot mineral bath soak this evening. Sitting on the bank of the Urubamba with a fellow hiker, watching the gurgling flow of water over rocks while waiting for the bus, we contemplate the power of the journey and tell stories of our lives, of the insights gained while hiking, and about connections between the mental exercises we've been doing and our challenges back home.

During the bus ride down ten hairpin turns on the way to an actual bed for the night, we all fall silent, barely energetic enough to take in the scenery passing the window, luxuriating in cushioned seating in a vehicle that moves under power other than our bodies. The feeling is short-lived, however, as we discover that the town of Aguas Calientes, our destination, is built on the side of a steep hill, and the hotel rests halfway up the slope atop a long flight of stairs.

Following a hot shower that feels like heaven and a leisurely dinner of pizza and soup in a local restaurant—where we're serenaded by two wandering mountain musicians who happen by with guitar and panpipes—we find ourselves climbing yet more stairs to the hot mineral springs that give the town its name. The dancing flames of many big candles surround us on stone walls framing the baths, a relaxing glow reflected in the hot water and each other's faces as we let the mineral salts do their work. Aching muscles gradually relax as we alternately sit and float, faces misted by steam, gazing at the diamond-spangled black velvet of a clear, star-filled sky.

AFTER A DELICIOUSLY DEEP SLEEP, we rise at the unbelievably late hour of eight in the morning—instead of the usual five thirty—lying between crisp white sheets, heads pillowed in softness and bodies swathed in blankets. It's hard to tear myself away from these creature comforts to do more hiking, but the women's temple awaits. Huayna Picchu holds the temple of the moon and a cave atop its rise above the main ruins. I can't miss that! At breakfast we're told that tonight, by the light of the full moon, we'll do ceremonies at sacred sites within the main ruins, another fascinating opportunity. After eggs, toast, and strong coffee, I tie boot laces once again and scramble to catch the bus in time to head back to the ruins.

Huayna Picchu rises steeply at the southern end of Machu Picchu. Entering from the north after crossing the ruins at its base, we begin to climb another steep path. The going is uneventful and not as treacherous as our guide suggested. The trail is clear and equipped with ropes for maneuvering past the steepest parts. Several members of the hiking party struggle nevertheless. Fatigue has taken its toll on everyone's strength and stamina. Having successfully maneuvered as a group through the significant challenges of the four-day hike, however, we walk now as a tribe, caring for and supporting each other up this last peak that only half the group is willing to attempt. I am humbled to be able once again to hike in a way that helps those who follow to link to whatever they can imagine of energy filaments in my wake, perhaps giving them at least an extra psychological boost, if nothing else.

Nearing the mountain's apex, the scene spreading itself beyond the narrow plateau where we stand is more dramatic than expected, including a wide view of the valley and Machu Picchu in detailed outline at the mountain's base. We sit briefly dangling feet over the precipitous drop. Then, as the only two women participating in this climb, a new friend and I become the anointed priestesses to guide the men through the birth canal cave of the women's temple in the traditional Incan way. I'm delighted to learn that the Inca gave equal reverence to the feminine aspect of their ancient culture, according to our guide. The larger ruin below is divided in half, representing male and female aspects of every human, honoring the importance of each to the sustenance of society. All grains were stored on the feminine side, the side where the nurturing, fertile, life-producing qualities of Earth are recognized and honored in the highly revered Pachamama stone, representing Mother Earth. The markets of the city are also found on the feminine side. Considering that we've also learned it was the Incan ability to store and distribute grain that made their empire so powerful for so long, it appears that this arrangement is more than a token concession to the sacred feminine.

Leading the men through the small, dark cave that gives the temple its meaning as an imagined birth canal, we emerge into the open air at the highest point of the ruins. Its prominence is significant, our guide tells us, because in Incan legends Machu Picchu represents the pinnacle of Earth's female energy pole, while Tibet in the Himalayas, directly opposite through the sphere of Earth, represents the male energy pole. He also says that this tale is replicated in Tibetan folklore, despite the impossibility that the two cultures communicated, except perhaps through stories passed down by nomads traveling down the mountainous spine of the Americas after crossing the Alaskan land bridge that no longer exists.

The three-hundred-sixty-degree view of the valley from atop Huayna Picchu's small collection of apex boulders is spectacular. We see the Urubamba entering the valley through a western cleft in the mountains, winding its way around the base; to the north is the trail we hiked yesterday, from the last lookout point to where it threads into Machu Picchu; to the east, the Urubamba river valley spreads wide in fertile fields that annually benefit from a generous spring flood. After passing through the valley, the river winds away again through another distant mountain cleft. To the south are yet more jungle-shrouded peaks across the Urubamba, hiding secrets only known to those on foot in that green tangle.

After pausing to drink our fill from both the glorious view and our water bottles, we gingerly descend the steep slope again without mishap, then make our way to a patio at some remove from the main ruins to eat a hearty four-course lunch and watch a couple of wild llamas graze nearby. Following lunch, my hiking partner and I find a cozy, shaded nook away from the tourists to take a siesta until a scheduled meeting time for meditation in a special circle of stones.

AT THE APPOINTED TIME, when the sun is beginning to sink behind the mountains, the ruins are quiet and nearly deserted as the few of us who opted in for this experience sit in a circle inside the stone ring believed to hold an energy vortex, a particularly strong point of connection between earth and sky in the Q'ero tradition. Their lore teaches that this meeting place of powerful male and female energy fields causes a kind of invisible tornado to emerge from earth's ley lines, which can be perceived by those open to the experience and sensitive enough to discern their subtle energies. The meditation we will engage in is intended to prepare us for moonlight ceremonies at sacred Incan sites throughout the main ruins later tonight when they are free of tourists.

Closing our eyes as we begin, we listen to our guide's calm voice as he encourages us to relax our bodies and empty our minds to sit very still and upright for twenty minutes. The peaceful sound of his voice guides us into meditative silence. I breathe easily, noticing how the air is filling my lungs, in and out, in and out, the rhythm of life. Feeling supported by the circle of others, I know they are present though their breathing is inaudible. It feels good to sit peacefully, despite the rocky ground. I relax gradually into the breath and the darkness behind my eyelids. After a while our guide stops speaking and there is hardly a sound.

As thoughts dissolve with the rhythm of the breath, a whirling funnel of grey light seems to materialize, spinning counter-clockwise within our meditating circle. Observing it peacefully, I wonder whether it's an image suggested by the story about the energy vortex or something I'm actually sensing. Not caring too much about which, I just observe and relax. Suddenly, that image is replaced by a clear, sharp view of the ruins as through open eyes, though mine remain closed. The ruins look just as they did as we first sat down, Huayna Picchu directly opposite the spot where I sit. Breathing and calm observing continue. Then the vision begins to alter almost imperceptibly. Two black shapes rise very slowly on the western and eastern sides of Huayna Picchu, looking very much like the mountains surrounding us except black as a starless midnight. They continue to steadily, slowly rise, holding my sharp attention until I realize they are not mountains but gigantic condor wings rising for flight at a huge bird's elbow-like joints. The combined spread of these wings is greater than the whole valley in which Machu Picchu sits. As they rise ever higher, their blackness blots out everything behind them. Finally there is nothing but their hovering darkness with Huayna Picchu between them.

My breathing and pulse begin to lose the peaceful rhythm. The hair on the back of my neck prickles, but I continue to hold attention on the vision that seems so real I can barely retain consciousness of our circle of meditators, although I feel the ground on which I sit and know that I'm safely anchored in physical reality. As I continue to watch with full attention, save for the sense of firm ground beneath me, I begin to see the great wings not as those of a bird but instead joined to the back of an immense, writhing snake with a head like a dragon. As I watch transfixed, the serpent coils and uncoils, moving toward me in slow-motion flight, suspended from its wings in the space between our meditation circle and Huayna Picchu. The snake's great yellowish cream-colored belly is revealed below the undulating curves of its green-brown back in the most fascinating and terrifying vision I've ever encountered.

I struggle to stay with the image, tempted to open my eyes into safety. The beast's huge, flicking red tongue darts in and out of a massive mouth. As I watch, it rears its head high into the sky. My breathing continues unevenly as its great black eyes fix me in their gaze. The head curls atop the long neck, then dives in dreamlike slow motion toward me, red tongue flicking and eyes like black pools. Pausing for a second or two perhaps five feet distant, its head still and body undulating and curving, suspended from those enormous wings, it examines me carefully. I can see the texture and shine of each greenish scale on its back and the cream-colored ones on its snake-like belly. Suddenly it opens its cavernous mouth as wide as my torso, revealing yard-long fangs in both upper and lower jaws, then lunges forward, sinking them into my neck and lower belly. I feel nothing of teeth in flesh, though a huge rush of energy jerks my spine erect and my chest forward and up. Just as the creature has clamped a firm hold, its body transforms into a swirling white vortex of energy so great I can hardly conceive of its size. I would later compare that energy to an experience of the fierce wind and night-like darkness of torrential rain that engulfed a sunny afternoon, as a Midwestern tornado skimmed so close to the city as to seem inseparable from the storm on its edge, through which I once drove in Minneapolis with my three-year-old daughter.

Each great wing transforms into another vortex feeding the central swirling energy mass fused with my own. For one eternal moment out of time, the creature's energy and mine are one, part of a cyclone connecting my torso to the sky. Everything around this electric mass turns bloodred and my body sways and vibrates with the intensity of the energy.

Our guide's voice breaks into consciousness, "When you're ready, come back to this place and open your eyes." With the sound of his voice, the image dissolves to my great relief. My spine slumps slightly, returning to a relaxed sitting pose. I pause long enough for my breathing to become even again. When the visual field behind my eyelids has remained in peaceful, familiar darkness for a moment or two, I open my eyes into the reassuring gentleness of late afternoon sunlight, a soft breeze, and the calm circle of fellow meditators. As the group begins to collect sweaters and backpacks to join the rest of our party for dinner, some members of the group share their experiences of a grey, energetic, counterclockwise-moving cyclone, and we soon realize it's an image that emerged for us all, though those details were not suggested beforehand. The details of my own experience, which I briefly try to describe, bring me unexpected shaking and tears. My hiking partner's embrace helps, as does our guide's effort to brush the energy out of my body with some quick, strong strokes of his hands down the outside of my jeans-clad legs.

His smiling comment, made with a twinkle in his eye, is "We don't know very many winged serpents, do we?"

I reply, "I didn't know *any* before this evening," trying to laugh through tears.

"There's Quetzalcoatl, the Mexican spirit of transformation, the snake who has moved around the medicine wheel and received its wings," he responds, also advising me to work with the image through drawing and free-form writing in the days and weeks to come, avoiding any immediate search for explanations.

I feel overwhelmed and very vulnerable, amazed that a meditative vision could have such an emotional impact. My hiking partner keeps his arm around me all the way down the hill. I breathe deeply and feel feet firmly planted on the ground as we walk, though deep inside something has changed.

That evening, following a rest in our comfy hotel rooms, our whole hiking party enjoys another excellent meal before heading out by the light of the stars to reenter the main ruins by special permission. As we stand on a plateau slightly above and to the north of the ancient city, we watch a silver-blue light grow behind the eastern mountain peaks of the surrounding bowl. Then, in an instant, the main body of the ruins just below becomes stunningly illuminated. The ethereal blue-white beauty of the first silent fingers of full moon light streams over the eastern peaks, leaving everything surrounding the ruins in darkness for several minutes, except the stars. Like a magical kingdom emerging suddenly from within the blackest part of the mountain night, Machu Picchu shimmers mysteriously in the moonlight.

Proceeding silently down a slight incline of stone steps into the ruins, we walk from one sacred site to the next by that magical light. The sky is so clear that quantities of stars are still visible despite the moonlight. Our guide proceeds to lead us through ceremonies at each of the power spots of Incan legend within the ruins. First, at the death stone, we experience a ritual honoring the transformation of the old self into the new, which he explains has always been the true purpose of this stone, as taught by Q'ero shamans, who firmly contradict Western academic interpretations of the site as a stone used for human sacrifice.

At the temple of the sun we feel the strong energy of the stones while meditating. I am relieved to have no visions this time. In the cave of initiation, where the spirits of Incan elders are said to linger, we honor their presence. We bring water to the spirit of the condor in its own namesake temple, opening to the possibility of a heightened energy as we each kneel to place our foreheads on the bird's ruff of sculpted stone.

The culmination of our nighttime rituals is a practice at the Pachamama stone. Fashioned in the shape of the mountain range directly behind it, the stone is believed by the Q'ero to hold the same nurturing, receiving, mulching energy that gives the earth the healing power to bring forth life, transforming old dead cells into new living forms. Every temple and sacred site in the Incan tradition serves as a focal point for the energy of the natural forces they represent, our guide explains, not in themselves idols of worship as they're commonly interpreted by Western academics. Instead these places are meant to be special focal points where humanity can sit in communion with specific aspects of universal energy, found and mixed together in everything everywhere in a multitude of ways. We all take turns standing against the flat, wide stone that stands over six feet tall and maybe twenty feet wide, opening to our love of the earth and the sense of gratitude and humility we share as we think of all that the planet provides to make living possible. We end the evening singing an old song about humanity's deep love for the earth, which has been passed down through the ages in Peru. This has truly been a night to remember, but as I drag an aching body toward the bus, all I can think of is the soft, warm bed waiting in the hotel.

Chapter Fourteen

The Art of Healing

While I'm flying home a week later, my life is already beginning to transform. I travel this time without my hiking partner. He is staying to help look for appropriate land on which to build a study center for native Peruvian traditions. My body is exhausted and my views of life and its meaning have been permanently altered. I carry a deep sense of wonder reverberating in memory from the hike to Machu Picchu and from several sacred sites where we camped and did ceremonies during the second week of our journey. The stark, raw beauty of the Andes and the deep sense of living as part of the natural world permeate my consciousness as I sit in this giant metal bird flying back to the States.

Returning to the usual patterns of home, I find an even more powerful contrast than anticipated between Peruvian and US cultures, heightened now by a deep awareness of how separated we in this country have become from the richness of Earth, the source from which every living being springs. I am at once relieved to return to the comfort of the *American* lifestyle and determined to continue on the road to creating living patterns that honor the multifaceted mystery of living earth in as reciprocal a relationship as I can muster within personal circumstances.

It's CLEAR that trying to return modern cultural practices to some semblance of those from ancient times will not alter Western culture's concept of humanity as separate from nature. However, slowing the pace of living to honor the richness of natural existence has great potential. Taking time to learn about the healing potential for body, mind, and spirit embedded in ancient, non-Western traditions still practiced today holds a healing balm missing from technological culture. Effective use of modern tools too often demands casting aside connections to wonder, enchantment, and imagination, as well as the heart's deep, emotional knowing. Rational analysis easily connects with transformative compassion when the heart and mind are instead free to function more as a unity than as consciously separated spheres of perception, honing their integrated power into the amazing gift it has the potential to be.

After returning from Peru, I spent many hours digesting the mental and emotional impact of the trip's experiences, primarily as background reflection during routine daily activities over the course of the following year. A watercolor and crayon painting that began as a family project with my two young daughters and hiking partner became one of the most helpful integration exercises in that process. The wisdom of the trip's guide in response to the disturbing meditative image I encountered at Machu Picchu was revealed as the project unfolded. Making art was a powerful healing tool in those first few weeks. The four of us had jointly created another playful painting a year earlier. We thought it would be fun to do it again, partly to reclaim a sense of family shortly after my hiking partner returned from his extended trip to Peru following our joint hiking experience.

To create the first painting, we had laid down sheets of newspaper on our apartment floor, taped down a four-by-four-foot sheet of white paper over them, then used crayons, markers, and watercolors to collaboratively create an abstract work of art. My hiking partner built a large plywood-backed frame for that first creation and hung it on a prominent living/dining room wall, where it was the much-admired focal point of the space. We had only two rules governing this kind of artistic effort. We were to draw and paint whatever spontaneously erupted through our bodies and minds as we used artistic tools to make scribbles, splotches, or recognizable images, refraining from negative judgment of our own or each other's work. We each participated in this way from one of the four sides of the paper and agreed to shift sides in a clockwise direction about every fifteen minutes. The second rule was that we could make whatever marks we wanted, using whatever art media we chose in whatever way inspired us, even if it meant adding to or altering—though not eliminating— each other's previous efforts on each side of the paper. We worked together in this way until the whole sheet was filled and we jointly agreed the masterpiece was complete. We had great fun with that first project, including lots of laughter and appreciation of each other's work.

The second joint painting effort turned out very differently. We began to work sometime during the early afternoon and at first it seemed to go as it had before, but after an hour or so my daughters lost interest and soon my hiking partner did as well. However, I became obsessed with the project, not wanting to stop working on it until dinnertime, which they all agreed was fine. Later, I gained everyone's permission to continue the work on my own, moving it onto the narrow screened-in porch in the back, which perched over the outer stairwell leading from a shared driveway to our second-story apartment. Tacking it to the large bulletin board we hung on the inner wall, I could step back to see the whole as I worked on elements of composition.

The experience felt akin to a scene from the movie *Close Encounters of the Third Kind*, in which the character played by Richard Dreyfuss can't stop building a model of a mountain in his living room, although thankfully mine did not involve bringing piles of rocky soil into my home. The scene that eventually emerged from my own feverishly driven painting and drawing—blending with the initial image created in community with my daughters and hiking partner—adequately depicted the essence of the encounter at Machu Pichu with the winged serpent. The fearsome beast was clearly evident, along with two mountain-like humps that were also giant wings amidst a wildly colored background of bright yellow, orange, red, green, blue, and black. The process of making the painting was healing in a way I couldn't explain. I felt as though those images had poured out onto the paper through my whole body, obliterating all sense of self and time as they came. The images flowed onto the paper somehow in a kind of subconscious torrent, accompanied by the feelings of fear and mystery that the encounter contained.

At a certain point I knew the work was finished. A sense of contented stability—a kind of peace with both the experience itself and this curious work of art—began to settle in. When the painting process had begun, I'd been unable to speak about that experience without triggering considerable fear. After completing the painting, I still had no desire to describe it in detail to anyone; however, mentioning it briefly no longer raised anxiety. Instead, the fear began to be replaced by a sense of mystery and wonder along with a new respect for the way the mind and body work as a unit, best served by paying close attention, with curiosity and focus rather than negative self-judgment, to where inspiration leads.

That fall, my hiking partner and I returned to the Providence Zen Center for the final weekend of our year-long study of Incan shamanic traditions. I brought the completed painting to show the group, using it as a means to explain why I had skipped the summer weekend following the Peru trip. It was my hope that the quality of the disorienting experience depicted there would be easily understood simply by looking at the art, erasing the need for much verbal explanation. That process was also healing, empowering me to own the value of the choice I'd made to follow an individual path outside the prescribed group process to which we'd all initially committed.

One of the monks who lived full-time at the Zen Center had a surprising and fascinating reaction upon seeing my painting. He had remained with us while the majority of monks were away on retreat, and he lead a skeleton crew who chose to stay to produce and serve meals, part of the periodic Zen Center practice of renting the space to groups like ours to make financial ends meet. This kitchen maestro was so moved by the painting that he wanted to buy it!

After the painting's presentation to the shamanic study group, our guide had suggested hanging it on the wall leading out of the kitchen into the courtyard behind the center, enabling everyone to have a chance to look at it more closely during the weekend. During one of the last study breaks on the final day of our stay, the talented monk chef encountered me standing by the painting. I was looking at it while trying to decide what to do with it following the end of the workshop, not really wanting to take it home. When he discovered that I was the one who had painted it, he told me that the images it contained had moved him to tears, and he described how, as an *American* soldier in Vietnam, he had encountered Buddhist practices among the villagers he was charged with protecting and later, moved by a vision that seemed to him to be depicted in my painting, chose to devote himself to the practice of Zen Buddhism. Immediately following the war he had begun studying with a group of monks in South Korea before returning to the US, where he devoted himself full-time to Buddhist practice at the Providence Zen Center. In response to his offer to buy the painting, I replied that it would be an honor for me if he would willingly receive it as my gift to him for the wonderful cooking that had sustained us all during our workshops. That response surprised and delighted him.

"Are you sure?" he asked.

"Nothing would make me happier," I responded, "than to know that this painting touched someone's heart so deeply that they would want to keep it." The mystery of connection between Earth, body, mind, and spirit continued to flow through such moments of serendipity from then on, as it always had, yet now I began to notice and acknowledge such times far more often than I had ever been able to before.

FOR WEEKS AFTER OUR RETURN TO THE STATES and completion of the course in Peruvian shamanism, I could barely tolerate thoughts of "the vortex vision" beyond describing it briefly to a few close friends. Only much later did I discover that the dream-like image I'd encountered on the trip was an introduction to a teacher who would lead me toward a new relationship with my own energy and authority, as you will soon see.

Frequent opportunities for free-form painting, dancing, and writing, in workshops and in recreational experiences, followed, offering fertile ground for the release of strong emotions in healthy, creative ways that became regular practices over time. I now could more easily release self-consciousness in these pursuits to unite with the creative process at the core of them all, and in so doing transform emotional energy into inspiration and wiser engagement with life afterward.

About a year after the trip to Machu Picchu, during a shamanic journey led in my own living room by my hiking partner and with a steady drumbeat, I met the beast again at Machu Picchu. This time it was flying into the valley from the west from a great distance. At first, I could barely make out what was flying toward me. It looked like some kind of huge white bird. As it flew around the base of Huayna Picchu, I watched as though perched on a rise to the north of the bowl holding Machu Picchu's ruins. While I observed closely, the white shape revealed itself to be the same dragon-like snake I had met while meditating at the energy vortex on the trip, although it was much smaller this time. Watching it fly around Huayna Picchu, I felt no fear, only a tremendous sense of peace, and understood internally somehow that the great snake was strangely my own natural power—not some fearsome beast but an entity that would support me if fully accepted, though conversely, that would destroy me if I ever again abandoned it.

THE GREAT SNAKE APPEARED ONCE MORE, much later, in a dream preceding a commitment made with the love of my life, whom I met in a wild, free-form barefoot dance a few years following the "vortex vision." At the time of this new dream, the two of us were about to move beyond our shared fear of yet another failed romantic commitment in order to let the deep connection we had instantly felt for each other evolve into all it could be. In that dream, we stood under a tree that appeared to be a great, wide, full maple outside a house of some sort. As we talked in the dream, out of the corner of my eye I saw a huge snake once again flying toward me. This time, however, there was no fear, and the snake was a normal snakelike color. It encircled the two of us in the space just beyond the outer branches of the tree. The snake's body was wider everywhere than we were tall, though still there was no fear, only a sense of peace and contentment. It was surely a good sign for this long-sought and deeply treasured relationship, which has since become an intimately connected and mutually supportive second marriage for the two of us.

DURING THE FINAL WEEKEND of the yearlong study of Incan shamanism, it had begun to dawn on me that my hiking partner and I were growing apart, although we didn't separate until a year later, following his return from a second trip to Peru that lasted more than a month. He accompanied our guide and a small group of others to bring veterinary medicine to the Q'ero people living high in the Andes. They traveled with a line of burros laden with related supplies to help sustain the llama herds so essential to Q'ero survival. Since he was a former anthropology student at Harvard, the opportunity to participate in such a project had been irresistible. When he finally returned, however, we sadly discovered that we had inexorably been pulled in opposing directions, despite the love and concern we still shared for each other and for my daughters. That realization required us, out of mutual understanding and love, to walk very different paths into the future, despite the deep emotional pain the separation caused us all.

FOLLOWING THAT NEW HEARTBREAK, I soon followed moments of serendipity to begin learning a new practice that further integrated insights gained on the Inca Trail. This new practice provided a disciplined channel for what sometimes felt like massive emotional energy experienced as nearly explosive restlessness. Shortly after my hiking partner departed for good, I began to learn ways to use my body's large reservoir of energy to inspire healing in others as well as myself. Studying to become a Five Element Shiatsu practitioner entailed learning therapeutic use of finger pressure on acupuncture meridians within various patterns of energy points mapped out in the body by Chinese Taoists more than twenty-five hundred years ago. Learning to effectively assist clients to rebalance their body's energy also included a course in anatomy from a Western perspective.

After completing the two-year shiatsu training and the accompanying supervised apprenticeship, I began to practice professionally. Three years as a shiatsu practitioner, using a combination of science, intuition, physical observation, and imaginative description of the elements of nature reflected in the body and psyche (as defined by Five Element Chinese Medicine), also helped me to heal parts of myself for which Western medicine had no words. My Five Element teacher often said that to give a shiatsu treatment was also to receive one. That was borne out in the meditative focus required to work on the body of another person with compassionate respect, using finger, hand, and arm pressure on acupuncture points and meridians, coupled with discussion of the body's response to the energetic quality of living patterns associated with their discomfort.

In addition to providing some relief from specific ailments causing discomfort for my client, my treatments were either physically relaxing or energizing, depending on their need, and a deeply relaxing and energizing experience for me as I let go of everything else to focus on the condition of the body under my fingers. Seeking to provide each client with individually tailored healing support, I used patterns of pressure and various qualities of touch to activate or calm energetic flows within the Five Element system of acupressure points, stimulating each body's ability to rebalance itself. Centering attention on the movements of the treatment pattern, while maintaining sensitivity to what the body revealed as I worked, required complete release of other thoughts and feelings in order to deeply engage the process. Working in this way also involved practicing several meditative modalities, including QiGong, Tai Chi, and sitting meditation, to sustain the healthy mental, emotional, and balanced energetic presence needed to provide effective healing support to clients. As I practiced these disciplines, the wildly energetic side of my psyche began to reintegrate with the rationally analytic one, which had so often used willpower to override intuitive messages.

During this time in shiatsu practice, I also discovered that sitting in circles of women, deeply listening and mindfully speaking of personal experience, helped strengthen awareness and confidence in the unique gifts women bring to society, too often undermined by Western cultural expectations. Regular participation in these circles began to make emotional space for my intuitive inner wild child to begin to reemerge from her metaphoric cave as living continued to unfold during five years of training and practicing in shiatsu massage. Finding my own experiences mirrored in those of other women in these circles gradually altered habits of thought through patient persistence, helping to lead my intuitive side back into a central role in daily life.

As the inner child gradually began to trust the adult I had become, and that adult came to understand the unique gifts the inner child had to offer, I increasingly trusted intuition to scout the way forward through life, reassigning the rationally conditioned aspect of consciousness to serve as administrator rather than dominating critic. Critical thinking began to act as equal partner to intuitive, emotional, and physical knowing, wonder, and inspiration, translating their wisdom into constructive speech and action. I came to understand that intuitive messages often required pausing long enough to meditatively listen to all the body could silently reveal before making or acting on any decision. This approach to living began to open new access to encounters with awe, mystery, and the deep beauty of nature, along with insights into the nature of life itself.

Ever since that chosen partnership between intuition and rationality began, rationally analytic consciousness has increasingly united with a growing capacity for patience to deeply listen and observe rather than reactively criticize or impulsively act. Emotionally centered intuition relaxed into its leadership role, allowing me to laugh, dance, sing, and act with imaginative abandon when appropriate opportunities arose and conversely to understand when to meld invisibly into everyday life to quietly watch and listen instead, depending on circumstances.

THE FIVE-YEAR SHIATSU JOURNEY I BEGAN in the mid-nineties served to provide a part-time profession while my daughters were still young enough to need a good deal of attention at home after school. Working independently allowed me time to support them in other ways also, like coaching my older daughter's soccer team and acting as co-leader for my younger daughter's Brownie troop. However, I eventually realized that shiatsu was not a career path that would sustain my spirit over the long haul or provide the financial support the Girls' Club would need as my daughters grew. Once again I missed the intellectual challenge of reading and writing, especially concerning various kinds of power and the ways in which society organizes itself around them.

Chapter Fifteen

Becoming the Change

What I consider now to have been a ten-year life transition period—from the end of identifying as the wife of my first husband to the beginning of a deeply centered sense of an independent self—culminated at the beginning of the new millennium in 2000. That period included graduation from the master's degree program at Tufts University's department of Urban and Environmental Policy in 1994, the year before my trip to Peru. Internet technology was still new at that time, though exponentially growing by the month.

In addition to the sole proprietor shiatsu practice that I learned, developed, and practiced between 1995 and 2000—shaping a business where I took my equipment with me to deliver treatments in the homes of my primarily women clients—I also worked with a couple of partners to gather two separate groups capable of and interested in leading organizational teams to function as boards of directors for potential nonprofit organizations. In the process I learned how to form such groups and which approaches worked and didn't. Both groups succeeded in presenting a series of programs over a period of several years. One of the two is still functioning, although neither chose to complete the work required to transform a voluntary association into a bona fide nonprofit organization.

The first such effort was an independent adult education project to design and deliver workshops capable of inspiring participants to explore ways to live more meaningful lives in their communities while shifting their lifestyle choices to better sustain natural systems. Presentations of practical sustainable living strategies were led by social and environmental activists, catalyzing breakout brainstorming discussions among workshop participants to develop local projects. These workshops were attended by town residents, including an assortment of public school, government, and business leaders in each town. The aim of the program was to drive development of new individual and community-based living patterns capable of supporting, rather than degrading, ecological systems. Five or six MetroWest communities around Boston hosted the workshops that the organization we called the Sustainable Living Institute led, attracting about fifty to seventy-five people to each event. I bowed out after the leadership group had solidified as a potential board, developed a replicable workshop model, and successfully delivered a couple of workshops because I was disappointed that the other project leaders didn't share a broader, more powerful vision of organizational growth beyond purely local activism.

A women's spirituality circle that still exists was the focus of the other start-up effort. Although it never became the certified nonprofit organization I initially envisioned—one strong enough to grow the capacity to support women in need internationally through large fundraising campaigns—it did develop into a unique hub of spiritual connection for an ever-evolving group of about twenty women. The group also contributed modestly to the needs of women beyond that circle for many years, making a joint financial contribution annually to a Nigerian school for girls and to the Greater Boston Food Bank. Sadly, I was again compelled to move on from a central leadership role in that group shortly after it was established in order to find a better way to financially support my children. Years later I returned to the group's continuing circle, as a participant, and continue to attend its quarterly gatherings for the deep, women-centered spiritual nourishment found there.

Learning from these start-up nonprofit development efforts augmented lessons learned in graduate school and through extensive volunteer community organizing activities, which had included a multiyear position on a nonprofit board of directors focused on environmental protection of Salem Sound during the early '90s. Eventually, a vision of a sole proprietor nonprofit development consulting practice began to take shape. Creative Initiatives was the name I gave to it as it coalesced in the first year of the new millennium, quickly morphing into a sixteen-year capstone to my years of activism. Through that work, I gained outside acknowledgement that all the hours dedicated to volunteer work since graduating from college had indeed been instrumental in creating the career path I'd imagined years earlier. That acknowledgement provided a deeper sense of self-respect and confidence than I could previously access.

Initiation of that acknowledgement came from an unlikely source in yet another example of the way serendipity influences life. An insightful résumé consultant opened that door to possibility. She offered me a free bonus session, as a gift of thanks for the sessions I paid her to provide my older daughter, with whom she worked to develop her college application materials in a program made available through the local high school. In preparation for our hour-long meeting, the consultant requested a chronological list of my educational and work experiences, including volunteer activities. When I showed her the list, I apologized, saying that most of the work I'd been paid to do was either so different or so long ago that it probably wouldn't work well in the résumé for the kind of position I'd asked her to help me achieve, explaining that everything else had been done as a volunteer. I couldn't imagine anyone thinking of the volunteer work as professional because it didn't hold the same status as paid work in the cultural story I had internalized. She took one look at my list and emphatically exclaimed that, to the contrary, it had the makings of a wonderful résumé for just what I aimed to do! She explained that the information in the list simply needed to be presented differently from the conventional résumé format. When combined more creatively, however, it demonstrated exactly the kinds of leadership and organizing skills needed to jump-start the consulting business I envisioned.

Thankfully she was right, which taught me one more lesson about the power of imaginative alternatives to conventional cultural approaches to just about anything, an insight that informed my consulting career from then on. As a result, I was able to assist the executive directors of numerous grassroots nonprofit organizations to strategically frame programmatic work, helping them to sustain and grow the organizational capacity necessary to successfully address public policy issues of social and environmental justice faced by their constituents, mostly at the community, state, and regional levels in New England. That collaborative process resulted in successfully raising more than seven and a half million dollars to support the essential projects of these groups.

THESE DAYS, living in the forest on the side of a mountain in Vermont and reflecting on writing skills gained before retiring in 2016, I realize it was the passion for telling compelling stories about the need and value of financial support for my clients' work that kept me going. That process delivered me to this place in life where my wildish nature has an even larger dreaming space to support it. The tools that the rational side of my conscious mind now uses to feed the writing practice resulting in these words have been honed through their continuous use because I developed the capacity to perceive and tell the same story in multiple ways as my practice solidified. The shape of any tale we tell ourselves or remember can change over time as original stories shift to become history. As each of us changes, so can our understanding of past events and our capacity to reimagine and tell new stories capable of creating wiser, more humane shapes for living as we learn and grow at every age.

As various circumstances developed and required me to adopt new living patterns, I came to understand that the most important task at such times is to pause in ambiguous moments before choosing action, for whatever length of time necessary, to pick up the crystal rock of that pivot point and turn it this way and that before deciding which reflection will best frame the next life choice. Once committed to a new course of action, moving at whatever pace allows enough similarly reflective moments remains important because the shape of the future never unfolds from one person's intentions, no matter how wise they may be, and always requires adjustments to envisioned goals before they transform from future dream into present reality. Major alterations to living patterns require resting spots along the way for looking around and determining whether the path you're on toward the top of any particular mountain of change leads in the direction your heart knows it needs to go or instead needs to branch off on a slightly different tack to avoid unexpected boulders. Taking the time to pause, even for a moment, before continuing on is a practice that has become a treasure for me, one deeply connected to the practice of listening—alone while meditating and also in conversation—for the heartfelt center of every spoken or silently imagined story, the one small spark capable of initiating the living moment into the wisdom of the world between worlds, where dreams live and give birth to everything we perceive and name as culture.

Chapter Sixteen

The Dance of Genes and Memes

Richard Dawkins' groundbreaking 2009 book *The Selfish Gene* describes in everyday language the scientific understanding of the developmental process of human origins gained in my lifetime. His book describes how our genes came to give us the ability to think and act as we do by "switching on" or not through various haphazard encounters with the environment. That includes the complex chemical soup of our bodies, the vehicles scientists widely speculate grew over a huge quantity of millennia as genes were forming, evolving from single-celled organisms swimming in the ocean, which eventually joined together to become intricately complex spiraling systems that allowed them to protect themselves and to thrive, systems commonly known today as DNA. Of course that soup also continues to change all the time through emotional reactions that invariably generate biochemicals or through the chemical makeup of what we eat, drink, and breathe that alters that soup from sources beyond the skin. We may think we're driving the cars of life we know as our bodies, but in fact our genes are steering most aspects of these incredibly complex living mechanisms. After all, our genes created those mechanisms by transforming every rare, minute flaw that mistakenly occurred into a new advantage, at least from our perspective as human beings.[1]

The thoughts and actions ignited by our genes give each of us unprecedented power to alter the environments in which we live, as well as the physical characteristics of the living Earth systems in which we reside, generally with little awareness of the immensity of that impact when all human actions are combined. Our minds and hands collaborate in fundamentally unique ways within the spiraling unfolding of life on Earth, and the spiral itself is continuously reflected as the ubiquitous shape within all that unfurling, from the first swirl of DNA when sperm and ova unite, to the formation of a baby's heart in the womb, newly opening leaves, the growing pattern of pinecones, nautilus shells, hurricanes, galaxies, and so much more. [2]

If we move to a cold climate, we no longer have to wait for natural processes to adapt our bodies the way animals do, slowly developing thicker coats of hair, more fat, or altered metabolisms. Instead, we make warmer clothing and build insulated houses with central heating systems. If we choose to fly, we study aerodynamics and build wings. If we want to step into the vacuum of space, we create ways to take essential life-support systems with us. And if we don't like our genetic constitution, we learn—as we are now beginning to do—how to re-engineer it. However, despite these most significant new capabilities of the living organisms known as human beings, most people don't consider technology to be part of nature. [3]

Looking around the earth today, it's easy to think that the human mind is the dominant creative force on the planet. And it's true that the whole panorama of planetary change, initiated by humanity as a result of the cultural stories we tell that differentiate us from every other creature, started as ideas in human minds. Most people think that humanity's creations are not part of biological evolution, however. Why not? We don't consider a beehive less natural than a bee, a beaver's dam less natural than a beaver, or a bird's nest less natural than a bird. Why should creations constructed using the know-how of human minds and hands be any less natural than human beings? The answer is that human creations, particularly the complex machines we've created, don't seem to be in harmony with the natural world. They must be unnatural in some way then, especially if human beings are separated from the natural world in the human imagination. Looking at living that way could be a major mistake, however. Maybe the real reason humanity's creations don't harmonize with nature is that the thinking behind them is out of sync with natural systems, due to psychological conditioning acquired from the culture that produced the industrial revolution, and the conditioning that educates us to imagine that we are masters over nature rather than agents within it. It's true that we often use our unprecedented creative potential in ways that seem to separate us from nature, often by unnecessarily destroying other kinds of life in the process. However, even if human creativity has become misguided on some level, its products and all the tools that shape them are made of natural Earth elements, so they can't really be considered unnatural.[4]

Richard Dawkins reminds us to notice that the evolution of technology directed by human minds and hands is reflective of natural systems, except that it catalyzes and develops changes in living Earth processes that would otherwise take millions of years or might never occur at all. The solar cell, for example, represents a method of capturing the sun's energy that can be compared in significance to the development of photosynthesis, though created in the blink of an eye by comparison. Radar, another good example, has allowed us to see in a new range of frequencies, a development as significant as the natural evolution of the eye, an essential organ for so many creatures. Through nuclear physics, we discovered how to create new chemical elements. The last time such a synthesis occurred in our area of the universe was in the supernova that preceded Earth's sun five billion years ago.[5]

A new theory has emerged in the last few decades to explain why the dynamic speed of evolutionary change has suddenly increased in such a short period of time, in terms of the age of the planet, jumping from the speed of physical processes slowly altering natural characteristics of species, land forms, ecosystems, climate, etc. to changes in Earth's natural systems centered instead in the more rapidly replicating realm of human ideas. That jump in the speed of change can be thought of as another giant leap in the evolutionary process of the living earth. In this story, humanity, the product of a long natural evolutionary process, has now become a conscious participant in the unfolding spiral of creation, exponentially speeding the forces of change that are literally and figuratively coalescing into mighty storms that require us to learn new ways to relate to living experience—that is, if we as a species are to survive the results of those storms.

Humanity appears to be inexorably altering biological evolution as a result of the increasingly rapid pace of cultural change. New pattern development today is also profoundly influencing our behavioral responses, playing out at lightning speed through the values our attitudes and actions transmit about the way we understand ourselves. Our thoughts, and how we can consciously direct them as we pay attention, are more important now than ever before because they can be so quickly and widely shared via technology. As such, it is not a stretch to say that, at the macro level, a wildly successful natural progression has led to preservation and replication of human life to the point at which our species has taken control of the living habitat required by all life on Earth.[6] Therefore, the quality of awareness we bring to living, along with the ways in which we communicate what that particular quality allows us to discover, quickly replicated in other minds through our technological communication networks, will determine life's next chapter.

Richard Dawkins defined this process: "*Memes* (discrete units of knowledge, gossip, jokes and so on) are to culture what genes are to life."[7] Like genes, memes pass from person to person, only much faster. Forty years ago there was no meme about personal computer use for work and entertainment. Today that idea is common sense. Memes can be seen as the basic units of cultural heredity. Like genes, they bind humanity together into stable, cohesive wholes. Some memes are useful. Ideas about how to lovingly raise children to reduce the incidence of childhood trauma are valuable and can profoundly improve everyone's quality of life. Others are less useful.[8] A meme that undervalues people of different cultures, races, classes, and sexes can spread contempt and violent strife throughout society. Such memes act like viruses, spreading from person to person with the capacity to infect all of society unless humanity's capacity for self-reflection is deeply engaged and widely supported. The different implications of spreading various kinds of memes could easily be seen in the year 2020 as global culture came to be dominated by humanity's political and social reactions to the COVID-19 pandemic.

In the same way that viruses in cells can cause genetic programs to switch on or off at the wrong times, resulting in lethal illnesses, without consciously taking time to slow down and reflect on the qualities that our own thoughts and emotional reactions foster in other minds and hearts in the culture around us, our minds can become vectors of infectious ideas that switch on destructive behaviors that spread as quickly as wildfire. However, with enough people paying careful attention to each thought and emotion and responding to any situation as compassionately and wisely as possible, there remains hope that the raging wildfires of the minds around them will begin to recede, leaving behind fertile ground for wiser, more just, and more life-nourishing cultural developments.

Trees have often been my best teachers. If a tree is to withstand a storm, it must be flexible, able to bend with the wind. A rigid tree will soon break or blow down. A strong, flexible tree must also have deep roots, a stable anchor connected to a wider community of trees through the fungal network below the soil. The same is true for humanity. If we are to survive accelerating change, we need to learn flexible stability equal to withstanding the increasing force of roaring winds of all kinds. We need to be able to let go of outdated assumptions and habits of thought that no longer serve us and find the inner freedom to see things with fresh eyes, as the gifted scholar of world religions, general systems theory, and deep ecology, Joanna Macy, described in her 1995 workshop I attended in Boston. That work was called Despair and Empowerment and has since transformed into a global network called the Work That Reconnects.

Deepening the capacity to reflect on the nature of personal experiences in order to see things in fresh, new ways can help us to respond more wisely and creatively to life's inevitable challenges. The capacity to reflect in this way, to become creatively flexible, also helps to stably anchor us in our bodies and communities so that when we meet the unexpected, we can more calmly respond rather than impulsively react.

THE TELLING OF THIS PERSONAL STORY has been intended to demonstrate in multiple ways how everything is completely intertwined and interconnected in mysterious ways. Hopefully my story reveals on some level how that interconnection is not a theoretical abstraction drawn from religious myth, dogma, bones, rocks, or theories of evolution. By contemplating and directly experiencing all that our bodies and minds encounter, a far wider and more varied expanse than could be accessed when I was born, anyone willing and able to consider such things has an opportunity to notice the myriad ways in which everything on Earth is deeply and inseparably intertwined in utterly tangible ways. This huge, interactive, interrelated system operates beyond human conscious direction, although it is influenced by all the choices we make while believing that we are somehow in control. From the atmosphere and the pull of the moon and the tides to the microbes living within and upon every inch of our bodies, functioning as part of our immune system at some points in life and as deadly predators attacking us at others, there is such a multiplicity of influences and chain reactions of both creation and destruction that one mind can't possibly conceive of how they all fit together.

Science has shown how our bodies are ever-evolving ecosystems within the ever-evolving ecosystems surrounding them and within the constantly transforming planetary and solar systems, galactic systems, and possibly even systems of multiple universes, according to some astrophysicists. All of this information is only now dawning on a broad enough plane of human awareness that the possibility is rising globally for individuals everywhere to choose to participate in intentionally evolving human consciousness and cultural systems from the inside out, one mind, heart, and community at a time.

Meditative and contemplative wisdom practices are today more widely available than ever before. The results they are reported to produce for broadening and deepening conscious awareness, increasing emotional and mental health and compassionate social connections, have begun to suggest a scientifically testable basis in fact through recent neurobiological research findings. When consistently practiced, they have already been documented to improve immune function, create an inner sense of well-being, and increase the human capacity for rewarding interpersonal relationships.[9]

These new explorations reinforce the growing body of knowledge that humanity has encountered on many levels during my lifetime, each pointing to the complete integration of all life on Earth with no part of which separate from any other. As challenging as that is to accept, everything, including the words I'm typing, the computer that contains them, and even the thoughts and feelings that seem utterly ephemeral, is connected to the immense, complex, ever-moving, changing natural system producing them, no matter how the mystery behind it all is characterized.

This dawning understanding of the physical connection of all that exists, coupled with the growing practices of meditation and mindfulness in so many applications not associated with any particular religion, gives me long-term hope for humanity. Of course these practices also support practical application of the kind, ethical teachings found at the taproot of world religions.

These internal practices are often first engaged to calm fear and pain, whether in medical, religious, or educational settings, because they offer effective ways to grapple with mental and emotional challenges. They can also be referred to as prayer, when prayer is conceived of as something that doesn't require words, even silently imagined ones. With the exponentially increasing speed of change, thrust to the forefront of perception by the Internet, perhaps these already widespread practices will facilitate a shift in human consciousness, refocusing its most powerful efforts toward supporting the living planet to sustain itself rather than continuing to view natural living forms as "things" and striving violently to preserve a destructive dream of a separate, ego-driven, human-centered hierarchy.

The process of moving toward a common vision of planetary regeneration cannot be legislated or forced. It won't come through rules and rational governmental policies, though such instruments may be catalysts for wide acceptance of new cultural practices to assist in bringing the evolving vision of humanity's regenerative role in the web of life into meaningful existence. The best of such policies will be used to codify the healing patterns that are rising to the surface of culture from within the myriad local efforts already afoot to do things differently, gaining increasing numbers of voices and energy from people able to reflect on the part their actions play in the larger living systems of Earth. Impossible, you say? I don't think so. Not after experiencing the shifts that have occurred at both individual and cultural levels over the course of my adult life.

FROM WHAT I'VE SEEN, one powerful way that hope for a kinder, more life-regenerating culture can continue to grow and the tipping point toward a widespread value of sustaining and regenerating planetary life can be reached is for every human being to reflect on and tell their heart's true story to the best of their ability. Maybe that's why memoir has lately become such a popular medium of creative expression in both written and oral forms. The ultimate importance of these stories is not contained in any one of them, just as the individual actions of one person will never be enough to counteract all the cultural forces of unconscious destruction. Each story, however, contains a unique thread of insight to help ignite the shift in consciousness we need the courage to make as a species in order to support planetary resilience. To make that shift, we also need the courage to let go of attachment to the outcome because we cannot know where the mystery of life behind everything will lead, and life inevitably includes beginnings and endings, births and deaths of all kinds. The rhythm of life and death is not to be feared, however. It is to be understood as part of the infinitely mysterious wonder that gives anyone the chance to be alive in a body at all. Learning the humble strength and courage that resides in a willingness to open our vulnerable hearts and minds to that truth, letting go of attachment to an identity wrapped only in the skin and bones of these bodies, is at the heart of the potential shift in human consciousness just over the horizon.

Who in the distant past would ever have imagined that we humans would have discovered and created all that we have in the past century? Those discoveries have risen not from one brilliant mind but from systems of minds working together in inspired, disciplined activity, probing every corner of being for answers to questions about everything from the shape and essence of the universe to the molecular makeup of the genetic code. How did the inspirations for the ideas that built those systems of integrated minds arise? They all came from some spark of insight and imagination ignited by some story, connected with some conscious perception, that had never before been able to dawn on a human mind. And there's no telling which story fed into which mind to flip the switch because we are not separate and there had to be innumerable stories and switches to get to where we now find ourselves.

Each moment of conscious attention and action is the only point of power any one of us has within the swirling processes of continual change. The more clearly and fully we can open awareness within every second of our personal dance on Earth—whether telling a story, washing the dishes, or confronting tragedy and pain—the more life-affirming our response can be, adding that one drop of wisdom over which we have control into the greater ocean of human activity. It is not our business to solve all the world's problems. It is our business to learn to be aware of as much as we can within the challenging moments of our individual lives and to act as wisely as we can. Doing what we can is all that can ever be done, and in the living web we are each positioned at unique junctures, all of which require attention and all of which have unique importance within the living flow. The more we pay attention, the more we will be able to observe and respond wisely to the process threads flowing through our own beings and grow them into their potential to benefit all lives unfolding together within this living Earth dance.

Chapter Seventeen

Eternity in the Moment

Philosophers today have starkly different answers to the question, why is there something rather than nothing? Some are sure there is a reason and we may be able to discover it. Others say there might be a reason, but we'll never know for sure because even the most intellectually gifted know too little to be able to discover it. Still others deem the question itself to be meaningless. Perhaps in the end the answer to why there is something rather than nothing can't be found in any of the usual rational approaches to philosophical mysteries, and can only be found in whatever way we each personally experience awe and wonder.[1]

As Jim Holt points out in his 2012 book, *Why Does the World Exist?* the mystery of existence is still a futile philosophical question to most people, explaining that pervasive opinion by quoting William James, who said, "from nothing to being there is no logical bridge." How can we know that, without trying to build one? Another bridge that seemed impossible to build until the day it was completed was the bridge between life and nonlife (molecular biology), which showed in detail how life indeed arises from nonlife. Today, those exploring the nature of consciousness are working toward the seemingly impossible bridge between mind and matter. Others are trying to unify physics by building a bridge between matter and mathematics. With such bridges under construction, are we beginning to see faint outlines of a bridge between Nothing and Something emerging from the mist?[2]

Any human brain can consciously choose where and how to place attention, no matter how constrained from outside. By repeatedly choosing to direct attention, rather than simply react to stimuli, brain synapses can be purposely solidified into new thought patterns, which are increasingly easy to replicate the more they are chosen. By attending reactively to the world without reflection, we unconsciously define meaning without ever acknowledging it, even to ourselves. However, every time a major break occurs in the expected/projected unfolding of life, attention patterns are disrupted, demanding mental shifts to new thought patterns capable of reweaving life's story. With disciplined reflection, after learning to at least periodically slow down reactive mental and physical activity, we can begin to encounter wonder and mystery in any moment, even in the depths of grief and pain. We now know that when consistently choosing kind, generous thoughts and actions over other possibilities that inevitably present themselves to our chattering minds, awareness gradually alters the structure and substance of our minds in that more compassionate direction. That process also facilitates access to enough contentment in any moment as it unfolds, allowing us to make wiser choices while meeting all of life's inevitable challenges.

THERE IS A FIFTY-THREE-YEAR-OLD WOMAN whose parents have died. Her hands are beginning to look like her mother's hands did as they aged. Her hair is greying at the pace her father's did. She hears their kind advice in the silence of her heart, loving wisdom that never leaves. She grieves deeply, even as she knows their deaths are blessings, ending the suffering of terminally diseased bodies. She watched them deteriorate through heart disease, cancer, dementia, and stroke, surviving at the end as mere husks of the lively, loving people who raised her. As she rises to read her eulogy to the large gathering in the Unitarian church of her teenage years, she recalls another time and other words she wrote and delivered in a wooded glade while celebrating fifty years of their marriage. Those words remain a constant song in her bones, saying:

Dear Mom and Dad,

Thank you for freeing the seed that became me. Your nurturing and pruning of the green shoots that sprang from that seed encouraged the blossoms of my imagination and intellect, and your deep and constant roots gave me insight into lasting love while providing shelter from life's storms. You have been great parents and I cherish you as true friends.

Thank you for encouraging me to run and climb freely, to roam woods and vale and rocky coast under my own guidance. Thank you for teaching me how to swim and ride the waves and for telling me the names of the flowers over and over again until I finally remembered a few. Thank you for piles and piles of pancakes, French toast, and pies of all kinds. Thank you for making table manners important and providing wonderful Sunday dinners where I could practice them, complete with jolly grandparents for company.

Thank you both for trying to answer all my "why?" questions and for giving me a great springy rocking horse for Christmas when I was six. Thank you for hikes in many woods and for driving across the country to show me how big and amazing is the USA. Thank you for taking me camping, for giving me dress-up clothes, and for watching my backyard plays. Thanks for letting me walk on the railing in Basking Ridge and do tricks on the grape arbor. Thanks for teaching me how to build snow forts, ice-skate, and dance the waltz. Thanks also for letting me crawl through drainpipes, roll down the hill in a barrel, smash rocks in the driveway with a hammer, and build tree forts, underground forts, and go-carts. Thanks for introducing me to improvisational dance and waking me up in the middle of the night to see the aurora borealis. Thanks for making a pinhole viewer to look at the solar eclipse. Thanks also for building me a sandbox and taking me to the Bronx Zoo and the museums in New York City, especially the spiraling Guggenheim and Museum of Natural History with all its dinosaur bones. Thanks for letting me ride the carousel in Central Park and slide down the big slide in Washington Square Park. Thanks for buying me sandwiches and cocoa that poured from the mouth of a golden lion at the Automat. Thanks also for letting me "do it myself." Thanks for driving me to endless gymnastics practices and activities of all kinds.

Thanks especially for listening to my problems and letting me cry on your shoulders. Thanks for umpteen philosophy discussion walks, and thanks for taking our family and a blanket out to the beach on a dark, clear night to lie down and look at the Milky Way and oh so many stars. Thanks for teaching me to pull myself together and jump back into the living fray after taking a little time to lick my wounds. Thanks for being there with energy, enthusiasm, and humor when my babies were born. Thanks especially for giving me my two longest standing friends, my sisters, and thanks for visiting me in Boston and letting me take care of you a little. Thanks for shipping me off to Italy when I seemed a bit confused, and thanks for letting me go back to Carleton when Pratt and New York City got the best of me. Thanks for putting a solar greenhouse on your home because I was selling solar greenhouse dealerships, and thanks for your interest and encouragement in all my projects. Thank you so much for giving me this life with such a generous dollop of opportunities to grow and experience joy in the world. I would not exist without this wonderful marriage of yours! Hurray for you! I love you now and forever with all my heart.

A SENSE OF WILDNESS returning to the heart is something I now seek every day by simply walking outside for an hour or so, opening all senses to the experience—particularly the qualities of light in the early morning or evening as the gloaming slants gold and orange sunbeams through tree branches—and listening to birdsong, frog song and insects greeting that change of light in the spring, summer, and fall or the wind murmuring through pines and the tingle of air brushing skin in the brisk cold of a New England winter. There is a deep sense of being part of the natural world that comes alive then. That experience is more than remembered joyful play, although that's where it began. It's also a physically experienced sense of relationship to the movement and wonder of living itself while letting go of controlled thinking as I move through natural environments, releasing preconceived notions moment by moment. When I was a child, that process came naturally. I unconsciously melded with nature when I played outside as a running, observing, listening, growing being, exploring and learning about my living body within the unity of every other living, growing body, whether plant, animal, or human. Discovering in middle age the deeply healing pathways of meditation and mindfulness and consciously nourishing the inner observer to which they naturally gave birth gradually led to words becoming more available to describe the physical sense of how this ever-changing body is only separated from every other element of nature by the written title: I.

Comfort through movement has been with me since birth, and through many kinds of joyful physical activity, I've developed a deep sense that the living force driving all our becoming is where wisdom resides. No combination of words and conditioned ethical rules holds the same quality of insightful wisdom for me as that which can be accessed by attending to all that can be perceived through the body, including the thoughts that rise and pass when each is simply noticed in concert with the physical and emotional sensations associated with them, in a practice I think of as listening to the body. Practicing this listening can either be done while pausing to sit or lie down silently or when moving in nature, attending to every element of the experience without grabbing onto any of them, allowing an unimpeded flow of it all, which often reveals new ways to imagine and respond to challenging situations life presents.

Experience tells me that the creative force igniting all living—beginning with the first atom that led to all natural being, including this body—can only be heard when words in the form of thoughts have quieted enough for the silent, wise knowing beneath them to emerge. Deepening the practice of slowing reactivity to increasingly respond mindfully, moment by moment, and remembering that creative force keeps a door open to receive and nourish every pinprick of inspired joy. Experiencing joy will be essential to resilience in the undeniably challenging times to come, as joy must also be fully intertwined with the pain and fear that are inseparable from the experience of human life and all the beginnings and endings every life contains.

Remembering that we are not separate, even in those beginnings and endings, can help to release the personal stories we often imagine to be universal truth in order to explain our inevitable experiences of human suffering, no matter who we are. Noticing that they are stories, no matter how true they feel, in order to move beneath their words to feel what our bodies are experiencing without the words, allows the pain of any situation to more quickly transform and release into its gift of wisdom as it mysteriously moves through these fragile, wondrous hearts. Cultivating this understanding with gratitude for the highly improbable opportunity to be alive in a human body is the best way I know to bring kindness and wisdom to Earth's dance that we all continuously do together. By continuing to learn how to be curious about, appreciate, and let go of feelings and stories associated with every moment of experience moving through our beings and releasing them into the wider dancing pattern of living creativity, all our thoughts, words, and deeds feed new networks of form that constantly emerge at points deep in the mystery of the future. And that mystery is also contained in every aspect of this very moment, right beside all that has ever been before.

Endnotes

Chapter One

1. Steven Pinker, *The Better Angels of Our Nature* (New York: Penguin Group, 2011).

Chapter Two

1. Lynne Kelly, *The Memory Code* (Sydney: Allen and Unwin, 2017).

2. Jared Diamond, *Guns, Germs, and Steel* (New York: W. W. Norton, 1997, 1999).

3. *Life* was a weekly magazine with photographic storytelling of general interest topics.

4. Andrew J. Cherlin, "The 50's Family and Today's," *New York Times*, November 18, 1981, National edition, *New York Times* Archive, 00031.

5. Cherlin, "The 50's Family and Today's."

6. Cherlin, "The 50's Family and Today's."

7. Cherlin, "The 50's Family and Today's."

8. Cherlin, "The 50's Family and Today's."

9. Cherlin, "The 50's Family and Today's."

10. Cherlin, "The 50's Family and Today's."

11. Cherlin, "The 50's Family and Today's."

Chapter Three

1. Eliza Griswold, "How '*Silent Spring*' Ignited the Environmental Movement," Web Site Edition, *New York Times Magazine*, September 21, 2012.

2. Linda J. Lear, *Rachel Carson, Witness for Nature*, Houghton Mifflin (New York: Houghton Mifflin 2009) Hoopla Digital eBook, 137 of 301.

3. Griswold, "How *Silent Spring* Ignited the Environmental Movement."

4. Maria Popova, "How to Save a World: Rachel Carson's Advice to Posterity" (excerpt from: Maria Popova, *Figuring*, New York: Pantheon Books, 2019) The Marginalian, accessed January 8, 2023, https://www.themarginalian.org/2019/04/12/rachel-carson-scripps-college-commencement/.

5. Popova, "How to Save a World: Rachel Carson's Advice to Posterity."

6. Popova, "How to Save a World: Rachel Carson's Advice to Posterity."

7. This whole paragraph, Popova, "How to Save a World: Rachel Carson's Advice to Posterity."

8. Lear, *Rachel Carson, Witness for Nature,* Hoopla Digital eBook, 174 of 301.

9. "In Today Already Walks Tomorrow," Scripps College News, Feature Stories, April 8, 2005, accessed January 8, 2023, https://www.scrippscollege.edu/news/features/in-today-already-walks-tomorrow.

10. Griswold, "How *Silent Spring* Ignited the Environmental Movement."

11. "A Day Like No Other: Commemorating the 50th Anniversary of the March on Washington," Exhibition Overview, Library of Congress, accessed May 22, 2021, https://www.loc.gov/exhibits/march-on-washington/overview.html.

12. "The Civil Rights Act of 1964: A Long Struggle for Freedom," The Day They Changed Their Minds, Exhibition Overview, Library of Congress, accessed May 22, 2021, https://www.loc.gov/exhibits/civil-rights-act/civil-rights-era.html.

13. "The Civil Rights Act of 1964: A Long Struggle for Freedom," Rosa Parks Being Fingerprinted, Rosa Parks Instructions for Bus Boycott.

14. "The Civil Rights Act of 1964: A Long Struggle for Freedom," The Day They Changed Their Minds.

15. "Publication of 'The Feminine Mystique' by Betty Friedan," Jewish Women's Archive, accessed May 22, 2021, https://jwa.org/thisweek/feb/17/1963/betty-friedan.

16. "The Publication of 'The Feminine Mystique.'"

17. "The Publication of 'The Feminine Mystique.'"

Chapter Four

1. Andrew Clark, "Jazz and Language," *Riffs and Choruses* (New York: Continuum International, Bayou Press, 2001), 459.

2. Danny Goldberg, "All the Human Be-In Was Saying 50 Years Ago, Was Give Peace a Chance," *The Nation*, January 13, 2017, https://www.thenation.com/article/archive/all-the-human-be-in-was-saying-50-years-ago-was-give-peace-a-chance/.

3. "Hippie," Wikipedia, accessed May 19, 2021, https://en.wikipedia.org/wiki/Hippie.

4. "Hippie," Wikipedia.

Chapter Five

1. David Mislin, "How Vietnam War Protests Accelerated the Rise of the Christian Right," The Conversation, *Smithsonian Magazine*, accessed June 30, 2021, https://www.smithsonianmag.com/history/how-vietnam-war-protests-spurred-rise-christian-right-180968942/.

2. Mislin, "How Vietnam War Protests Accelerated the Rise of the Christian Right."

3. Mislin, "How Vietnam War Protests Accelerated the Rise of the Christian Right."

4. Mislin, "How Vietnam War Protests Accelerated the Rise of the Christian Right."

5. Mislin, "How Vietnam War Protests Accelerated the Rise of the Christian Right."

6. Mislin, "How Vietnam War Protests Accelerated the Rise of the Christian Right."

7. Mislin, "How Vietnam War Protests Accelerated the Rise of the Christian Right."

8. Adrian Desmond and James Moore, *Darwin* (New York: Viking Penguin, 1991), 34–35.

9. Desmond and Moore, *Darwin*.

10. Roger E. Salhany, *The Origin of Rights* (Toronto: Carswell, 1986), 32.

11. John R. Thelin, *A History of American Higher Education* (Baltimore: Johns Hopkins University Press, 2004), 46–47.

12. Julian Huxley, *The New Divinity: Essays of a Humanist* (New York: Harper and Row, 1964).

13. Edward J. Larson, *The Remarkable History of Scientific Theory* (New York: Modern Library, Penguin Random House, 2004), 246–253.

14. Larson, *The Remarkable History of Scientific Theory*, 3.

15. This entire paragraph, Huxley's Popularizing Synthesis, 1942, Modern Synthesis (20th Century), Wikipedia, accessed May 27, 2021, https://en.wikipedia.org/wiki/Modern_synthesis_(20th_century).

16. "Edward O. Wilson, PhD: Father of Sociobiology," Academy of Achievement, Sept. 27, 2017, accessed May 29, 2021, https://achievement.org/achiever/edward-o-wilson-ph-d/.

17. "Edward O. Wilson On the Importance of Diversity," Egon Zehnder, January 1, 2017, accessed May 29, 2021, https://www.egonzehnder.com/insight/edward-o-wilson-on-the-importance-of-diversity.

18. Susan Murphy, *Minding the Earth, Mending the World* (Berkeley: Counterpoint Press, 2014).

Chapter Six

1. Mark Johanson, "What Happened to the Hippie Trail? The Legacy of the Asia Overland Route," Culture, *International Business Times*, June 2, 2012, https://www.ibtimes.com/what-happened-hippie-trail-legacy-asia-overland-route-701219.

2. Johanson, "What Happened to the Hippie Trail?"

3. Michelle Goldberg, "The Roots of Mindfulness," Community, *Tablet*, October 8, 2015, https://www.tabletmag.com/sections/community/articles/the-roots-of-mindfulness.

4. Johanson, "What Happened to the Hippie Trail?"

5. Johanson, "What Happened to the Hippie Trail?"

6. Kate Daloz, "The 'Back to the Land' Movement." *Utne Reader,* September 2016, reprinted from *We Are as Gods: Back to the Land in the 1970s on the Quest for a New America*, https://www.utne.com/environment/back-to-the-land-movement-ze0z1609zfis.

7. Daloz, "The 'Back to the Land' Movement."

8. Daloz, "The 'Back to the Land' Movement."

9. Tom Hayden, "The Port Huron Statement," Students for a Democratic Society, June 15, 1962, https://images2.americanprogress.org/campus/email/PortHuronStatement.pdf

10. Daloz, "The 'Back to the Land' Movement."

Chapter Seven

1. John W. Dean, *The Nixon Defense: What He Knew and When He Knew It* (New York: Penguin Group, 2014), 610–620.

Chapter Eleven

1. Robert F. Kennedy, "Day of Affirmation Address, University of Capetown, Capetown, South Africa," John F. Kennedy Presidential Library and Museum, June 6, 1966, https://www.jfklibrary.org/learn/about-jfk/the-kennedy-family/robert-f-kennedy/robert-f-kennedy-speeches/day-of-affirmation-address-university-of-capetown-capetown-south-africa-june-6-1966.

2. Hana Muslic, "A Brief History of Nonprofit Organizations (And What We Can Learn)," Nonprofit Hub, October 27, 2017, accessed June 9, 2021, http://nonprofithub.org/starting-a-nonprofit/a-brief-history-of-nonprofit-organizations/.

3. Muslic, "A Brief History of Nonprofit Organizations."

4. Muslic, "A Brief History of Nonprofit Organizations."

5. Steven Rathgeb Smith, "Government and Nonprofits: Turning Points, Challenges, and Opportunities," *Nonprofit Quarterly*, September 21, 2009, https://nonprofitquarterly.org/government-and-nonprofits-turning-points-challenges-and-opportunities/.

6. Smith, "Government and Nonprofits: Turning Points, Challenges, and Opportunities."

7. Lester M. Salamon, "The Rise of the Nonprofit Sector," *Foreign Affairs*, 73, no. 4 (July/August 1994), https://doi.org/10.2307/20046747.

8. Paul Hawken, *Blessed Unrest* (New York: Viking Penguin, Penguin Group, 2007), 2–8.

9. Smith, "Government and Nonprofits: Turning Points, Challenges, and Opportunities."

10. Muslic, "A Brief History of Nonprofit Organizations."

11. Smith, "Government and Nonprofits: Turning Points, Challenges, and Opportunities."

12. Smith, "Government and Nonprofits: Turning Points, Challenges, and Opportunities."

Chapter Twelve

1. Paul H. Ray, PhD and Sherry Ruth Anderson, PhD, *The Cultural Creatives: How 50 Million People are Changing the World* (New York: Harmony Books, Crown, 2000), 170.

2. Ray and Anderson, *The Cultural Creatives: How 50 Million People are Changing the World.*

3. Ray and Anderson, *The Cultural Creatives: How 50 Million People are Changing the World*, 171.

4. Peter Dreier, "The Fifty Most Influential Progressives of the Twentieth Century," *The Nation*, September 15, 2010, https://www.thenation.com/article/archive/fifty-most-influential-progressives-twentieth-century/.

Chapter Sixteen

1. Richard Dawkins, *The Selfish Gene* (London: Oxford University Press, 2009), 12–18.

2. Jan Boeyens and Francis Thackeray, "Number Theory and the Unity of Science," *South Africa Journal of Science*, November 2014, https://cyberleninka.org/article/n/1149813/viewer.

3. Dawkins, *The Selfish Gene.*

4. Dawkins, *The Selfish Gene*.

5. Dawkins, *The Selfish Gene*.

6. Dawkins, *The Selfish Gene*.

7. Richard Dawkins, second definition of *meme*: an idea, behavior, style, or usage that spreads from person to person within a culture, merriam-webster.com, accessed January 13, 2023, https://www.merriam-webster.com/dictionary/meme.

8. Dawkins, *The Selfish Gene*.

9. Daniel J. Siegel, *The Mindful Brain: Reflection and Attunement in the Cultivation of Well-Being* (New York: W. W. Norton & Company, Inc., 2007), 189–208.

Chapter Seventeen

1. Jim Holt, *Why Does the World Exist?* (New York: W. W. Norton, 2012), 28–29.

2. This whole paragraph, Holt, *Why Does the World Exist?* 30.

Acknowledgments

There are far too many people to acknowledge here, whose presence in my life made it possible to experience, reflect, write, and organize this book—teachers of all kinds, some with academic degrees and others not old enough to know what it means to be a teacher. Then there are all the nonhuman teachers of equal importance. As a result, I have limited this list to those who directly impacted the writing process, first and foremost my husband, Bill Abel, an open-minded, open-hearted confidante, unparalleled supporter and first editor of choice. Other key people include Sarah Ehinger and Andy Migner, two readers of early drafts who provided loving encouragement that strengthened my resolve. Annie Gray, Susan Douglass, and Dirkje Legerstee read early drafts and drilled down deeper to provide ongoing insight and inspiration that buoyed my spirit over challenging terrain. They, along with Lyndsay Granveau and Rebecca Pfister, my writing group sisters, Kinny Perot and Joan Liggett, my walking partners, and my friend and mentor Francie Nolde built confidence in the authority of my own experience. Olivia Thomes, Linda Hoffman, and Olivia Hoblitzelle's willingness to review the book's final draft and consider writing endorsements gave me courage. Allyson Machate, Julie Haase, Michele Rubin, Emily Hitchcock, and associates of The Writer's Ally brought deep professional expertise from the publishing world to my fingertips, teaching, advising, and collaboratively shaping the book you hold in your hands. I will be forever grateful to every one of these people for the parts they played in a life-changing process.

About the Author

Jane Gallagher is a writer who lives with her husband in the green woodlands of Vermont's mountains. She retired in 2016 from nonprofit development consulting to New England's nonprofit organizations working to address social and environmental injustices at the local, state, and regional levels. A mother of two and grandmother of three, she holds a BA in Political Science and International Relations from Carleton College in Minnesota and an MA in Urban and Environmental Policy from Tufts University in Massachusetts.